ESSENTIALS OF
NEUROPSYCHOLOGICAL ASSESSMENT

Lawrence C. Hartlage, Ph.D., received his doctorate from the University of Louisville in 1968 and has diplomates in clinical psychology from the American Board of Professional Psychology and in neuropsychology from the American Board of Professional Neuropsychology. He has served as President of the National Academy of Neuropsychologists and the American Psychological Association Division of Clinical Neuropsychology, and as coeditor of the *International Journal of Clinical Neuropsychology.*

Michael J. Asken, Ph.D., received his doctorate in clinical psychology in 1976 from West Virginia University. Most recently he was Assistant Director for Preventive Medicine and Health Psychology at the Department of Family Medicine at Polyclinic Medical Center of Harrisburg, Pennsylvania, where he was involved in the training of residents from 1976 to 1986. Dr. Asken is currently in private practice with the Cowley Associates medical group. He also holds an appointment with the Department of Behavioral Science, College of Medicine, The Pennsylvania State University, Milton S. Hershey Medical Center, in Hershey, Pennsylvania, and is an adjunct associate professor of psychology at Lebanon Valley College in Annville, Pennsylvania. He is the author of over 30 publications in the areas of health psychology and family medicine.

J. Larry Hornsby, Ed.D., received his doctorate from the University of Georgia in 1973. He has served as the Director of Behavioral Medicine for the Department of Family Medicine, Medical College of Georgia since 1976. Dr. Hornsby has published over 25 journal articles and several book chapters.

Essentials of Neuropsychological Assessment

Lawrence C. Hartlage, Ph.D.
Michael J. Asken, Ph.D.
J. Larry Hornsby, Ed.D.
Editors

SPRINGER PUBLISHING COMPANY
New York

Springer Publishing Company, Inc.
536 Broadway
New York, NY 10012

87 88 89 90 91 / 5 4 3 2 1

Library of Congress Cataloging-in-Publication Data

Essentials of neuropsychological assessment.

　Includes bibliographies and index.
　1. Neuropsychological tests.　2. Brain—Diseases—
Diagnosis.　I. Hartlage, Lawrence C.　II. Asken,
Michael J.　III. Hornsby, J. Larry.　[DNLM:
1. Neuropsychological Tests.　2. Neuropsychology.
WL 103 E78]
RC386.6.N48E87　　　1987　　　616.8'0475　　　87-4819
ISBN 0-8261-4470-5

Printed in the United States of America

Contents

Contributors

Erin D. Bigler, Ph.D.
Austin Neurological Clinic and
Department of Psychology
University of Texas at Austin
Austin, Texas

Kathleen Lou Edwards, B.S.
Department of Psychiatry
School of Medicine
University of Pittsburgh
Pittsburgh, Pennsylvania

Lawrence J. Lewandowski, Ph.D.
Department of Psychology
Syracuse University
Syracuse, New York

William D. MacInnes, Ph.D.
Departments of Medicine and Radiology
School of Medicine
Creighton University
Omaha, Nebraska

Michael F. Martelli, Ph.D.
Neuropsychological Services of Virginia
Inc. and Psychology Service, Shelter-
ing Arms Hospital
Richmond, Virginia

Kimford J. Meador, M.D.
Department of Neurology
School of Medicine
Medical College of Georgia
Augusta, Georgia

F. T. Nichols, M.D.
Department of Neurology
School of Medicine
Medical College of Georgia
Augusta, Georgia

David C. Osmon, Ph.D.
Department of Psychology
University of Wisconsin
Milwaukee, Wisconsin

Edward A. Peck, III, Ph.D.
Independent Practice and
Neuropsychological Services of
Virginia and Department of
Psychology
Virginia Commonwealth University
Richmond, Virginia

Douglas E. Robbins, Ph.D.
Department of Psychosocial
Medical Psychology
Lakeshore Hospital
Birmingham, Alabama

Valerie Stephens, M.S.
Neuropsychological Services of Virginia
    Inc. and Department of Psychology
Virginia Commonwealth University
Richmond, Virginia

Dennis P. Swiercinsky, Ph.D.
Independent Practice
Mission, Kansas

Ralph E. Tarter, Ph.D.
Department of Psychiatry
School of Medicine
University of Pittsburgh
Pittsburg, Pennsylvania

Greta N. Wilkening, Psy.D.
Departments of Pediatrics and
    Neurology
The University of Colorado Health
    Science Center
Denver, Colorado

J. Michael Williams, Ph.D.
Department of Psychology
Memphis State University
Memphis, Tennessee

Preface

Scarcely more than a decade ago neuropsychology was a relatively exotic specialty whose practitioners were typically found only in neurology programs in medical schools and tertiary hospital settings. The vast majority of these practitioners, who worldwide numbered at most a few hundred, primarily tended to be involved in assessment of severe neurological or neurosurgical impairments; for the most part they used the Halstead–Reitan Neuropsychological Battery as their major assessment tool. Perhaps reflecting the status of neuroimaging, at that time crude by today's standards, a major focus of much assessment was on lesion localization.

Today's neuropsychology is different in many ways. The number of trained neuropsychologists has shown a rather dramatic increase, with membership in the American Psychological Association Division of Clinical Neuropsychology currently in excess of 2,000. The increased number of trained neuropsychologists has resulted in their much greater availability not only in hospital settings, but also in private practice, community mental health programs, and university settings. There is increased variability in approaches to assessment, with approximately one-third of practitioners using the Halstead–Reitan Battery, one-third using the (relatively new) Luria–Nebraska Neuropsychological Battery, and one-third using some other combination of tests (Seretny, Gray, Hartlage, & Dean, 1985). The focus of assessment, once limited to lesion localization in severely neurologically impaired patients, now encompasses broader issues, including such diverse areas as learning problems, behavior disorders of associative and personality types that may have neuropsychological substrates, and a broad area referred to as "behavioral neuropsychology." Perhaps reflecting the range of this latter area, a recent title, *The Neuropsychology of Individual Differences* (Hartlage & Telzrow, 1985), approaches the topic of individual differences in development, perception, temperament, and general cognitive ability from a neuropsychological perspective, with neuropsychological substrates discussed as possible determinants of individual differences for each.

For the neuropsychology practitioner, a number of implications result from the changes of the past decade both in neuropsychology and in related fields. The increased availability of neuropsychology practitioners has made neuropsychological services much more visible. Increasing recognition of neurological substrates of much behavior, and of the behavioral correlates of such neurological insults as closed-head injury (e.g., Goethe & Levin, 1984), has led to the recognition that neuropsychology has relevance for a wide range of behavior anomalies and problems. Finally, the contributions of research in such related areas as individual differences, normal aging processes, and learning problems suggest that neuropsychology may have relevance for helping understand behavior along a considerable age continuum, and along a continuum ranging from the apparently normal to the severely impaired.

This volume is intended for the neuropsychology student or beginning practitioner as an introduction to the diverse aspects of clinical neuropsychology, with special reference to how neuropsychology may relate to the issues likely to be encountered in practice.

The volume should also enable the non-neurologically trained practitioner to appreciate the range and types of clinical problems for which neuropsychology may make contributions toward diagnosis or management. The book also discusses some of the conceptual and methodological approaches to the assessment of neuropsychological substrates of problems likely to be encountered in practice.

Chapter contributors were solicited on the dual criteria of recognized expertise in their respective areas and the ability to communicate this expertise in clinically relevant form to professionals whose involvement with neuropsychology is at a developmental stage. Toward this goal, the editors have sought to preserve the richness of the individual clinical perspectives of the authors so that the practitioner will recognize that there is no absolute standard, procedure, or battery that represents the essence of neuropsychology.

REFERENCES

Goethe, K. E., & Levin, H. S. (1984). Behavioral manifestations during the early and long-term stages of recovery after closed head injury. *Psychiatric Annals, 14* (7), 540–546.

Hartlage, L. C., & Telzrow, C. F. (Eds.). (1985). *The neuropsychology of individual differences*. New York: Plenum.

Seretny, M., Gray, J., Hartlage, L. C., & Dean, R. (1985, August). *Survey of current issues in neuropsychology*. Paper presented at the meeting of the American Psychological Association, Los Angeles, CA.

1

Neuropsychology: Definition and History*

Lawrence C. Hartlage

Within the last decade, clinical neuropsychology has gained increasing recognition as a discipline with relevance to such diverse practice areas as family medicine, neurology, neurosurgery, psychiatry, and psychology, as well as to such research areas as behavior, learning, and individual differences. With practice origins evolving from attempts to separate functional from organic origins of disordered behavior, such referral questions continue to constitute a significant focus of neuropsychology, although the scientific basis of clinical practice and methodologies used have progressed well beyond the ability to resolve such questions as, "Is this problem neurological or psychogenic?"

NEUROPSYCHOLOGY AND OTHER ASSESSMENT APPROACHES

In a number of ways, clinical neuropsychology can be viewed as representing a synthesis of the best features of neurological and psychological examination procedures, whereby the systematic neurological assessment of functional cortical systems is combined with the precise scaling of psychometric measure-

*Acknowledgment is made to the National Endowment for the Humanities for support of research at the Archives of the History of American Psychology, summer 1984; to the Bearce Museum, University of Akron, repository of the Archives of the History of American Psychology; and to Dr. John Poppleston, director of the Archives, for help and assistance with the collection of data relative to the history of neuropsychology.

ment. An example of assessment of upper extremity motor function may help illustrate this point. In the traditional neurological examination, grip strength may be assessed by instructing the patient to grip the examiner's hand or fingers "as hard as you can." While there is no doubt that a skilled clinician can readily identify either gross bilateral weakness or asymmetry of strength by this method, the measurement is usually subjective or, at best, quantified on a "plus four" scale, on which continuum the differentiation between 2+ and 3+ may vary for a given patient examined by different clinicians.

In the neuropsychological examination, grip strength is assessed by a dynamometer, which produces a quantifiable score in kilograms or pounds. While providing much greater likelihood of agreement among clinicians concerning the absolute strength level, it also provides a much more sensitive baseline for sequential comparisons. In the case of a patient with suspected neuromuscular degeneration, for example, the course and rate of decline may be detected with considerably more precision than even an experienced clinician may detect over intervals of several weeks or months.

Assessment of upper extremity fine-motor coordination represents another good illustration. Traditional clinical assessment of such function may take the form of having the patient rapidly oppose index finger and thumb, or thumb and fingers in succession, and depends on the examiner's skill and experience to detect either asymmetry or bilateral slowness. Neuropsychological examination of this same function would likely involve having the patient depress and release a counter with calibrated resistance over a given (e.g., 10 seconds) time period. In addition to providing a quantified record, this procedure can help detect subtle impairments in either rate or symmetry. In serial evaluation of patients whose disease (or treatment) may affect oscillation rate over time, these quantified baseline data can detect such changes to quite a sensitive degree, even when measured by different examiners.

It is in the assessment of higher cognitive functions that neuropsychological assessment may provide even greater sensitivity than traditional mental status examinations. While traditional clinical measures, such as fund of information, ability to calculate serial sevens, or similar tasks, are obviously relevant for detecting gross instances of dementia, dyscalculia, or dysphasia, they have a number of limitations in the precise identification of which functional system is impaired or to what extent it is impaired.

Through neuropsychological evaluation, possible dyscalculia can be assessed by comparing calculation abilities to other mental abilities. This helps determine whether problems with calculation represent a specific deficit or exist as part of more global problems in higher mental function. Similarly, dysphasia may be assessed by comparing performance on measures of receptive language with performance on associative and expressive language measures. Neuropsychological evaluation may also help identify subtle receptive problems by comparing the patient's verbal performance on visual, as opposed to auditory, presentation of stimuli. Dementia may show subtle early signs; by comparing performance on word-finding and fund-of-information tasks, and by using measures with comparable difficulty level, the type of dementia may be identified with greater precision. For the purpose of determining or estimating prior levels of mental function, neuropsychological approaches may compare performance on tasks measuring abilities relatively resistant to deterioration (e.g., word recognition) against performance on tasks measuring abilities more likely to show deterioration (e.g., short-term memory or complex problem solving) to develop hypotheses concerning whether current cognitive functioning differs from prior levels, and if so, to what extent.

Clinical neuropsychology has thus far been described in terms of how it may compare with traditional clinical neurological or mental status examination procedures. In comparison with traditional clinical neurological assessment, clinical neuropsychology differs on one essential dimension when related to the presumed neurological substrates of behavior being measured. As measured by traditional clinical psychology measures, such functions as intelligence are not assumed to depend on specific neurological or other substrates; rather, they are defined in behavioral terms, that is, "intelligence is what is measured by an intelligence test."

Specifically, a patient's performances on given samples of behavior are collected to reach a conclusion concerning intellectual or personality functions, without any specific hypothesized rationale being necessary for items to be considered valid. The Minnesota Multiphasic Personality Inventory, as an illustrative personality measurement instrument, has no theoretical basis for either its scale or for its individual items. Clusters of responses, which on empirical study were found to classify individuals with given behavioral characteristics, are used as validity or character scales, without presuming to relate to any underlying substrate or etiology. Thus, while traditional clinical psychology measurements can describe and in some cases predict behavior, this descriptive or prognostic function does not focus on determinants in the form of biological substrates. Neuropsychology, on the other hand, uses measures that presumably assess either (1) specific anatomic loci (e.g., left posterior frontal lobe motor strip or right anterior parietal lobe sensory strip functional systems) with respect to presumed anatomic loci (e.g., rhythm sense) or (2) constellations of functional systems (e.g., short-term visual-spatial memory, long-term verbal memory) that have implications for specific aspects of brain function.

THE PRACTICE AND SCIENCE OF NEUROPSYCHOLOGY

Neuropsychology and traditional clinical psychology may well use many of the same diagnostic instruments, but the purpose for their use and implication for diagnosis differ on the dimension of referral to neurological substrates of findings. A traditional clinical psychologist may use a test of dominant-hand, fine-motor coordination to determine whether an individual could perform a given job requiring such coordination, while the focus of the neuropsychologist on this measure would more likely involve the functional integrity of the contralateral cerebral hemisphere motor strip. The practice of clinical neuropsychology could thus be defined as the scientific application of psychological and psychometric measurement procedures in the assessment of behaviors related to the central nervous system.

The science of clinical neuropsychology could, in a similar fashion, be defined as a body of scientific knowledge related to brain–behavior relationships that uses measurement procedures developed on the basis of psychological research for the description and diagnosis of behaviors mediated by the central nervous system. Many clinical neuropsychologists are, in fact, also clinical psychologists (Hartlage, Chelune, & Tucker, 1981), although the reverse is much less common. For individuals whose professional field is not psychology, the distinction between clinical psychologists and clinical neuropsychologists is further obscured by the fact that, after attending a few days' workshop in clinical neuropsychology, many clinical psychologists have begun to use some clinical neuropsychology assessment procedures in their clinical psychology practice. By analogy, although a cardiologist uses a stethoscope, anyone who learns how to use a stethoscope does not automatically become a cardiologist.

Even among those with specific training, knowledge, skill, and experience in clincal neuropsychology, there is no common agreement concerning the "right way" to do adequate neuropsychological assessment. In three national surveys of practicing clinical neuropsychologists, for example, it was found that approximately one-third tend to use the Halstead–Reitan Neuropsychological Battery (HRNB), one-third use the Luria–Nebraska Neuropsychological Battery (LNNB), and one-third use a variety of measurement instruments not classifiable as a standardized battery (Hartlage & Telzrow, 1980; Hartlage, Chelune, & Tucker, 1981; Seretny, Gray, Hartlage, & Dean, 1985).

In spite of the diversity of approaches to assessment, there is a fairly strong agreement among practitioners concerning which abilities need to be assessed for developing a comprehensive neuropsychological profile. The difference in assessment approaches represents a variety of causes, involving such factors as tradition; the particular approach with which the neuropsychologist has greatest familiarity; level of training; and, to some extent, the time available for each neuropsychological assessment. With respect to tradition, the Halstead–Reitan Battery has been in use in evolutionary forms for nearly 40 years and has been the major battery used over time. Perhaps related to its venerability and the promulgation of training workshops by Reitan, many practitioners have become familiar with its use.

In recent years, Golden and his colleagues (Golden, Hammeke, & Purisch,

1980) have made available a variety of workshops involving the Luria–Nebraska Battery, to the point where it is probably safe to say that approximately equal numbers of professionals have become familiar with the LNNB as with the Halstead–Reitan Battery. Although there are no definitive data concerning the relationship between a practitioner's level of training and the choice of an assessment approach, there is a likelihood that less experienced practitioners may feel more secure in the use of a standardized battery. In this respect, the LNNB is probably easier to learn, administer, and interpret. With respect to time required for administration, the LNNB is also probably the least time consuming: a fact that may make the LNNB especially appealing to practitioners who work in institutional settings, where time constraints on individual evaluations represent an important consideration.

HISTORICAL DEVELOPMENT OF NEUROPSYCHOLOGY

The foundation of modern clinical neuropsychology had its origins in the work of nineteenth-century researchers who presented evidence of relationships between brain damage in given cortical areas and impaired function in given adaptive behaviors (Broca, 1865/1960; Jackson, 1874/1932). In spite of this localized empirical basis, early neuropsychology in the United States addressed global brain function as its primary focus.

Work in the United States during the first half of the twentieth century was concerned for the most part with attempts to discriminate patients with brain damage from other groups, which typically involved either psychiatric patients or presumably normal populations. There was relatively little concern for differentiating the type of brain damage resultant from such disease causes as trauma, neoplasm, or vascular insult. Further, the areas or even extent of damage to cortical or subcortical structures were not addressed as a major concern; rather, the emphasis was on detecting whether the patient suffered from brain damage.

The lack of measures of nonsurgical criteria during this period may have been a factor contributing to the relatively crude and nonspecific approaches to the assessment of brain–behavior relationships. Before the advent of computerized approaches, tomograms and electroencephalograms provided only relatively crude data. This left only the neurological examination as a nonsurgical criterion measure against which psychological tests, possibly related to brain function, could be evaluated.

Neurological thinking during this era was influenced by "mass action" concepts of brain functioning, which tended to deemphasize a strict localizing approach to diagnosis. The neurosurgical cases available for validation of novel psychological approaches to diagnosis were limited, and, even in major research centers, limited numbers of surgical cases suitable for study were available each year (Halstead, 1952). Thus it was much easier to study "brain damage" as a unitary phenomenon, rather than collect data relative to possible specific psychological test correlates of lesions in given cortical areas. To study a single phenomenon, i.e., brain damage, during the twentieth century, neuropsychological research focused on the use of a single test, such as the Bender Gestalt, Benton Visual Retention Test, or Graham Kendall Memory for Design Test.

Approximately concurrent with the Second World War, two major forces contributed to the growth and refinement of neuropsychology. The large number of head injuries involving both concussive and penetrating wounds related to military action required diagnosis and treatment and provided a ready source of patients for study. Further, the emergence of clinical psychology as a profession, with special interest in measurement of abnormal human mental conditions, resulted in the availability of a cadre of trained individuals who could evaluate the neurologically related problems of veterans requiring care.

Prominent among such researchers and practitioners was Ward Halstead, who, in 1947, published a monograph concerning observations on several hundred cases with special reference to frontal lobe damage (Halstead, 1952). Using a combination of 10 indicators (tests), he was able to identify differences between patients with brain lesions that had been (subsequently) surgically verified and those with normal controls, at the p.00001 level of confidence (Halstead, 1952). Although some attempts were made to relate psychological test results to lesions in given brain areas, the main success of Halstead's measures was in differentiating frontal cortical damage from frontal subcortical or nonfrontal cortical damage. It was a student of Halstead's, who, in 1955, based on a modification of Halstead's battery, was able to relate patterns of psychological test findings to lateralization of cerebral damage (Reitan, 1955). Subsequently, Reitan and his co-workers were able to relate findings from the modified Halstead (Halstead–Reitan) Battery to such discrete aspects of brain lesions as lateralized motor deficits (Reed & Reitan, 1969); temporal lobe damage (Reitan, 1955); abstraction ability (Reitan, 1959); dysphasia (Reitan, 1960); aging (Reitan, 1967); sensorimotor functions (Reitan, 1971); and cerebrovascular lesions (Reitan and Fitzhugh, 1971).

The approach used by Reitan was sufficiently successful that it was widely regarded as the benchmark of neuropsychological assessment for nearly two decades. Scholars and researchers from the United States, Canada, and Europe who studied with Reitan at his Indiana University Medical Center Laboratory during the 1950s and 60s returned to their hospitals and universities, thus increasing the popularity of his approach. Their own research efforts, building on the skills developed in Reitan's laboratory, helped shape the course of human clinical neuropsychology throughout much of the Western hemisphere (e.g., Boll & Reitan, 1972; Davis & Reitan, 1967; Doehring & Reitan, 1962;

Fitzhugh, Fitzhugh & Reitan, 1961; Klove & Reitan, 1958; Matthews & Reitan, 1963; Reitan & Shipley, 1963; Reitan & Tarshes, 1959; Wheeler & Reitan, 1962).

It was not until the mid-1970s that an alternative battery approach to neuropsychological assessment began to challenge the Halstead–Reitan Battery. Originally developed by Annelise Christianson from her observations of A. R. Luria's neurological examination procedures, this approach received considerable recognition in the United States in the form of a standardized battery developed by Golden and his associates (Golden, Hammeke, & Purisch, 1980) as the Luria–Nebraska Neuropsychological Battery (LNNB). Based essentially on Luria's theories of functional systems, this 269-item battery could be administered in approximately two hours (as opposed to the six to eight hours typically required for the Halstead–Reitan Battery); it also provided 11 objective scales, e.g., motor, left and right sensorimotor, and memory, each with independent cutoff scores that made interpretation and reporting considerably easier than with the Halstead–Reitan Battery.

Although initially subjected to considerable skepticism and attack (Adams, 1980; Spiers, 1981), by 1980 the LNNB had become the neuropsychological assessment approach of choice for 31% of U. S. neuropsychologists, as compared with 38% usage of the Halstead–Reitan Battery (Hartlage, Chelune, & Tucker, 1981). In the period since then, the Luria–Nebraska appears to have maintained its popularity relative to the Halstead–Reitan. A 1985 survey shows 31% of neuropsychologists using the LNNB, while 34% are still using the Halstead–Reitan (Seretny, Gray, Hartlage, & Dean, 1985).

CURRENT TRENDS IN CLINICAL NEUROPSYCHOLOGY

As noted, the use of standardized batteries, such as the Halstead–Reitan or the Luria–Nebraska, accounts for approximately two-thirds of the diagnostic approaches in current neuropsychological practice. Neuropsychologists who do not use one of these standard batteries tend to use an array of tests that, although standardized to some extent, may vary according to the diagnostic issues or in presenting problems for the individual patient (Hartlage, 1984; Hartlage & Hartlage, 1977; Lezak, 1976).

Whatever approach to assessment is used, there appears to be a shift in diagnostic focus from emphasis on lesion localization toward integrating findings from assessment of brain–behavior relationships into broader contexts. Neuropsychologists are increasingly relating findings from their assessment to such issues as vocational potential, career choice, and optimal instructional strategies for individuals; they are also developing approaches for studying how given levels of therapeutic medication or environmental neurotoxins may affect neuropsychological functioning. While the diagnostic focus remains on the individual patient, findings are being applied to such broader issues as the choice of the least behaviorally toxic drug for treatment of such problems as epilepsy or the exposure levels to potential neurotoxins that may be tolerated without neuropsychological impairment.

In addition to a changing focus on assessment, there is emerging an increased involvement in treatment, with nearly half of practicing neuropsychologists engaged in some type of cognitive rehabilitation or retraining activities (Seretny, Gray, Hartlage, & Dean, 1985). Although the research concerning cognitive rehabilitation is in its infancy, this appears to be an area of very rapid growth and one that can be expected to represent an important facet of neuropsychological practice.

Another trend in clinical neuropsychology involves a shift away from medical school and university settings. During the early years of neuropsychology in the United States the majority of practitioners were in academic settings, but in recent years there are considerably more neuropsychologists in independent practice than there are in medical schools and universities (Seretny et al., 1985). This probably reflects both an increase in the numbers of neuropsychologists and an increasing demand for their services as independent practitioners.

Whatever the cause, there has been a shift to settings wherein intervention and consultation to service providers in nonmedical specialties is much more common. An example of the increasing emphasis on consultation to and interaction with nonmedical service providers is the emerging involvement of neuropsychologists in forensic work. Plaintiffs' attorneys increasingly are consulting with neuropsychologists concerning such issues as sequelae of head injury and exposure to neurotoxic chemicals. In the 1985 survey mentioned above, neuropsychologists indicated an average involvement in five litigated cases per year (Seretny et al., 1985).

With the increasing number of neuropsychologists in practice, and with pressure for definition of the field from such diverse sources as hospital staff privilege committees and legal demands for specification of qualifications, there has been an increased emphasis on the credentialing of neuropsychologists. Although essentially all practicing neuropsychologists are required to be licensed by their respective state psychology licensing boards, such licensure by no means can be considered as evidence of competence in neuropsychology. Accordingly, two national professional credentialing boards in neuropsychology have been established. The American Board of Professional Psychology has established a subsection dealing with clinical neuropsychology, and the American Board of Professional Neuropsychology deals exclusively with specialists in neuropsychology. This latter board provides a two-tiered certification, with the diploma awarded to neuropsychologists who manifest exceptional competence and certification awarded to neuropsychologists who demonstrate intermediate competencies or establish experience in the field.

SUMMARY

In terms of an operational definition, clinical neuropsychology involves the professional application of psychological tests, modified neurological assessment procedures, clinical observation, and anamnestic data toward the formulation of diagnostic and treatment conclusions related to the functional status of the central nervous system. Obviously, in given diagnostic or treatment settings, and among individual practitioners, a somewhat broader or narrower focus may apply: it is with the range of variability among the settings and practitioners in mind that the field of neuropsychology has begun to attempt a definition of who is versus who is not a neuropsychologist in terms of national certification boards.

The development of neuropsychology has evolved from the lesion localization focus of the late nineteenth century toward a more behaviorally oriented focus. This evolution is reflected in a gradual shift from a concern limited to frank neurological pathology toward a broader emphasis that also includes studying subtle neurological substrates of behavior in mild deviations from normal, and even in looking to neurological organization as a determinant of individual difference in such domains as learning, temperament, and personality. Another manifestation of the greater behavioral orientation of human clinical neuropsychology involves the emergence of cognitive remediation or retraining as a part of neuropsychology practice.

With the advent of advanced neuroimaging procedures, such as computerized axial tomography, magnetic resonance imaging, and positron emission tomography, and with advances in electrophysiology, the use of neuropsychological assessment as a means of localizing brain abnormalities gave way to its use of comprehensive quantified description of how given brain abnormalities affect behavior. It is likely that current practices in neuropsychology will continue to adapt to changes in related fields.

REFERENCES

Adams, K. (1980). An end of innocence for behavioral neurology? Adams replies. *Journal of Consulting and Clinical Psychology, 48*, 522-524.

Boll, T. J. (1985). Developing issues in clinical neuropsychology. *Journal of Clinical and Experimental Neuropsychology, 7*(5), 473-485.

Boll, T. J., & Reitan, R. M. (1972). Motor and tactile-perceptual deficits in brain-damaged children. *Perceptual and Motor Skills, 34*, 343-350.

Broca, P. (1960). Remarks on the seat of the faculty of articulate language, followed by an observation of aphaesia. In G. von Bonin (Trans.), *Some papers on the cerebral cortex*. Springfield, IL: C. C. Thomas. (Original work published 1865).

Davis, L. J., & Reitan, R. M. (1967). Dysphasia and constructional dyspraxia items, and Wechsler verbal and performance IQ's in retardates. *American Journal of Mental Deficiency, 71*, 604-608.

Dean, R. S. (1985). Foundation and rationale for neuropsychological basis of individual differences. In L. C. Hartlage & C. F. Telzrow (Eds.), *The neuropsychology of individual differences* (pp. 7–39). New York: Plenum.

Doehring, D. G., & Reitan, R. M. (1962). Concept attainment of human adults with lateralized cerebral lesions. *Perceptual and Motor Skills, 14,* 27–33.

Fitzhugh, K. B., Fitzhugh, L. C., & Reitan, R. M. (1961). Psychological deficits in relation to acuteness of brain function. *Journal of Consulting Psychology, 25,* 61–66.

Golden, C. J., Hammeke, T., & Purisch, A. (1980). *A Manual for the Luria-Nebraska Neuropsychological Battery* (rev. ed.). Los Angeles: Western Psychological Services.

Halstead, W. (1952). The frontal lobes and the highest integrating capacities of man. *Halstead papers.* M175, p. 26. Akron, OH: Archives of the History of American Psychology.

Hartlage, L. C. (1984). Neuropsychological assessment of children. In P. A. Keller & L. Ritt (Eds.), *Innovations in clinical practice* (Vol. III) (pp. 153–165). Sarasota, FL: Professional Resource Exchange.

Hartlage, L. C., Chelune, D., & Tucker, D. (1981, August). *Survey of professional issues in the practice of clinical neuropsychology.* Paper presented at the meeting of the American Psychological Association, Los Angeles.

Hartlage, L. C., & Hartlage, P. L. (1977). The application of neuropsychological principles in the diagnosis of learning disabilities. In L. Tarnopol & A. M. Tarnopol (Eds.), *Brain function and reading disability* (pp. 111–146). Philadelphia: University Park Press.

Hartlage, L. C., & Telzrow, C. F. (1980). The practice of clinical neuropsychology in the U.S. *Clinical Neuropsychology, 2*(4), 200–202.

Jackson, J. H. (1932). On the density of the brain. In J. Taylor (Ed.), *Selected writing of John Hughlings Jackson* (Vol. II). London: Hodder and Stoughton. (Original work published 1874).

Klve, H., & Reitan, R. M. (1958). The effect of dysphasia and spatial distortions on Wechsler, Bellevue results. *Archives of Neurology and Psychiatry, 80,* 708–713.

Lezak, M. D. (1976). *Neuropsychological assessment.* New York: Oxford University Press.

Matthews, C. G., & Reitan, R. M. (1963). Relationship of differential abstraction ability levels to psychological test performance in mentally retarded subjects. *American Journal of Mental Deficiency, 68,* 235–244.

Reed, J. C., & Reitan, R. M. (1969). Verbal and performance difference among brain injured children with lateralized motor deficits. *Perceptual and Motor Skills, 29,* 747–752.

Reitan, R. M. (1955). Discussion: Symposium on the temporal lobe. *Archives of Neurology and Psychiatry, 74,* 569–570.

Reitan, R. M. (1959). Impairment of abstraction ability in brain damage: Quantitative versus qualitative changes. *Journal of Psychology, 48,* 97–102.

Reitan, R. M. (1960). The significance of dysphasia for intelligence and adaptive abilities. *Journal of Psychology, 56,* 355–376.

Reitan, R. M. (1967). Psychological changes associated with aging and with cerebral damage. *Mayo Clinic Proceedings, 42,* 653–673.

Reitan, R. M. (1971). Sensorimotor functions in brain-damaged and normal children of early school age. *Perceptual and Motor Skills, 32,* 655–664.

Reitan, R. M., & Fitzhugh, K. B. (1971). Behavioral deficits in groups with cerebrovascular lesions. *Journal of Consulting and Clinical Psychology, 3,* 215–223.

Reitan, R. M., & Shipley, R. E. (1963). The relationship of serum cholesterol changes on psychological abilities. *Journal of Gerontology, 18,* 350-356.

Reitan, R. M., & Tarshes, E. L. (1959). Differential effects of lateralized brain lesions on the Trailing Making Test. *Journal of Nervous and Mental Disease, 129,* 257-262.

Seretny, M., Gray, J., Hartlage, L., & Dean, R. (1985, August). *Survey of current issues in neuropsychology.* Paper presented at the meeting of the American Psychological Association, Los Angeles.

Spiers, P. A. (1981). Have they come to praise Luria or to bury him?: The Luria-Nebraska controversy. *Journal of Consulting and Clinical Psychology, 49,* 331-341.

Wheeler, L., & Reitan, R. M. (1962). The presence and laterality of brain damage predicted from responses to a short form aphasia screening test. *Perceptual and Motor Skills, 16,* 681-761.

2
Brain–Behavior Relationships

Lawrence J. Lewandowski

Over the past hundred years, a tremendous amount of brain-related research has been conducted. It is not possible to review all of the relevant research studies over this time period. Instead, an attempt will be made to bring the reader up-to-date with regard to present knowledge about the functioning of the human brain.

EARLY THEORIES

The history of beliefs about the workings of the human brain is both humorous and enlightening. For example, Aristotle and other early Greek thinkers suggested that the heart was the central control organ in the body that directed human behavior. Centuries later this viewpoint gave way to Galen's ventricular hypothesis. Galen, as well as others after him, argued that the internal chambers or ventricles of the brain were warehouses for the development of psychic spirits, which were necessary for executing behavior. This view went virtually unchallenged for over a thousand years, before scientists began to take a closer look at the brain matter itself (Clarke & Dewhurst, 1972).

From the Renaissance to the beginning of the nineteenth century, many different thoughts about brain structure and function were ventured. One viewpoint that found strong popularity, yet was short-lived, was that of phrenology. Phrenology was a practice advocated by Gall and Spurzheim (ca. 1820) that encouraged predictions about an individual's psychological faculties based upon the shape of his or her skull. The underlying premise of this practice was that brain areas underneath certain skull protrusions were more highly developed in certain people. Correlations were made between people with similar skull protrusions and psychological characteristics. Before long, phrenologists were identifying different areas of the skull with various psychological faculties. Dozens of phrenology maps were developed, each new one more complex than the last. It was this undisciplined practice of relating brain area to psychological function that fueled the strict localization movement.

SCIENTIFIC PROGRESS

Throughout the early 1800s, the issue of whether the brain was highly localized was heatedly debated. In 1861, a French physician named Broca presented clinical evidence that the function of speech was localized in the third frontal convolution of the left hemisphere. Since that historical claim, hundreds of clinical and experimental neuropsychological studies have been conducted. In 1870, Fritsch and Hitzig reported a landmark paper on the electrical excitability of the cerebrum. Applying electrical stimulation to the cortex of dogs, they successfully mapped the sensory and motor cortex in both hemispheres. Their secondary finding indicated that when the remaining two-thirds of the cortex was stimulated, no measureable behavioral change resulted. Quite naturally, this remaining two-thirds of the cortex was referred to as "silent areas." Since that time considerable research in medical and behavioral science has been conducted in an attempt to determine what goes on in those "silent areas."

It should be clear that beliefs about brain function have been erroneous much of the time and for hundreds of years. But despite all the misinterpretations and controversies, scientific discoveries have advanced brain science greatly, particularly over the last 25 years. Our present knowledge of brain anatomy, function, and pathology is more extensive and accurate than one would have projected in 1960. Yet history has taught us that there is much to learn about the workings of the brain; and the pursuit of scientific fact will remain a slow, evolving process.

LURIA'S THEORY

There are a variety of theories dealing with how the brain is organized and how it operates. For example, Hebb's (1949) cell assembly theory and MacLean's (1978) theory of the triune brain attempt to explain brain function from both a micro- and macroscopic perspective. No theoretical account of brain function is as complete as that proposed by Alexander Luria. Luria's views on brain function are widely quoted and have been useful in conceptualizing both research and clinical work. He has derived his ideas from investigations of adults with brain pathology. His ideas are highlighted primarily in two books, *Higher Cortical Functions in Man* (1966) and *The Working Brain* (1973).

As opposed to a strict localization view of brain structure and function, Luria proposes a more dynamic conceptualization of brain function. He suggests that conscious behavior is made up of a system of brain-related activities. He calls this complex composition of brain activities a "functional system." In other words, a function such as speaking or writing is mediated by a coordinated set of brain activities. An inability to speak or write would indicate a breakdown somewhere within the functional system. One would need to do further assessment in order to determine what part of the functional system best accounts for the disability. Luria also suggests that no specific brain area completely controls a given function. Therefore, if a particular brain area is damaged, a variety of behavioral disruptions may result. This phenomenon is referred to as "pluripotentiality." This term highlights the interdependence and communication between various brain structures. Hence, the notion of a functional system refers to a network or chain of brain substrates that are intricately linked to one another. The breakdown of a specific link in the chain will determine the qualitative aspects of behavioral deficits related to that functional system.

Units of the Brain

In order to operationalize Luria's notion of functional systems, one must have some overall sense of what is going on in various parts of the brain. Based on previous research and current thinking, Luria has proposed a comprehensive theory about how the brain is organized and what types of functions are subserved by specific brain units. Luria contends that the human brain is made up of three main blocks or functional units. All mental activity, and thus every functional system, draws from each of these three units.

Arousal

The first unit described by Luria is the arousal unit. This unit is comprised of a network of diffuse interacting structures at the brain stem and thalamic levels, also referred to as the reticular activating system. The arousal unit is primarily involved in filtering sensory input and adjusting the arousal level or tone of the cortex. It is crucial to one's ability to attend or respond to stimuli. Dysfunction in this unit can cause sleep disorders, difficulties in screening incoming stimuli, hyper- or hyporesponsiveness to situations, and lack of attention or concentration. Structures in the arousal unit are linked hierarchically to other brain areas, particularly the prefrontal cortex. Ontogenetically, this first brain unit develops very early. Damage to this unit in an adult may greatly affect vegetative functions and the ability to attend and adapt sufficiently to the environment. Developmental disturbances to this unit within the first year of life may have less drastic effects on the individual, but seem to cause problems of attention, hyperactivity, and inadequate filtering of information (Golden, 1981).

Sensory Reception and Integration

The second unit of the brain is the sensory reception and integration unit. This unit essentially identifies cortical brain areas posterior and inferior to the central sulcus. Within this second unit, Luria describes a suborganization that is hierarchical in nature. This same suborganization is applied to the parietal, temporal, and occipital lobes. The foundation of this unit is the primary zone, or primary projection area, within each of these three lobes in both hemispheres. The primary zone of the parietal lobe, for example, is located along the post-central gyrus and is chiefly responsible for the reception of somatosensory input, including touch, pain, temperature, and proprioception. The primary zone of the temporal lobe is located along the superior temporal gyrus. This is the primary projection area for auditory information. The primary zone of the occipital lobe is located in the posterior portion of each hemisphere. This zone is the primary projection area for incoming visual stimuli. Note that these primary zones within each lobe are modality specific. The specificity of cells in these primary zones has been well detailed in other sources (e.g., Hubel & Wiesel, 1963).

The secondary zone within each lobe is located adjacent to the primary zone. Here the degree of modal specificity is somewhat less, and the structure is composed of neurons that associate with other brain areas, including homologous areas of the contralateral hemisphere. In general these secondary zones, or association areas, are involved in the analysis, coding, and storing of information. For example, within the function of vision the secondary (association) area in the occipital lobe seems to be involved in temporal, spatial, and featural analysis of the visual stimulus. In the parietal lobe the secondary (association) area is involved in gnostic tactual functions; in other words, knowing what an object is by feeling it, and also knowing where your arm is located in space from the perception of moving it. Similarly, the association area in each temporal lobe serves to analyze auditory information.

At this secondary zone level, one begins to see an increase in hemispheric differentiation. The secondary zone of the left temporal lobe is more involved in the perception of speech sounds, while the right hemisphere appears to be more involved in the analysis of nonspeech sounds, particularly aspects of rhythm, pitch, and tone. In general, these secondary zones or association areas are involved with one's ability to recognize incoming stimuli, detect and analyze the information, and associate the information to previous experience.

Another zone within this second brain unit is the tertiary zone, located at the juncture of the parietal, occipital, and temporal lobes. In this zone, data from different sensory sources are integrated. There is much less modal specificity. In fact, this zone has been identified as multimodal or crossmodal in function.

The principal role of the tertiary zone is information organization, particularly as it relates to the simultaneous processing of information. It is in this zone that one achieves a high degree of analysis of incoming information. Here information from a particular modality, such as visual information, can be related to tactual or auditory input, and all information can be converted to symbolic representations. Disruption of the tertiary zone in either hemisphere tends not to produce overt sensory deficits, but instead yields deficits in higher levels of perceptual and cognitive functions, such as those associated with reading, writing, mathematics, and construction.

It should be pointed out that the three zones within this second brain unit are both developmental and hierarchical in nature. Whereas the primary zones develop early in life and deal with the reception of modality-specific information, the tertiary zones develop later in life and are involved in more complex, less modality-specific mental operations.

Programming, Regulation, and Verification of Activity

Luria refers to the third unit of the brain as that involved with programming, regulation, and verification of activity. While this brain unit receives orienting and sensory information from the other two brain units, it is essentially involved with motor output, planning, and evaluation of behavior. It, too, is described in terms of a suborganization.

The primary zone of this unit is the motor cortex located anterior to the central sulcus. This area of the brain is known to exert major control over motor impulses sent to the contralateral side of the body. The secondary zone or premotor area lies anterior to the motor strip. It is involved with preparing motor programs by analyzing, organizing, and sequencing motor acts, and then applying spatial and temporal analysis to ongoing movement. Corballis (1983) has suggested that the left hemisphere is preeminent in the execution of motor programs regarding both speech and limbs. The tertiary zones of this third brain unit lie in the most anterior part of the brain, the prefrontal lobe, and are also modality nonspecific.

In fact, the prefrontal lobe has many efferent and afferent connections with the other brain units. Luria (1973) and others have suggested that this brain area plays an important role in the formation of intentions and programs, as well as in planning and regulating the most complex forms of human behavior. In addition to planning, executing, and evaluating behavior, the prefrontal lobes are involved with selective attention, concentration, mental flexibility, and personality functioning such as the regulation of mood, judgment, and drives. Once again, this brain unit has both a hierarchical and developmental organization. The primary motor cortex is fully functional quite early in life, while the tertiary zones in the frontal lobe subserve much more complex functions and seem to develop gradually in childhood and adolescence.

Luria's theoretical formulation is rather macroscopic in nature. For example, he does not describe the functions of the nerve cell or the neurophysiologic mechanisms involved in memory. Nevertheless, most brain scientists have found Luria's model of brain function to be helpful in integrating research findings and understanding brain–behavior relationships.

CEREBRAL SPECIALIZATION

Throughout the twentieth century and, in particular, the last 20 years, there has been a dramatic growth in brain-related research. For the most part, brain scientists have been investigating brain structure–function relationships. Many discoveries have indicated that the two cerebral hemispheres, and certain relative areas within them, seem to be specialized for the execution of specific psychological functions. Although the research is far from conclusive, some of the widely held views regarding brain–behavior relationships merit discussion.

Anatomic and Functional Differences

Perhaps the most popular area of research in neuropsychology has to do with the investigation of anatomic and functional differences between the hemispheres. Studies involving split-brain subjects, hemispherectomy patients, sodium amytal testing, blood-flow analysis, evoked-potential recording, dichotic listening, visual half-field presentation, lateralized lesions, and simple sensory and motor functions have all yielded converging evidence regarding certain aspects of hemispheric functioning. In the most general sense, the left hemisphere is viewed as being the speech-producing hemisphere for most people, while the right hemisphere has been linked to certain nonspeech functions, such as visual ideation and visual-spatial organization. It is important to keep in mind that lateralization of functions is a relative, not an absolute, concept. It appears that both hemispheres are to a large extent capable of handling functions that may be better executed by a particular hemisphere. In fact, there are those who think that the hemispheres of the brain start out as equipotential and that left-hemispheric language specialization is imposed on brain organization (Moscovitch, 1977).

In addition to the question of how the hemispheres become specialized, there is considerable controversy over when the hemispheres become specialized. Some investigators, such as Lenneberg (1967) and Bryden and Allard (1978), have argued that increasing development in hemispheric specialization occurs as a child ages. Others, such as Kinsbourne and Hiscock (1977), have suggested that hemispheric specialization is essentially determined at birth and only changes qualitatively with age. Despite these controversies, few people would argue that anatomic and functional differences do exist between the hemispheres.

The homuspheres are similar at primary zone level

Behavioral Indices of Hemispheric Specialization

There are several behavioral indices of hemispheric specialization that are likely to be encountered by a clinician. At the level of primary zones, the two hemispheres are relatively symmetrical in structure and function. The neurological design in these primary zones is highly specific, such that a stroke or similar trauma to the left hemisphere motor strip will result in a right-sided hemiparesis. In a similar manner, a trauma to the right hemisphere motor strip will result in a left-sided hemiparesis. Damage to the entire primary zone of the left occipital lobe will result in a right visual field loss, while damage to the entire primary zone of the right occipital lobe will result in a left visual field loss. Damage to the primary zone in the left parietal lobe will result in sensory loss on the right side of the body, while damage to the right parietal primary zone will result in sensory loss on the left side of the body. Impairment to the primary auditory cortex in either temporal lobe, however, will only result in a mild sensory hearing loss in the contralateral ear. The sparing of auditory function under these conditions is due to a greater degree of bilateral neural representation for audition.

Secondary Zones - there is more homotheric asym'y

The secondary zones in the four lobes of the brain are more diffusely organized neurologically. Because of this diffuse organization there is more functional asymmetry between the hemispheres and more communication between hemispheres, that is, more interhemispheric transfer. These secondary zones are for the most part modality specific; thus the secondary zone of the occipital lobe receives information from the primary zone of the occipital lobe.

The function of this secondary zone includes the perception of visual information. The task of the secondary zone is to synthesize visual stimuli into a recognizable whole. Disturbances in this part of the brain have been known to result in visual agnosia, that is, an inability to recognize such things as simple objects, colors, or faces (Williams, 1970). Such agnosias are fairly rare and usually involve damage to the subcortical white matter and/or corpus callosum in addition to the occipital cortex. It appears that the inability to name objects, colors, or persons is more apt to result from a left occipital lesion, whereas difficulty in pictoral recognition is related to right occipital damage (Kolb & Wishaw, 1982).

Lesions involving the secondary zone of the left parietal lobe tend to

Visual agnosis - inab. to recognize such simple things as objects of faces

produce an inability to name objects from touch. It is assumed that tactile input, particularly from the right side of the body, is analyzed and coded in this secondary zone. In terms of the right parietal secondary zone, a lesion will tend to produce asterognosis, or tactile recognition errors, particularly with the left hand (Semmes, Weinstein, Ghent, & Teuber, 1960).

Damage to the secondary zones of the temporal lobes tends to result in disorders of auditory perception. These disorders include a disability in differentiating acoustic stimuli and in processing different combinations of sounds. The left hemisphere seems to be more involved with the synthesis of speech sounds and the linguistic aspects of auditory input, such as phonemic and semantic qualities. The right temporal association areas seem to be more involved in the acoustic properties of music, as well as nonverbal memory (Luria, 1973). Both temporal lobes have been shown to be involved in aspects of visual perception as well as emotion. The most discussed function of the temporal lobes involves the language processing of the left hemisphere. Damage to the association areas of the left hemisphere may produce a variety of auditory-language problems, including verbal memory loss, poor comprehension, and aphasia. *Tertiary Zone + Brain damage*

The areas of the temporal, parietal, and occipital lobes that border one another are referred to as tertiary zones. The zones are not modality specific, but rather crossmodal in nature. In these areas information of all forms is synthesized. In both hemispheres these zones are attributed with human cognitive processing. In the left hemisphere, damage to the tertiary zone could impair reading, writing, calculating, visual-motor construction, and language processing. Damage to the right tertiary zone is apt to result in visual-spatial difficulties found in drawing, building, dressing, writing, and moving. Secondarily, disturbances of memory and personality are found frequently with tertiary-zone damage. *Premotor Area + Lesion*

The premotor region of the frontal lobes includes an area known as Broca's area. Broca's area has been identified as the principal site of the motor control for speech. Other areas of the premotor region are involved in complex body movement. These areas that generate motor programs are refined by the extrapyramidal system. Lesions in this area could disrupt fluidity of movements and result in a disorder such as apraxia. Apraxia, or the inability to reproduce motor movement, seems to be primarily a left-hemisphere dysfunction. *Prefrontal + Lesion*

Lesions to the prefrontal regions, or tertiary zones of the frontal lobes, will affect motor programming and inhibit complex motor behavior. Damage to the left side may induce rigid, inflexible, or stereotypic behaviors, as well as problems with verbal fluency and attention. Damage to the prefrontal regions also has been related to personality changes. Lesions of the left prefrontal lobe have been linked to symptoms of depression, apathy, reduced sexual interest, and decreased verbal output, while lesions to the right prefrontal lobe have been related to such symptoms as immature behavior, lack of tact and social judgment, coarse language, inappropriate sexual behavior, and increased motor output. In general, damage to the frontal lobes has been linked to problems with memory, spatial orientation, and sequencing. These latter problems do not appear to be hemisphere specific and may result from lesions in either frontal lobe.

Luria has suggested that the frontal lobes are the last structures to have developed, both phylogenetically and ontogenetically. It is with this in mind that assumptions are made about the significance of the frontal and prefrontal areas of the human brain and how they set humans apart from lower species. One must not assume that the frontal lobes exclusively subserve the most complex aspects of human behavior. In fact, higher-level mental functions, such as memory, thought, reasoning, and emotion, have been difficult to pinpoint from a neuroscience perspective. Because these functions are so easily disrupted with lesions in any part of the brain, it is safe to say that elaborate networks, or "functional systems" as Luria would call them, are involved in the execution of complex functions.

Cognitive Functioning in Left and Right Hemispheres

Through various types of research, including lesion studies, sodium amytal testing, and blood-flow analysis, investigators have compiled a mosaic of left- and right-hemisphere cognitive functioning. Although far from conclusive, current knowledge suggests the following assumptions. The left hemisphere is the language-producing side of the brain, which is logical and analytical in nature; in most people the left hemisphere is involved in sequential solutions to problems; and the left side of the brain seems to be more concerned with detail and more directly associated with skilled, fine-motor movements. In contrast, the right hemisphere is more ideational and more pictorial than verbal in nature. It prefers a mode of simultaneously synthesizing and integrating information. The right hemisphere seems to be less concerned with details than it is with getting the big picture. The right hemisphere is more musically inclined and more apt to take governance in gross-motor activities, particularly as to how the body arranges itself in space. Its approach to problems and problem solutions tends to be more impulsive and holistic. In a sense, these are caricatures that have been derived from years of studying human hemisphere asymmetries. Obviously these cognitive styles of each hemisphere are exaggerated. Even in persons with only one hemisphere, it is doubtful that they would manifest all of the above-mentioned characteristics to a great degree. However, studies have indicated that people vary in terms of these hemisphere styles, and present custom finds clinicians referring to people as left-hemisphere and right-hemisphere individuals.

CHARACTERISTICS OF BRAIN PATHOLOGY

It is an understatement to say that the relationship between the brain and behavior is very complex. The overview presented above is far too simple compared with the actual effects of brain pathology. Clinicians are often reminded that neurological patients do not behave in accordance with the textbook. There are many reasons why an understanding of the behavioral affects of brain damage is not straightforward. *Diagnostic Issues*

Lezak (1983) mentions a number of diagnostic issues that are important in assessing a patient with neurological problems. The first issue to consider is the type or nature of the neuropathology. The type of pathology can include such things as a space-occupying tumor, a penetrating laceration of tissue, a hemorrhagic insult, or even a biochemical deficiency. Circumscribed damage to cortical tissue will tend to produce specific deficits, while widespread tissue disease, including that of white matter, will yield a greater range of behavioral impairment, particularly if chemical and electrical activities are disrupted.

Another diagnostic variable to be considered when studying neuropathology is the extent or severity of the disorder. Obviously there are differences between a minor head injury, such as hitting one's head on a door, and head injury from a car accident, in which the skull is fractured and unconsciousness results. Similarly, vascular accidents, tumors, and disease processes can all vary in extent or severity. In some cases, the more brain tissue damaged or diseased, the more extensive the functional impairment. The presence of prolonged coma, rapid deterioration, and disturbance of vegetative functions are other indications of the extent and severity of neuropathology.

An important consideration when assessing the effects of neuropathology is the location of the brain damage. A large tumor in the right frontal lobe may impair functions only to a subtle degree, whereas a small lesion around Broca's area in the left hemisphere may severely affect speech and right-sided motor functions. As previously discussed, damage in particular parts of the brain often results in predictable types of behavioral impairment. Therefore, knowing the location of a lesion may help the patient better understand his or her weaknesses and aid in future management. Of course, location is of utmost concern to the neurosurgeon, particularly when working near speech centers, the visual cortex, or motor-control areas.

A diagnostic variable that is important for the patient's outcome is the velocity of the neuropathology. In a sense, velocity refers to the rate of onset of the pathology, its present status, and its eventual course. Certain types of pathology, such as cerebral palsy, originate at or before birth and are static disorders, in which no further neuropathology occurs. In other examples of neuropathology, such as a stroke, the trauma occurs suddenly but the damage resolves over time, some more quickly than others. Certain types of tumors and degenerative diseases, such as Parkinson's disease, multiple sclerosis, and

Alzheimer's disease, are progressive in nature. Once again, the rate of progression is variable and often difficult to assess in terms of a patient's prognosis. Another significant diagnostic consideration is the difference in neuropsychological outcome between congenital and acquired neuropathology. For example, there are qualitative differences in functioning between children who are born with hydrocephalus, cerebral palsy, or other brain anomalies, and children (particularly after age five) or adults who acquire brain injury later in life. The former tends to affect functioning in a more general than specific manner. Others have written extensively on this subject (see Spreen, Tupper, Risser, Tuokko, & Edgell, 1984).

The variables discussed thus far are very important in determining a patient's overall impairment and outcome. However, one cannot overlook other patient variables that affect the recovery from neuropathology. Some of these patient variables include age and sex, family medical history, and present and previous health status.

Other factors that contribute to the overall picture of a patient with neuropathology and that combine to determine a patient's resulting functional status may include handedness, motivation, and family support. Perhaps this is why the assessment and treatment of patients with neuropathology is such a challenging endeavor. In order to understand better the interactions of these clinical variables, as well as the brain–behavior relationships previously discussed, it is worthwhile to review some major neuropathological disorders and their characteristics.

TYPES OF NEUROPATHOLOGICAL DISORDERS

Vascular Disorders

One of the leading causes of brain disorder after the age of 50 is vascular disorder. The most common of these disorders is the cerebral vascular accident commonly referred to as stroke. A stroke can result from a variety of vascular problems, including thrombosis, embolism, or aneurysm. In general, a stroke refers to a severe restriction in blood flow that denies needed oxygen and nutrients to areas of the brain. The temporary and reversible decrease in blood flow to a portion of the brain is called ischemia. When blood flow and oxygen to the brain are decreased for a long period of time, changes in cell function can occur and tissue can die. This form of pathology is called infarct. Depending upon the severity of the stroke, an infarct of varying size may result. Generally speaking, the larger the infarct, the more severe the consequences.

A thrombotic stroke results from the gradual occlusion of a blood vessel by the buildup of fat deposits on the vessel wall. Usually, thrombotic strokes are preceded by small strokes or transient ischemic attacks (TIAs). TIAs also can occur as a result of vascular changes accompanying a migraine headache.

Usually, any neurological symptoms from TIAs clear within hours. Most frequently the occurrence of TIAs signals the gradual occlusion of arteries and can act as a forewarning of a future stroke. An embolism refers to an obstruction of a blood vessel by some foreign particle, clot, or fatty deposit that usually flows from another area of the body and gets lodged in a brain vessel. In such cases, the restriction of blood flow is immediate and without warning.

Another form of stroke involves hemorrhage. This can occur from a rupture of an aneurysm, whereby a weak vessel wall becomes distended and eventually bursts. This type of stroke also has a sudden onset. The results of this stroke depend on the severity of the bleed. When massive bleeding occurs the condition may be fatal.

Most of the time strokes will affect cortical functioning, usually on only one side of the brain. Given the nature of the vascular network, the stroke may affect a fairly large area of the brain. It is for this reason that strokes often impair motor functioning on the side of the body contralateral to the damage. As swelling subsides and other physical changes take place following stroke, recovery begins. Some recovery of sensory, motor, and cognitive functioning is almost always found, yet complete recovery seldom occurs. Left-hemisphere stroke is the most common cause of aphasia in adults. There seems to be a greater tendency toward bilateralization of function in left-handers and females, which makes some of them more resilient in speech following stroke (Castro-Caldas, Ferro, & Grosso, 1979).

Head Injuries

Head injury is becoming an increasingly common form of brain damage, particularly among children and young adults. Most head injuries are caused by vehicular or industrial accidents and other violent acts. Onset is usually sudden, and the cause of the injuries is frequently known. There are two types of head injuries, which are commonly referred to as open- and closed-head injuries. Open-head injuries involve lacerations, wounds, or penetration from skull fragments. Closed-head injuries result from a blow to the head that does not penetrate the skull. These injuries range from minor to severe. Minor head injury is characterized by a brief loss of consciousness without demonstrable neurological changes. After such an injury, higher mental functions may be impaired for a period lasting hours, depending upon a number of factors. Some suggest that subtle changes in functioning following a minor head injury are long lasting (Levin, Benton, & Grossman, 1982).

The duration of unconsciousness or length of coma can serve as an index of the severity of the injury. In cases of prolonged coma, the reticular formation is usually involved. If the brainstem structures have been damaged to a significant degree, the injury may be fatal or leave the patient in a nonfunctional state. These severe closed-head injuries are often accompanied by hematoma, hemorrhage, and swelling. One perplexing aspect of closed-head injury involves the site of the trauma and the resulting behavioral impairment. A blow to the head in one particular area may cause the brain inside the skull to crash against the opposite side of the skull. It is not uncommon for the damage to occur in both places or in the area opposite the blow. This effect is called a contre-coup. This effect can explain how a rather focal blow to the head may cause diffuse and bilateral brain dysfunction, particularly when the trauma results from a great deal of momentum on impact or head rotation.

As discussed earlier, closed-head injuries may result in memory loss, slowed thinking processes, decreased ability to concentrate and make decisions, and inability to perform complex mental operations. The study of minor closed-head injury is presently receiving great research interest and appears to be unveiling subtle neuropsychological deficits, even after slight head injuries (Rimel, Giordour, Barth, Ball, & Jane, 1981).

Neoplasms

Another category of neuropathology is tumor. Intracranial tumors, or neoplasms, appear in many varieties (see Bannister, 1978). A meningioma, for example, is an encapsulated tumor that is easily separated from nervous tissue with good results. Generally, such noninvasive tumors of the nervous system tend to be benign. Tumors that are brain invasive, or space occupying, tend to exert more of an effect on cerebral functioning. Several of these tumors belong to the family of gliomas.

The glioblastoma multiforme is a rapidly growing tumor that occurs most frequently in middle age. Onset is fairly acute, and the average survival period is about one year, even with surgery. With this tumor, behavioral manifestations occur rather quickly and are initially focal. However, within weeks or months the cerebral involvement extends and disrupts many different functions.

A medullablastoma is a rapidly growing tumor of the vermis of the cerebellum found almost exclusively in children. It characteristically metasticizes to the surface of the central nervous system via the subarachnoid space. The survival expectancy is one to two years.

An astrocytoma is a slow-growing cystlike mass that occurs more commonly in adults. The cerebellum is a frequent site of an astrocytoma. Given the slow growth rate, the onset of symptoms may be gradual and subtle. Once discovered, these tumors are treatable, with survival periods ranging from five to twenty years.

Oligodendrogliomas are slow-growing tumors that calcify and become solid, usually found in adults. These are also treatable, with a fairly good prognosis. As with other gliomas, there is usually negative change in cerebral functioning associated with the presence of the tumor. Even after successful surgery or therapy, there is generally residual impairment.

Metastatic tumors usually arise from carcinomas in some other part of the body, usually of the lung, breast, thyroid, or gastrointestinal tract, which spread to the brain. These tumors generally metasticize within the brain such that treatment only postpones the inevitable outcome. When multiple tumors exist, particularly in both hemispheres, the assessment task is complicated. In such cases, however, rapid mental deterioration usually occurs.

In general, the presence of a tumor may initially give rise to subtle, affective, cognitive, sensory, and/or motor dysfunction. Due to tissue invasion, intracranial pressure increases and headache is a common symptom. Fatigue, nausea, and mental confusion may also occur. Tumors tend to produce focal effects in terms of both motor and cognitive deficits. Depending upon the site, size, and type of tumor, various functional problems will be reported. Seizures represent a common problem both pre- and postoperatively. Almost always, the course is one of continuing deterioration, unless treatment is successful.

Degenerative Diseases

There are many degenerative diseases of the central nervous system. Among these are various forms of dementia, neuromuscular disorders, cerebellar ataxia, and demyelinating disease. Dementia refers to diffuse deterioration in mental functioning, particularly involving memory and thought processes, as well as emotion and conduct. Presenile dementias, such as Pick's and Alzheimer's diseases, are progressive disorders that afflict adults, usually between 40 and 60 years of age. Atrophy of the cerebral cortex is found in both diseases. While Pick's disease generally affects the frontal temporal lobes, Alzheimer's disease is more diffuse. Both conditions are sometimes misdiagnosed as psychiatric disorders. Both slowly progress until death occurs, usually within 10 to 20 years.

Senile dementia involves cerebral changes with old age in the absence of specific neurological disorders. Autopsy often reveals small brain size, a thinner than normal cortex, deep sulci, and dilatated ventricles. Neuronal cell degeneration can be seen microscopically. The accompanying mental changes may be sweeping. A loss in recent memory ability is one of the first things reported. Impaired thought processes in judgment, reasoning, and abstraction are commonly present. Affect often becomes unstable, while delusions and hallucinations may occur. Attention, concentration, and activity level are usually affected. Arteriosclerosis, hardening of the arteries, may be a concomitant factor.

The other diseases that are known as subcortical dementias are Parkinson's and Huntington's diseases. Parkinson's disease primarily involves degeneration of cells in the substantia nigra associated with abnormally low concentrations of the neurotransmitter dopamine. Symptoms of the disease include increasing rigidity and tremor, loss of facial expression, disturbed posture and gait, monotone voice, and gradual motor weakness. Tremors are worse at rest and characterized by pill-rolling movements of the fingers. The response to medical treatment is variable, but some medications have had positive effects. The extent of cognitive and psychological changes associated with Parkinson's disease has not been fully detailed. Huntington's chorea is a hereditary disease associated with movement disturbances and mental deterioration. The disease attacks the basal ganglia and cortex, usually beginning during early adulthood. The actual cause of the disease is unknown, though it is assumed to be chemical rather than structural. The first symptom is usually the presence of rapid, jerky movements, which progress to the limbs, and dysarthria of speech. Mental changes develop a few years after onset of the chorea and progress to dementia. The disease is fatal in about 15 years.

Primary demyelinating diseases represent another category of neuropathology. Among the most well known of these diseases is multiple sclerosis (MS). MS is a slowly progressive neurological disorder that begins in early adulthood. It is characterized by multiple lesions of the central nervous system, in which the myelin sheath around nerve axons is broken down. The demyelination occurs most frequently in the spinal cord, but also in the white matter of the brain. There is no known cause underlying the disease. Clinical symptoms often involve impaired visual acuity and/or motility. The typical symptoms include motor and sensory losses, which may go into remission but usually worsen. The course of the disease is unpredictable, and diagnosis can be difficult. There may be cognitive changes in some cases, but mental deterioration is not usually associated with the disease. A similar neuropathology is amyotrophic lateral sclerosis (ALS), or Lou Gehrig's disease. ALS results from motor neuron degeneration, beginning usually in the cord and moving up to the brainstem; it sometimes involves the motor cortex. The course is progressive, and eventually the muscular atrophy affects the control of vital organs, leading to death. There are no specific cognitive or psychological deficits associated with ALS.

Infectious Diseases

A category of central nervous system pathology that tends to be progressive in nature has to do with infection. There are different types of infectious disorders, among which is a condition known as herpes simplex encephalitis. Of those who survive this rare disease, most have lost brain tissue in the frontal and temporal lobes as well as subcortical structures. The behaviorial manifestations of this pathology include poor impulse control, lack of goal-directed activity, and inappropriate social behavior, as well as memory and thinking disturbances. Another type of infectious brain disturbance is a brain abscess. Brain abscesses are usually caused by the spread of bacterial infection from the ear, sinus, blood stream, or infected head injury. They can be confused with tumors because they produce focal signs and many similar symptoms, such as intracranial pressure, headache, and papilledema. Treatment may involve surgery and/or chemotherapy. Due to the actual death of nerve cells, there is usually some functional loss associated with the site of the abscess.

Toxic Disorders

The last category of neurological disorders has to do with toxic conditions. Perhaps the most well-known toxic disorder is alcohol induced, a severe form of which is called Korsakoff syndrome. Korsakoff syndrome is chiefly a memory disturbance that involves a lack of ability to consolidate, retrieve, and utilize new information. It results from the degeneration of the dorsal medial thalamic nucleus and is produced by chronic alcoholism. Oscar-Berman (1980) delineated other aspects of cognitive and motivational impairment, including slowed mental processing, premature responding, and diminished ability to use cues or profit from mistakes. She suggests that the multiplicity of deficits observed in alcoholic Korsakoff patients can be linked to a multiplicity of sites of brain damage. The effects of other toxic substances on brain function have been poorly delineated as yet. Experiments with animals have shown considerable changes in brain tissue and behavior, particularly when animals are subjected to high levels of metal or various chemical intoxications. Various other studies have investigated the effects of industrial toxins on employee brain function.

There are many more neuropathological disorders that could be discussed. It is hoped that this brief review of some of the major disorders is helpful in applying brain-behavior concepts. The hundreds of different neuropathological disorders, each with its own etiology and all interacting with the many variables discussed earlier, make neuropsychology a stimulating field for research, assessment, and patient management.

CONCLUSION

In this chapter an attempt has been made to present an overview of past and present thoughts about brain function. A theoretical framework borrowed from Luria was described and used as a basis for explaining brain-behavior relationships. At a more specific level, findings regarding hemispheric specialization and regional specialization of function were discussed. Each of the lobes within a cerebral hemisphere was described in terms of primary, secondary, and tertiary zones as defined by Luria. It was pointed out that, generally, the more complex the function, the more complex is the neurological substrate that executes the function. Therefore functions such as memory, thought, reasoning, and emotion tend to be diffusely organized in the brain, and lesions in many places throughout the brain may disturb these functions. This issue became more clear in a discussion of brain pathology characteristics associated with tumors, dementia, head injury, stroke, and demyelinating diseases. Also, major variables that clinicians must consider in assessing patients were discussed. The interaction of these variables as exemplified by categories of brain pathology served to illustrate how difficult neuropsychological assessment can be and how much research is still needed in this area.

The study of neuropsychology, or brain–behavior relationships, has gone beyond the "strip-mining" stage. Scientists and clinicians are digging deeper to unravel mysteries of the human brain and its functioning. Modern medical technology, using such devices as computerized axial tomography (CAT), magnetic resonance imaging (MRI), positron emission tomography (PET), and brain electrical activity mapping (BEAM), as well as clinical experimental neuropsychological studies, continue to improve the foundation of knowledge concerning brain and behavior. Research with normal and brain-damaged humans and animals is providing converging information that has been helpful in our understanding and treatment of a number of neuropathological disorders. It appears that brain science will continue to make rapid growth. It is to be hoped that these new developments will replace old ideas, so that views about the brain will continue to improve, rather than lie in error for centuries at a time, as was once the case.

REFERENCES

Bannister, R. (1978). *Brain's clinical neurology* (5th ed.). New York: Oxford University Press.

Bryden, M. P., & Allard, F. (1978). Dichotic listening and the development of linguistic processes. In M. Kinsbourne (Ed.), *Asymmetrical function of the brain* (pp. 392–404). Cambridge, England: Cambridge University Press.

Castro-Caldas, A., Ferro, J. M., & Grosso, T. J. (1979, June). *Age, sex, and type of aphasia in stroke patients.* Paper presented at the meeting of the International Neuropsychological Society, Noordwijkerhout, Holland.

Clarke, E., & Dewhurst, L. (1972). *An illustrated history of brain function.* Oxford, England: Sanford.

Corballis, M. C. (1983). *Human laterality.* New York: Academic Press.

Golden, C. J. (1981). The Luria–Nebraska children's battery: Theory and formulation. In G. Hynd & J. Obrzut (Eds.), *Neuropsychological assessment of the school-age child* (pp. 277–302). New York: Grune & Stratton.

Hebb, D. O. (1949). *The organization of behavior: A neuropsychological theory.* New York: John Wiley and Sons.

Hubel, D. H., & Wiesel, T. N. (1963). Receptive fields of cells in striate cortex of very young, visually inexperienced kittens. *Journal of Neurophysiology, 26,* 994–1002.

Kinsbourne, M., & Hiscock, M. (1977). Does cerebral dominance develop? In S. J. Segalowicz & F. Gruber (Eds.), *Language development and neurological theory* (pp. 125–166). New York: Academic Press.

Kolb, B., & Wishaw, I. (1982). *Fundamentals of human neuropsychology.* San Francisco: Freeman Press.

Lenneberg, E. (1967). *Biological foundations of language.* New York: John Wiley & Sons.

Levin, H. S., Benton, A. L., & Grossman, R. G. (1982). *Neurobehavioral consequences of closed head injury.* New York: Oxford University Press.

Lezak, M. D. (1983). *Neuropsychological assessment.* New York: Oxford University Press.

Luria, A. R. (1966). *Higher cortical functions in man.* New York: Basic Books.

Luria, A. R. (1973). *The working brain.* New York: Basic Books.

MacLean, P. (1978). A mind of three minds: Educating the triune brain. In *Education and the brain* (pp. 308-342), 77th Yearbook of the National Society for the Study of Education, Part II. Chicago: Chicago University Press.

Moscovitch, M. (1977). The development of lateralization of language functions and its relation to cognitive and linguistic development: A review and some theoretical speculations. In S. J. Segalowicz & F. Gruber (Eds.), *Language development and neurological theory* (pp. 193-211). New York: Academic Press.

Oscar-Berman, M. (1980). Neuropsychological consequences of long-term chronic alcoholism. *American Scientist, 68,* 410-419.

Rimel, R. W., Giordour, B., Barth, J. T., Ball, T. J., & Jane, J. A. (1981). Disability caused by minor head injury. *Neurosurgery, 9,* 221-228.

Semmes, J. S., Weinstein, L., Ghent, L., & Teuber, H. L. (1960). *Somatosensory changes after penetrating brain wounds in man.* Cambridge, MA: Harvard University Press.

Spreen, O., Tupper, D., Risser, A., Tuokko, H., & Edgell, D. (1984). *Human developmental neuropsychology.* New York: Oxford University Press.

Williams, M. (1970). *Brain damage and the mind.* Harmondsworth, England: Penguin.

3

The Neurological Examination As It Relates to Neuropsychological Issues

Kimford J. Meador
and
F. T. Nichols

The medical specialty with which neuropsychologists have closest interface is likely to be neurology. Whether the neuropsychologist evaluates patients on referral from neurologists or wishes to obtain neurological evaluations on patients already evaluated with neuropsychological procedures, it is important to be aware of the context and content of the neurological examination in order to bring the unique contributions of each to bear on the most appropriate evaluation of a given patient.

It is obvious that both the context and content of the neurological examination differ from those of neuropsychological evaluation procedures. Even when there is overlap, the focus of these items is on different issues. While in comparison with the neuropsychological examination, the neurological examination may be lacking in precise quantitative measurement of diverse aspects of cognition, it provides information relative to noncognitive functions not covered by the neuropsychological examination. Further, the neurological examination addresses issues of etiology, such as infections, genetic disorders, metabolic problems, and a variety of other phenomena that typically are not addressed by neuropsychological assessment procedures. Thus, the issue is not so much which examination approach is the more sensitive to central nervous system problems, as it is to what extent the neurological and neuropsychological assessments contribute to an understanding of the given patient in his or her medical social milieu.

HISTORICAL PERSPECTIVE

The neurological examination has developed from a series of observations linking specific cerebral lesions with associated patterns of deficits (i.e., signs and symptoms). Historically, the first recorded observation of this type was approximately five millennia ago. The Edwin Smith surgical papyrus translates the writings of an Egyptian physician from about 3500 B.C. This narrative probably represents the first report not only of aphasia, but also of a seizure:

> A man having a wound in his temple . . . perforating his temporal bone . . . ; if thou ask of him concerning his malady, he speak not to thee, . . . copious tears fall from both his eyes, . . . if thou puttest thy fingers on the mouth of the wound . . . , he shudder exceedingly . . . (McHenry, 1969).

Hippocrates noted the importance of the brain in cognitive function, referring to the brain as the organ of "intellect" and the "guiding spirit" (Luria, 1980).

> Men ought to know that from the brain, and from the brain only, arise our pleasures, joys, laughter and jests, as well as our sorrows, pains, griefs and tears. Through it, in particular, we think, see, hear, and distinguish the ugly from the beautiful, the bad from the good, the pleasant from the unpleasant. . . . It is the same thing which makes us mad or delirious, inspires us with dread and fear, whether by night or by day, brings sleeplessness, inopportune mistakes, aimless anxieties, absent-mindedness, and acts that are contrary to habit (McHenry, 1969).

Hippocrates also reported the association of right hemiparesis and aphasia: "A woman . . . became unable to articulate and the right arm was paralyzed . . ." (McHenry, 1969).

However, an appreciation of the brain as the seat of cognitive functions was not generally accepted until many years later. This helps explain the persistent allusions in our language to the association of the heart with the emotions. If the views of Hippocrates had been accepted earlier, a different organ might be revered on St. Valentine's day.

In the second century A.D., Galen made one of the first crude attempts to localize mental phenomena in the structures of the brain. According to his theory, the frontal lobes were the seat of the soul and the source of animal spirits. Vital bodily humors from the liver were transported in the blood to the *rete mirabile*, where they were converted into psychic humors as they entered the brain. Throughout the Middle Ages, the concept that cognition was localized in the substance of the brain vied with the concept that psychic humors in the ventricles controlled mental function. This idea of ventricular localization was probably derived from Herophilus (ca. 300 B.C.) and persisted well into the Renaissance. Even Leonardo da Vinci depicted this ventricular/humoral theory in a drawing of the human head.

The genuine scientific beginnings of functional localization in the brain awaited the nineteenth century. At times it reached ridiculous proportions in the school of phrenology, which assigned a variety of complex cognitive functions (e.g., wit, love of parents, prudence, sexual love, etc.) to specific portions of cerebral gyri. On the opposite extreme, the holistic view contended that the brain functioned as a single unit. By the end of the nineteenth century, the localizationists held the upper ground through a series of striking observations.

In 1861, Paul Broca described a man with a lesion centered in the left frontal operculum, which actually extends beyond Broca's area proper. In all likelihood, the lesion was produced by a series of infarctions secondary to meningovascular syphilis. The patient has been referred to by the eponym of Tan because the extent of his verbal output was "tan-tan." In this setting of severe motor aphasia, the patient's comprehension was remarkably intact. This observation led Broca to conclude that the motor engrams for language were located in the posterior one-third of the left inferior frontal gyrus. Thirteen years later, Carl Wernicke described another patient who was the antithesis of Broca's case. Wernicke's patient exhibited a severe comprehension deficit combined with intact verbal fluency. The lesion was in the region of the posterior one-third of the left superior temporal gyrus. Wernicke concluded that the sensory engrams for language were located in this region. Ferrier's demonstration of the differential patterns of motor movement produced by electrical stimulation of the cortex furthered the concept of localized function. In the later nineteenth century, Golgi and Cajal demonstrated that the brain was not a homogenous mass, but made up of discrete cellular elements. Later, the full spectrum of cerebral cytoarchitectural differentiation became apparent, implying regional differences in function.

These and other observations provided strong support to localizationism and laid the foundation for the modern neurological examination. In the early twentieth century, the balance of opinion between localizationist and holistic views swung back toward the holistic view under the weight of experimental evidence of diffuse distribution of certain functions (e.g., Lashley's experiments on localization of memory), but more recently the pendulum of opinion has begun its swing back toward localizationism. As is often the case when two schools of scientific thought mount strong conflicting arguments, the truth lies somewhere between the two views. Any theory of brain function is at best a metaphorical description. Each description is valid in its predictive capacity and in its ability to explain and offer insight into brain mechanisms. Each metaphor is inadequate to the extent that it fails to explain brain mechanisms and to the degree that it focuses attention away from certain aspects of brain function. The fallacy of strict localizationism is that externally observed behavioral symptoms occurring in association with focal cerebral lesions are used as a basis for assigning specific complex behavioral functions to discrete anatomical locations. As Hughlings Jackson so aptly pointed out, the localization of a symptom associated with a lesion in a circumscribed area of the brain is not synonymous with localization of the particular function. Sir Charles Sherrington also viewed brain function as a dynamic process across a distributed neuronal network. His description of 80 years ago echoes the current view:

> It is as if the Milky Way entered upon some cosmic dance. Swiftly the brain becomes an enchanted loom where millions of flashing shuttles weave a dissolving pattern, always a meaningful pattern though never an abiding one; a shifting harmony of subpatterns. (Jastrow, 1983)

BASIS OF THE NEUROLOGICAL EXAMINATION

Our present concept of brain mechanisms views neurobehavioral function as an analysis and synthesis of information coded as specific temporo-spatial patterns of neural activity occurring across a network of neural assemblies. Neural activity encompasses not only propagated electrical discharges, but also postsynaptic potential and neurochemical, membrane, and cellular (DNA/RNA/protein) changes. While the brain's highly differentiated cytoarchitecture and a mass of experimental data strongly suggest that individual cellular columns and local neural assemblies perform different processing roles, overt behavior is always the function of the activity in a network of neurons including both cortical and subcortical structures. A lesion at any one point in the network may shut down the processing capacity of the entire network. Furthermore, lesions at different points in the network may produce similar behavioral deficits. A single neuron or a group of neurons may be involved in many neuronal networks, depending on the task demands. The symptoms, signs, and behavioral deficits produced by a discrete lesion are the product of a pattern of deficits produced by overlapping networks that are functionally unable to "rewire" around a common set of damaged neuronal tracks and analyzers. That pattern is the key to the neurological exam. Through the pattern of deficits (i.e., signs and symptoms), the physician is able to localize the lesion, generate differential diagnoses, provide prognosis, and direct therapy.

More than any other portion of the physical examination, performance of the neurological examination varies with the individual patient and disease state. The physician uses a neurological examination based on a skeletal framework that is shaped and expanded depending on the patient's history and the results of the ongoing examination. During the history and exam, the physician should be constantly searching for performance discrepancies, pathological signs, and neurological asymmetries that can be fitted into a pattern of deficits consistent with known brain mechanisms and disease states. In this chapter, the neurological examination is described as it relates to neuropsychological issues and disease.

GENERAL PHYSICAL EXAMINATION

The general physical exam is an important accompaniment to the neurological exam in patients with altered mental status. For example, systemic diseases such as hypoxia, hypertension, hypoperfusion, uremia, and liver failure can all affect cognition. Vital signs may give clues as to the best places to look for organic causes of altered mental status:

Pulse: Tachycardia and bradycardia may impair cerebral perfusion, while arrhythmias (e.g., atrial fibrillation) may impair perfusion as well as predispose to embolic phenomena. Pulsus paradoxus may be seen with severe obstructive pulmonary disease or in pericardial effusion with tamponade.

Blood Pressure: Elevated blood pressure suggests the possibilities of malignant hypertension, intracerebral hemorrhage, and increased risk of cerebral infarction. Orthostatic hypotension may produce mental clouding, dizziness, and symptoms of vertebro-basilar insufficiency.

Respiration: Tachypnea may be seen with hypoxia, other pulmonary problems, sepsis, or severe liver disease. Hypoventilation may accompany severe brain injury or respiratory failure of other causes. Cheyne-stokes respiration is commonly due to CNS causes but may also be seen in older patients and in congestive heart failure. Kussmal respirations may result from an acidosis (especially diabetic ketoacidosis). Apneustic breathing is seen with brainstem dysfunction.

Temperature: Elevation of temperature generally implies an infectious process that may directly involve the brain (e.g., meningitis, encephalitis, brain abscess) or secondarily affect the brain (e.g., sepsis, pneumonia, subacute bacterial endocarditis). Hypothermia may be seen in patients suffering from exposure, hypothyroidism, and drug intoxication.

The skin should be examined for cyanosis or edema as evidence of cardiopulmonary disease. The presence of petechiae suggests abnormal platelet function and an increased hemorrhagic risk. Splinter hemorrhages suggest embolic phenomena. The stigmata of phakomatoses (e.g., telangiectasia, facial angiomas, ashleaf spots, cafe-au-lait spots, and neurofibromas) might indicate specific intracerebral structural abnormalities. The skin, especially of the head, should be examined for evidence of contusions, which suggests direct brain injury or subdural/epidural hematomas. Auscultation of the head and neck should be performed. Cranial arterial bruits may be indicative of an arteriovenous malformation. A venous bruit interior to the external auditory canal raises the possibility of increased intracranial pressure. The bruit is abolished by light pressure over the ipsilateral jugular vein or by valsalva maneuver. A bruit over the carotid suggests the presence of vascular disease. The ears are examined for the presence of otitis media, raising the possibility of associated brain abscess, and for the presence of blood behind the tympanic membrane (i.e., Battle's sign), which frequently accompanies basilar skull fractures. The examination of the nose includes checking for the presence of cerebrospinal fluid rhinorrhea (which predisposes to recurrent meningitis) and for neoplastic sources (which is usually seen in diabetes and may directly invade the brain). Pain on percussion over the frontal or maxillary sinuses suggests sinusitis and the possibility of associated brain abscess. Examination of the mouth and throat may reveal infectious or neoplastic sources. Paleness of the mucous membranes will be present in severe anemia. The neck should be examined for suppleness; a stiff neck suggests meningeal irritation such as is seen with infection or subarachnoid hemorrhage. The size of the thyroid gland should be assessed, as both hyperthyroidism and hypothyroidism may produce abnormalities in cognition. Auscultation and percussion of the chest may reveal pulmonary dysfunction such as pneumonia, congestive heart failure, obstructive airway disease, tumor, and effusions. The cardiovascular exam should assess rate, rhythm, rubs, clicks, murmurs, cardiac size, and function in order to rule out hypoperfusion, hypoxia, and/or embolic sources (e.g., subacute bacterial endocarditis [SBE] and other valvular disease). The abdominal exam should specifically check liver size, as an enlarged liver raises the possibility of metastatic disease, alcoholic hepatitis, or infectious hepatitis with resultant hepatic failure and encephalopathy. Gastric resection or malabsorption will predispose the patient to dementia secondary to nutritional deficiencies (e.g., Korsakoff's syndrome). The abdominal exam may also reveal neoplastic sources.

THE NEUROLOGICAL EXAMINATION

The Mental Status Examination

The neurological examination proper classically begins with the mental status exam. The first item is the level of consciousness, which is rated as alertness, stupor or lethargy (i.e., depressed, but arousable), semicoma (i.e., responds to pain), or coma (i.e., no response). In addition to these general labels, it is always preferable to state specifically the patient's response (e.g., responds to pain with purposeful movement) Orientation should be noted to person, place, and time. Again, it is preferable to record the patient's specific answers. For instance, a patient disoriented only to the month would be at a much higher level than a patient who thought that the year was 1936.

The assessment of memory is divided into three parts: (1) immediate memory, which is essentially a measure of attention; (2) recent memory, which is the capacity to learn or make new memories, and (3) remote memory, which represents the long-term memory store. Remote memories are relatively resistant to disease. Remote memory may be spared to a large degree, while recent memory is impaired in a variety of diffuse encephalopathies or early in idiopathic degenerative dementias. A recent memory disorder may exist in relative isolation following focal lesions in the mesial temporal lobes, septal nuclei, and dorsomedial thalamus. Immediate memory and cognitive capacity to some degree are tested by digit spans. In general, a normal person should be able to repeat seven random digits forward and five digits backwards (i.e., recall five digits in reverse of the order given). Recent verbal memory may be assessed at the bedside by giving the patient four objects to remember (e.g., horse, apple, table, 43). The patient should repeat the four objects to insure that he has understood the test items. Other verbal items in the examination are presented and serve as a distractor. Three to five minutes following verbal distraction, the patient is asked to recall the four objects, and the number correctly remembered is recorded (e.g., two of four objects at five minutes). If the patient fails to recall the objects, then a second trial, or cuing, may be used further to delineate the deficit. While recent verbal memory may be disordered in a variety of diffuse disease states, it may be specifically impaired by lesions of the left (i.e., dominant) temporal lobe. In contrast, lesions of the right temporal lobe may preferentially decrement visuospatial recent memory. When the diagnosis or exam suggests right-temporal pathology, the encoding of visuospatial memories may be tested easily at the bedside in patients with otherwise intact visuospatial skills by having them copy a figure such as a Rey-Osterrieth complex figure (Lezak, 1983) and then reproduce the drawing immediately and at a 30-minute delay. This is a very sensitive test for right frontal temporal dysfunction. Remote memory may be assessed to a large degree via details in the personal history. If a more objective measure is desired at the bedside, one might ask the patient to name the last five presidents. However, the socioeducational pitfalls of using this single question as a measure of remote memory must be borne in mind.

In the vast majority of patients, the left cerebral hemisphere is dominant for propositional language. Thus assessment of propositional language may be thought of essentially as a measure of left cerebral function. This will even hold true for most sinestrals (i.e., left-handers) and ambidextrous persons, although to a lesser extent. They will tend to show an increase of mixed cerebral dominance, and, in a small minority, right cerebral dominance for language. One should keep in mind that our division of left and right cerebral functions is based on the general population. The distribution of various functions may vary with an individual, especially if there is a prior history of cerebral damage in childhood or personal/family history of sinestrals. *Lng. assess*

At least six components should be tested in the language assessment: naming, repetition, comprehension, fluency, reading, and writing. Naming should be tested by having the patient name several common objects (e.g., watch, shirt, door, etc.) and parts of objects (e.g., watchband, sleeve, penclip, etc.) Repetition is tested by having the patient repeat a phrase such as "no ifs, ands, or buts." This phrase is particularly difficult because of the string of prepositions. If the patient is unable to repeat the sentence, then a simpler sentence or single words may be tested. Comprehension is assessed to a large degree during the history taking and other components of the exam. It may be specifically stressed by using multistep commands or sentences with complex syntax, such as "point to the door after you point to the ceiling." In some cases, aphasics who are unable to comprehend commands external to the body will be able to carry out midline body commands, such as "close your eyes" or "stick out your tongue." One should be careful not to give visual cues when giving these commands. Speech fluency may also be assessed during the history taking and other components of the exam. Specific testing for fluency may include the Benton Word Fluency Test, in which the patient is asked to write or repeat as many words beginning with a certain letter (excluding proper names) as he can in one minute. The letters commonly used are *S*, *T*, or *A*, and the patient should be able to name at least 10 words in the one-minute time span. Assessment of naming, repetition, comprehension, and fluency will allow the examiner to classify the patient's aphasia according to standard nomenclature. When all four functions are severely impaired, the patient's deficit is classified as a global aphasia. A motor (i.e., Broca's, anterior, or nonfluent) aphasia is characterized by impaired fluency and repetition with relative sparing of comprehension and, perhaps, naming. If speech output is not completely destroyed, remaining speech will be effortful and lacking connecting words, such as prepositions. While Broca's area is the posterior one-third of the inferior frontal gyrus, a classical Broca-type aphasia actually requires a larger lesion. Lesions restricted just to Broca's area proper produce an acute marked decrease in speech output from which the patient usually recovers in the course of a few days to weeks. A permanent motor aphasia requires a lesion extending beyond Broca's area to include the underlying white matter and adjacent peri-Sylvian cortex. *Wernike*

A sensory (i.e., Wernicke's, posterior, or fluent) aphasia typically spares speech fluency. Comprehension, naming, and repetition are impaired, while speech output flows effortlessly with normal rhythm. In the more severe forms, the patient becomes incomprehensible, juxtaposing meaningless phrases and neologisms to form a "word salad." In contrast to Broca's aphasia, a contralateral hemiparesis is absent or minimal. The patient with Wernicke's aphasia is at times misdiagnosed as schizophrenic because of comprehension problems, neologisms, and lack of gross motor weakness. Such a mistake can be avoided by careful observation for neurological signs frequently associated with lesions in the left cerebral hemisphere (i.e., apraxia, Gerstmann's syndrome, right visual field deficits, and subtle neurological deficits such as a slight facial weakness, drift, reflex asymmetries, or pathological reflexes).

Although repetition is impaired with lesions anywhere in the primary language area (i.e., peri-Sylvian region of the dominant hemisphere), repetition is most severely impaired *relative* to other language functions with lesions of the arcuate fibers connecting Wernicke's and Broca's regions (i.e., the so-called conduction aphasia) or occasionally with lesions of Wernicke's area. Repetition is relatively intact in the transcortical aphasias, which spare the primary language area. Such a condition may exist following a cardiopulmonary resuscitation that results in infarction of the watershed areas. If comprehension and naming are spared along with repetition, the language deficit is classified as a transcortical motor aphasia. This isolated loss of fluency may be present in diffuse dementias (e.g., Parkinson's disease), akinetic states, or lesions of either frontal lobe (left greater than right). If fluency is spared along with repetition, the deficit in comprehension and naming is classified as a transcortical sensory aphasia, which is typically produced by lesions posterior to the primary language area. Naming may be disrupted in relative isolation with lesions in the vicinity of the temporoparietal-occipital junction on the left. It may also be disordered in diffuse disorders or dementias such as Alzheimer's disease.

One should remember that the standard aphasia classifications are based on aphasias produced by chronic cortical lesions. The patient examined in the acute phase may not fit classical patterns and may evolve over time into a more classic picture. Subcortical lesions (e.g., thalamic) may also produce aphasias, and these do not fit the standard localizations.

Finally, reading and writing should be assessed separately because dissociated deficits of reading or writing may occur, as in apraxia or in alexia without agraphia. At the bedside, simple command sentences may be used in this context. Having the patient read proper names and having the patient write his own name are very poor measures for testing because they are diffusely represented and almost reflexively engrained. In alexia without agraphia, the lesion disconnects the primary language area from the primary visual cortex. For instance, the lesion in Dejerine's original case of alexia without agraphia had produced destruction of the left calcarine cortex along with the splenium of the corpus callosum.

Apraxia is a disorder in the execution of learned movements that cannot be explained by the degree of weakness or sensory loss. Since handedness and language dominance are linked in the majority of the population, it is not surprising that apraxia would be produced by lesions to the left hemisphere. Lesions to the left parietal region are specifically prone to produce apraxia in both hands. Lesions of the anterior callosal fibers or in the subcortical white matter in either frontal lobe may produce an isolated left-hand apraxia. Manual apraxia should be tested by asking the patient to pantomime a task such as hammering, using a screwdriver, or flipping a coin in the air. The apraxia may improve with imitation of the examiner's movements or by use of the real object. In severely aphasic patients, the use of a real object may be the only way to test for the presence of apraxia. Buccofacial apraxia for items such as sucking on a straw or blowing out a match may be seen following lesions of the left dorsolateral frontal lobe.

The constellation of findings including acalculia, agraphia, right/left confusion, and finger agnosia, which are frequently referred to as Gerstmann's syndrome, has been attributed to lesions of the left angular gyrus. This syndrome is very rarely seen in isolation, but its components may frequently accompany other deficits following lesions in this region. Again, it is the pattern of symptoms that is important, in that isolated components of this syndrome might be produced from lesions in the opposite hemisphere (e.g., dyscalculia and right/left confusion).

Evaluation of right cerebral cognitive function should begin with assessment for the neglect syndrome. Just as the left hemisphere may be thought of as dominant for language functions, the right hemisphere may be thought of as dominant for some attentional and intentional mechanisms. Thus lesions to the right cerebral hemisphere may produce the neglect syndrome, which, in its severest form, includes anosognosia (i.e., denial of disease or weakness) and even denial of body part. The patient may even ignore all stimuli from his left hemispace. In milder forms, the patient may admit his weakness but show a lack of concern (i.e., anisodiaphoria). He may only ignore stimuli from the left hemispace when given double simultaneous stimuli from both sides (i.e., extinction). This neglect may be seen in any sensory modality, but is most consistently present to tactile stimuli. In addition to the attentional disorder, the patient may exhibit an intentional disorder, especially following lesions of the basal ganglia or the mesial or dorsolateral frontal lobes. For example, the patient will bisect lines consistently to the right of midline. He may also exhibit a left hemibody akinesia or contralateral motor neglect. A modification of the test for tactile extinction is used to test for motor neglect. Instead of having the patient answer "left," "right," or "both" when touched on his hands with his eyes closed, ask him to raise the hand opposite from the hand touched. In other words, he is to raise his right hand when touched on the left, the left hand when touched on the right, and both when simultaneously touched on both hands. In motor neglect, the patient will fail to raise the akinetic arm (usually the left) when touched bilaterally.

Visuospatial constructional skills are frequently disordered following right cerebral lesions, even in the absence of the neglect syndrome. Having the patient draw a cube, a cross, or a square will test these skills at progressively lower levels of difficulty. Stereognosis and graphesthesia are also disordered following parietal lesions (right or left). Stereognosis is the ability to recognize objects by touch alone; graphesthesia is the ability to recognize numbers or letters written in the palm or on the fingertips. Prosody has to do with the intonation of language. Emotional prosody may be tested by having the patient identify the emotional tone of a nonsense sentence given in a happy, sad, mad, or indifferent voice. Prosody may be impaired following right cerebral lesions and specifically spared in aphasics with left cerebral lesions.

Frontal lesions produce the paradox of a patient who has both difficulty initiating tasks (e.g., akinesia or decreased word fluency) and difficulty stopping or alternating tasks (e.g., perseveration). Due to the plasticity of the frontal lobes, frontal lesions can be particularly silent, especially if due to a slowly progressive or chronically static process. Luria figures, go/no-go tasks, and fist/edge/palm task are sensitive to frontal dysfunction. The Luria figures include copying of repeated M's and N's or of loop figures. Typically the patient will perseverate and lose the pattern. A common go/no-go task would be to ask the patient to raise two fingers in response to the examiner's raising one finger, and to raise a fist when the examiner raises two fingers. The examiner then gives random alternating strings of the two signals. In the fist/edge/palm task, the patient is repeatedly to perform the sequence of alternately placing his hand in the fist, edge, and palm positions. Frontal patients have a great deal of difficulty maintaining the task and alternating the responses at the appropriate times. One should keep in mind that these "frontal" signs may be produced by not only focal frontal lobe lesions, but also by diffuse dementias (e.g., Alzheimer's disease) or by focal subcortical lesions (e.g., thalamus).

Finally, the mental status exam should include assessment of the patient's affect and thought processes. A flat affect may be seen in diffuse encephalopathies, frontal lobe pathology, or disorders of the ascending dopaminergic tracts (e.g., Parkinson's disease). This flat affect may be part of a symptom complex known as abulia. Abulia is characterized by flat affect, inertia, akinesia, apathy, and perhaps bradykinesia. Most dramatically, there is slowness of response and lack of spontaneous motor or cognitive activity. Depression may produce cognitive dysfunction or be the result of neurological disease. At times a catastrophic depressive response may be seen following left cerebral lesions, and a euphoric or "laissez-faire" affect may follow right cerebral lesions. Psychotic symptoms in an adult without prior psychiatric history are particularly suggestive of an organic process, especially if visual hallucinations are present or if the thought disorder does not fit a typical schizophrenic pattern. An organic psychosis may be a function of metabolic disorders, diffuse dementias, or focal brain lesions (e.g., right frontotemporal or midline lesions). Acute confusion and delayed psychosis have been reported separately in patients with focal right-hemispheric lesions. In conjunction with other experimental evidence, the association of focal right-hemispheric lesions with psychosis and with aprosody suggests a unique role for the right cerebral hemisphere in interaction with the limbic system for the processing of emotional stimuli.

CRANIAL NERVE EXAM

A complete listing of the cranial nerve exam is in the exam outline (Table 3.1). Cranial nerve deficits in conjunction with ataxia and crossed motor/sensory deficits are helpful in localizing lesions to the brainstem and posterior circulation. Nystagmus in the primary position or vertical nystagmus (if present in the absence of drugs such as anticonvulsants, benzodiazepines, and ethanol) is particularly suggestive of a process in the posterior fossa.

Defects in eye movements may point to a specific diagnosis in a dementing disease. For example, impaired upgaze is seen in Parinaud's syndrome, and impaired vertical or horizontal gaze (especially downward) is typical of progressive supranuclear palsy. A combination of a recent memory disorder with impaired vertical gaze raises the possibility of Wernicke's encephalopathy (i.e., thiamine deficiency) or peri-thalamic injury secondary to top of the basilar artery embolic infarction. Deficits in the cranial nerve exam may also point to hemispheric lesions. For example, gaze preferences (toward destructive lesions and away from active seizure foci), visual field defects (e.g., a superior quadranopsia with contralateral temporal lobe lesions or an inferior quadranopsia with parietal lesions), or central facial weakness may result from hemispheric lesions.

Particular attention should be given to the fundiscopic exam for evidence of vascular disease [e.g., hemorrhages, exudates, and arteriovenous malformation (AVM) crossing defects] and increased intracranial pressure (i.e., papilledema). If papilledema is questionable, spontaneous venous pulsations at the center of the disk indicate the presence of normal intracranial pressure as long as glaucoma is absent. If spontaneous venous pulsations are not seen, no specific statement concerning intracranial pressure can be made in the absence of papilledema, as spontaneous venous pulsations may be absent in normals.

The examination of the pupils should assess size, reactivity, and symmetry. Both pupils are normally the same size. While up to 15% of normals may have asymmetric pupil size, anisocoria (difference in the size of the pupils) should prompt further evaluation. If one pupil is large and unreactive there may be a third cranial nerve palsy (such as may be seen with expanding intracranial masses) or parasympathetic nerve injury. If one pupil is smaller and less reactive than the other, the lesion involves the sympathetic nervous system, raising the possibility of brain injury, superior thoracic lesions (e.g., Pancoast tumors), or carotid artery occlusion or dissection. If both pupils are large and minimally reactive, there may be anticholinergic intoxication or brainstem

TABLE 3.1 Outline for the Neurological Examination

General physical examination:	Skin — petechiae, cyanosis, neurofibromatoses, etc.
	Head — deformities, bruits
	Neck — supple without masses or bruits
	CVS — rhythm, murmurs
Mental status examination:	
Level of consciousness:	Alert and 0 × 3 (alert/stupor or lethargy/semicoma/coma)
Memory — Immediate:	digits: 7 forward and 5 reverse
Recent:	4/4 objects at five minutes
Remote:	5/5 presidents, personal history intact
Left cerebral:	Language intact to naming, repetition, comprehension, and fluency.
	Thurston greater than 10 (S, T, A)
	Reading and writing intact
	Gerstmann's syndrome absent (acalculia, agraphia, right/left confusion, finger agnosia)
	Praxis normal
Right cerebral:	No neglect
	Stereognosis and graphesthesia intact
	Visuospatial construction intact
	Prosody intact
Frontal:	Luria figures, go/no-go tasks, fist/edge/palm task
Psychological:	Thought processes intact
	No predominate affect
Cranial nerves:	CNs I–XII intact (see below)
	CNs: I — smell intact bilaterally
	II — PERRLA; VFs intact OU (fundi benign with spontaneous venous pulsations)
	III, IV, VI — EOMs full; no nystagnus
	V — facial sensation, corneals and masseters intact
	VII — facial musculature symmetric; taste intact
	VIII — hearing intact AU
	IX, X — gag intact; Uvula midline
	XI — sternocleidomastoids (SCM) and trapezius 5/5
	XII — tongue midline
Motor: 5/5 Rating	Normal bulk, tone, and strength in all groups
	Coordination intact to FTN, HTK, RAM, and tandem gait.
	Gait normal
Reflexes:	DTRs 2+ and symmetric
	No pathological reflexes
	(Hoffman, palmomental, grasp, Meyerson's, snout, and Babinski)
Sensory:	Intact to pinprick, light touch, vibration, and position

injury. If both pupils are small and minimally reactive, narcotic intoxication or pontine injury may be present.

MOTOR EXAM

Muscles should be evaluated on the basis of bulk, tone, and strength. Tone may be decreased (as in lesions of the cerebellum or acute lesions in the cortex) or increased. Important forms of hypertonicity include: (1) "lead-pipe" rigidity, as seen in the contralateral extremities in chronic lesions of the motor cortex; (2) "cogwheel" rigidity, as seen in parkinsonism; (3) spasticity (or clasp-knife rigidity), as seen in cerebral palsy; (4) paratonia, Gegenhalten, or frontal rigidity (i.e., a fluctuating hypertonia seen in frontal lobe disease or diffuse dementias). A good general screen of muscle strength in the extremities would include the deltoids, biceps, triceps, wrist extensors, handgrip, interossei, hip-flexors, quadriceps, hamstrings, and the dorsal and plantar flexors of the foot. Strength should be graded on a 0 to 5 rating scale in the following manner: 0 for absence of movement, 1 for trace movement, 2 for movement but inability to move against gravity, 3 for movement against gravity but lack of resistance, 4 for weakness but movement against gravity with resistance, 5 for normal strength. Obviously the grade 4/5 encompasses the largest group and may be subdivided into 4– and 4+ in order better to denote the degree of weakness or to indicate asymmetries. Minimal weakness may be best demonstrated by a downward or pronator drift of the outstretched arms. Coordination should be tested by finger to nose, heel to shin, and rapid alternating movements. If possible, routine gait and tandem gait should also be tested. Coordination is typically thought of as a cerebellar test, but it may be disordered in a variety of cortical and subcortical lesions. Motor speed should be observed for slowed initiation of movement (i.e., akinesia) and slowed movement after initiation (i.e., bradykinesia). The two symptoms commonly occur together and may result from dysfunction in frontal, striatal, or dopaminergic systems.

EXAM OF REFLEXES

Deep tendon reflexes (DTRs) should be elicited at the biceps, triceps, brachioradialis, patellar, and Achille's tendons. DTRs should be graded on a four-point scale in the following manner: 0 for no reflex, 1 for trace movement, 2 for normal reflex, 3 for hyperactive reflex, and 4 for the presence of clonus. Asymmetries in reflexes should be noted. Testing of pathological reflexes should include the Babinski, Hoffman, palmomental, grasp, and snout reflexes. If present, the Babinski indicates dysfunction in the corticospinal tract and the

Hoffman simply indicates hyperreflexia. The remaining reflexes (i.e., grasp, snout, and palmomental) are the so-called frontal lobe reflexes, which actually are more commonly seen in diffuse diseases such as senile dementia of Alzheimer's type. Meyerson's sign (i.e., gabellar tap) is also classified as a frontal-lobe reflex but most commonly is seen in Parkinson's disease.

SENSORY EXAM

Examination of sensation should include pinprick, light touch, vibratory, and position-sense testing. While cortical lesions may produce hypesthesia, the sensation of pain will be maintained with lesions above the thalamus. Sensory deficits that exactly divide the midline are rare and may indicate a conversion reaction; however, subcortical lesions (e.g., thalamic) may produce such a pattern. Deficits in vibratory and position sense are most commonly produced by peripheral neuropathies or lesions of the posterior columns (e.g., B_{12} deficiency or Lues).

SUMMARY

In closing, one should remember that no single sign or symptom is diagnostic or even localizing in and of itself. The pattern of deficits helps the examiner determine the location of the lesion and ultimately points to the etiology. Formal neuropsychological testing can complement the neurological examination by confirming a suspected pattern of cognitive dysfunction, further delineating the neurobehavioral deficits and documenting in detail the pattern of capacity and incapacity. The results not only have a role in legal and rehabilitative perspectives, but also can assist in difficult diagnostic problems.

REFERENCES

Jastrow, R. (1983). *The enchanted loom.* New York: Touchstone.
Lezak, M. D. (1983). *Neuropsychological assessment* (2nd ed.). New York: Oxford University Press.
Luria, A. R. (1980). *Higher cortical functions in man.* New York: Basic Books.
McHenry, L. C. (1969). *Garrison's history of neurology.* Springfield: Charles Thomas.

SUGGESTED ADDITIONAL READINGS

Adams, R. D., & Victor, M. (1985). *Principles of neurology.* New York: McGraw-Hill.
DeJong, R. N. (1982). Case taking and the neurological examination. In A. B. Baker & L. H. Baker (Eds.), *Clinical neurology* (pp. 1–87). Philadelphia: Harper & Row.

DeMeyer, W. (1980). *Technique of the neurologic examination.* New York: McGraw-Hill.

Heilman, K. M., & Valenstein, E. (Eds.). (1979). *Clinical neuropsychology.* New York: Oxford University Press.

Heilman, K. M., Watson, R. T., & Greer, M. (1977). *Differential diagnosis of neurologic signs and symptoms.* New York: Appleton-Century-Crofts.

Kandel, E. R., & Schwartz, J. H. (Eds.). (1982). *Principles of neural science.* New York: Elsevier/North-Holland.

Kertesz, A. (1983). *Localization in neuropsychology.* New York: Academic Press.

Pribram, K. H. (1971). *Languages of the brain.* New Jersey: Prentice-Hall.

4

Assessment of Cortical Functions

Erin D. Bigler

The assessment of cortical functioning relates to the evaluation of cognitive abilities that depend on higher-order cerebral processes. Some of these functions are lobe specific (e.g., motor functions of the frontal lobes), some are hemispheric dependent (e.g., verbal–abstract reasoning abilities that are dependent on the dominant hemisphere vs. spatial-perceptual functioning dependent on the nondominant hemisphere), some are system dependent (e.g., receptive and expressive aspects of language), and some are dependent on integrative whole-brain functions (e.g., intellect, reasoning). The approach to assessing these various functions thereby requires a variety of special techniques, as will be outlined in this chapter. The emphasis of this overview will be on screening techniques that permit the delineation of underlying cortical/cognitive dysfunction.

FUNCTIONS AND ASSESSMENT BY LOBE

When discussing the various functions of each lobe, it should be kept in mind that the subdivisions of the cerebrum into frontal, temporal, parietal, and occipital lobes were done prior to the development of histological techniques and, accordingly, the classification is not dependent on underlying neuronal microstructure or specific functional anatomy. Rather, the divisions are made because of major visual landmarks (e.g., Rolandic fissure, Sylvian fissure—see Figure 4.1). However, out of convention, the frontal, temporal, parietal, and

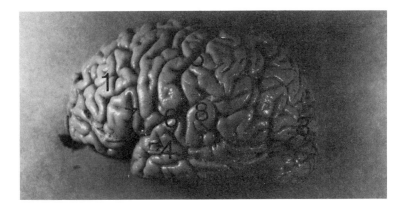

FIGURE 4.1 Lateral view of the left cerebral hemisphere. 1—Frontal lobe; 2—parietal lobe; 3—occipital lobe; 4—temporal lobe; 5—central sulcus; 6—Sylvian fissure; 7—Broca's area; 8—Wernicke's area.

occipital lobe classification distinctions will be used. Where appropriate, the various functional features within each lobe will be discussed in terms of motor, sensory, language, memory, personality, and visual-spatial functions.

Frontal Lobe

Motor Function

The precentral gyrus (see Figure 4.1) houses the cell bodies for the direct cortical spinal (pyramidal) tract, with the axonal fibers coursing downward via the internal capsule, through the cerebral peduncle, down the lower brain-stem—where decussation occurs before termination and synapse with the lower motor neuron occurs in the spinal cord. Damage to the precentral gyral area or the subcortical white matter projection system (prior to decussation) produces a contralateral spastic hemiplegia. Damage, just anterior to the precentral gyrus, will produce some paralysis, typically less severe than with direct precentral damage and frequently with less spasticity. Damage to the prefrontal cortex may not produce paralysis, but usually there will be a decrease in coordinated and integrative motor control and possibly some loss in strength. Also, with extensive, typically bilateral frontal damage, primitive reflexes (e.g., suck, grasp, rooting) may be released and elicited.

Tests. Hemiplegia is quite obvious on clinical examination, and, associated with the paralysis, some degree of spasticity is usually present. When such obvious motor signs are not present, the motor exam should include measurement of grip strength (there should be equal to slightly greater strength in the dominant hand in comparison to the nondominant), finger dexterity (rapid index-finger-to-thumb tapping, alternating sequential finger-thumb tapping), and rapid alternating movements (alternating palm-fist, alternating vertical-horizontal hand movements [see Christensen, 1979]). Formal assessment of finger oscillation speed can be obtained with the finger oscillation test (Reitan & Davison, 1974), and strength of grip can be assessed with a hand dynamometer. Integrative motor control can best be evaluated by the motor examination outlined by Luria (1966) and formalized by Christensen (1979).

Language

Dominant-hemisphere frontal lesions may affect expressive language abilities. Focal lesions in the inferior frontal operculum (Broca's area, see Figure 4.1) may result in impaired expressive language characterized by dysarthric, effortful speech that is telegraphic and, typically, agrammatical. In association with the expressive language deficits, there is typically contralateral paralysis. With severe damage to this area, there may be a complete loss of expressive speech. Despite the marked deficits in expressive language with frontal lesions, comprehension, in comparison, may be relatively preserved. If Broca's area is spared, but surrounding regions are damaged, an interesting clinical picture may emerge. This is the so-called transcortical motor aphasia (Albert, Goodglass, Helm, Rubens, & Alexander, 1981; Benson, 1979), in which the patient has absent or deficient spontaneous speech, but repetition is relatively preserved. For example, the patient may be able to repeat, "it is a cold, snowy day outside," but when asked to comment about the weather outside, the self-generated response from the patient may be quite devoid of content (e.g., the patient may respond only with "cold, snow"). Confrontation naming may also be affected with frontal lesions of the dominant hemisphere. Either nondominant or dominant hemisphere frontal lesions may affect speech prosody (Ross & Rush, 1981).

Tests. Considerable information concerning language disturbance can be gathered during astute clinical observation and interviewing of the patient. Any language evaluation needs to include a separate assessment of word articulation, word fluency, reading, spelling, writing, and comprehension. However, a quickly administered aphasia survey, sufficient for screening purposes, is the Reitan–Indiana Aphasia Screening Test (Reitan, 1984; Reitan & Davison, 1974). If, through either clinical observation and/or aphasia screening, language disturbance is noted, then more comprehensive language examination may be needed to document fully the extent of language disturbance. There are several excellent comprehensive language batteries, such as the Western Aphasia Battery (Kertesz, 1982), the Boston Diagnostic Aphasia Examination (Goodglass & Kaplan, 1972), and the Porch Index of Communicative Abilities (Porch, 1967).

Intellectual Functions

Damage to the frontal regions typically affects intellectual functions in some fashion (Damasio, 1985; Stuss & Benson, 1983). Well-learned or overlearned behaviors frequently are quite resistant to frontal lobe damage, though, whereas new learning and particularly complex reasoning and problem solving are impaired. The following case illustrates this point quite well. M.M. survived a self-inflicted gunshot wound to the head in which the 4-10 shotgun blast essentially obliterated the anterior 5-7 cm. of both frontal lobes. During a previous psychiatric hospitalization approximately six months before the self-inflicted gunshot wound, a Wechsler Adult Intelligence Scale (WAIS) had been obtained which yielded the following results: VIQ = 96, PIQ = 85, FSIQ = 91. When retested approximately seven months postinjury, there was actually a slight increase in his Verbal IQ score (VIQ = 103), a slight reduction in Performance IQ score (PIQ = 76), and no change in measured Full-Scale IQ (FSIQ = 91). However, despite no significant changes in measured intellectual abilities, the patient demonstrated a classic frontal lobe syndrome (Benson & Blumer, 1975; Freemon, 1981). The patient displayed attentional deficits and vacillation in concentration, being easily distracted and misdirected. Marked deficits in terms of complex reasoning and problem solving, as well as judgment, were present. He was very apathetic, with little or no self-directed motivation (i.e., he would stay in bed for hours if allowed to; when watching TV, he would sit and watch for hours without changing a channel or showing any curiosity about what might be on other channels).

This case demonstrates that much of what is assessed by formalized intelligence tests actually is based on well-established and well-learned information and may not be affected by frontal damage. When tested on tasks that tap new learning and abstract reasoning, such patients typically are found to be very dysfunctional. Judgment and social behavior typically are affected, as was the situation in the case presented above. This type of cognitive inflexibility and behavior syndrome is commonplace with frontal damage (Benson & Blumer, 1975, 1982).

Tests. The WAIS (see review by Wechsler, 1958; or revised edition, Wechsler, 1981) is the most well-established and thoroughly researched assessment tool for measuring current intellectual levels (Bigler, 1984). However, the limitation, as pointed out above, centers around the fact that the WAIS tends to assess well-learned abilities and not the patient's adaptive intelligence, particularly on tasks that require new learning. Because of this, it is frequently instructive to examine performance on the various subtests rather than actual IQ scores, since several of the WAIS subtests are more sensitive to intellectual deficits than others. Studies (reviewed by Russell, 1979) have shown that the Information and Vocabulary subtests typically are least affected by cerebral dysfunction and most resistant to cerebral injury, whereas the Block Design,

Digit Span, and Digit Symbol subtests may be more affected when brain injury occurs. Knowing this relationship, the Information and Vocabulary subtest scores in the nonaphasic brain-injured individual actually may provide some general estimate of the patient's premorbid level of intellectual ability; in comparison, the results on the Digit Symbol and Block Design subtest may be reflective of the degree of the patient's decline.

Patients with brain damage in frontal regions (and, in many cases, irrespectively of the location) tend to give concrete responses. This can be assessed by asking the patient to interpret various proverbs. For example, if asked to explain what the following statement means—"you shouldn't change horses in the middle of the stream"—the concrete frontal lobe-damaged patient may respond with "because you would get wet," or "because you can't do it," rather than the more abstract response, such as "one should persist until they accomplish their goal." The patient with frontal lobe damage may not even be able to appreciate the significance or meaning of the more abstract response, even if it is explained to them. Formal testing for deficits in cognitive shifting, problems with deficits in concept generalization, abstract reasoning, and complex problem solving can be assessed by using some of the following tests: Category Test (Reitan & Davison, 1974), Wisconsin Card Sorting Test (Berg, 1948; see Lezak, 1983, for update and modifications of this procedure), Raven Coloured Progressive Matrices (Raven, 1962), and Stroop Word Color Test (Stroop, 1935; see Lezak, 1983, for review of applications).

Personality

A wide spectrum of behavioral changes may develop following damage to the frontal areas (Blumer & Benson, 1975; Damasio, 1985; Freemon, 1981; Stuss & Benson, 1983). There is, however, no clear correspondence between a frontal lesion site, emotional response, and behavioral change. The differences may range from subtle to marked. The most common findings are a lack of drive/ motivation, lack of initiative, diminished spontaneity, and disregard for social amenities. Inappropriate jocularity and excessive silliness/giddiness, as well as emotional lability, are commonplace. The frontal areas are frequently the site of damage identified in head injury, and the accompanying behavior change may be associated with such damage. Similar behaviors may be associated with the early behavioral changes seen in a variety of degenerative disorders (e.g., Alzheimer's disease) and are most common in such patients after the fifth decade of life. Frontal neoplastic or vascular disease may also produce such behavioral effects.

Tests. There are no formal psychometric tests designed to measure personality change in the brain-damaged individual. Therefore, this is best accomplished by careful history taking, with consideration of the chronology of the change. In giving such a history, patients with frontal lobe disease are notoriously poor historians; accordingly, a spouse or close relative is an invaluable source of information. Lezak (1978) suggested that in head-injured individuals there may be five identifiable areas of personality change. These are listed in Table 4.1. While these changes were noted with traumatic disorder associated with frontal damage, similar observations have also been made about individuals with frontal lobe involvement secondary to a variety of etiologies (Bigler, 1984; Stuss, & Benson, 1983), and this description by Lezak is most fitting for the clinician's guideline in the evaluation of personality change.

Memory

Memory functions are frequently affected with frontal lobe damage, but the relationship between memory processes and frontal lobe functioning is not well understood. Some speculate that the memory difficulties are mainly related to the frontal lobe syndrome effects (e.g., diminished concentration, impaired motivation, lack of attention to detail, etc.) and deficits in new learning and, thus, that they are not a true memory disorder (Damasio, 1985). However, there are a variety of important limbic system and thalamic projections into frontal regions (Brodal, 1981), and such interconnections are thought to perform some regulatory role in memory processing (Squire & Butters, 1984). Accordingly, in patients with damage restricted to the frontal

TABLE 4.1 Possible Areas of Behavioral/Personality Change
Following Frontal Lobe Damage

Capacity for social perceptiveness
Increase in self centered behavior
Diminution or loss of self criticisms
Loss of ability to show empathy
Capacity for self-control
Random restlessness
Impatience and impulsivity
Learned social behavior
Diminution or loss of initiative
Impaired judgment
Increased social dependency
Ability to learn
Mental slowness
Rigidity of thought
Reduced learning capacity
Emotion
Irritability
Silliness
Lability of mood
Apathy
Change in sexual behavior

regions who display memory deficits in which motivational and other frontal lobe syndrome features are not considered to be the primary cause, impairment of memory functioning is most likely due to disruption of frontal-thalamic-limbic interconnections. Tests for evaluating memory will be outlined in the temporal lobe section.

Temporal Lobe

Motor Function

The temporal lobe is not involved in direct motor control; but with damage to the posterior association areas of the temporal region, and in particular the region of the temporal-parietal junction, an apraxia of movement may develop (Heilman, Rothi, & Kertesz, 1983). Ideomotor apraxia is the most common type and involves the failure of carrying out, on command, a previously learned motor act; such findings may be observed in buccofacial, upper and lower extremities, or truncal musculature. The command that is to be carried out is a simple, straightforward motor act (e.g., facial musculature—"show me how you drink from a straw, blow out a match"; limb musculature—"throw a ball, comb your hair, kick a ball, crush out a cigarette"), and the deficit in performance is not related to impaired comprehension (i.e., aphasia) or paralysis. It should be pointed out, though, that patients with such apraxia frequently have some degree of dysphasia; accordingly, it is sometimes difficult to rule out fully that comprehension deficits are not contributing to the movement disorder. Ideational apraxia represents a higher-order disturbance in the execution of the sequence of motor planning (e.g.,"show me how you would pour a drink into a cup and stir it") and is most typically seen with bilateral disease. Constructional praxic deficits, most directly revealed by paper and pencil drawing of familiar figures (see Figure 4.2), also may be found with temporal lesions; but they are more commonly seen with temporal-parietal or parietal lesions, particularly with nondominant parietal involvement.

Sensory

The auditory system terminates in the upper extension of the superior temporal gyrus. Damage to this area produces a classic Wernicke's aphasia (fluent paraphasic speech associated with impaired comprehension, naming, reading, and writing). Posterior to and surrounding Wernicke's area is the large temporal association cortex, and damage in this area also results in disturbed language functioning (see the following section on language). While these patients usually do not display an actual deafness (cortical deafness typically is seen with involvement of the bilateral superior temporal gyrus), they may display contralateral auditory inattention when auditory stimulation is presented simultaneously to each ear. (The methods for administration of double

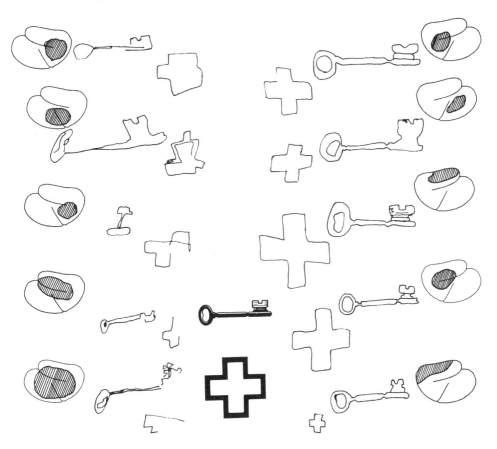

FIGURE 4.2 The left-hand columns depict the copying of a Greek cross and key (presented at bottom, center) by patients with damage to the left cerebral hemisphere (extent of damage depicted by shaded area). The right hand columns depict similar drawings but by patients with right cerebral damage. Note the considerable greater degree of constructional dyspraxia with right hemisphere damage in comparison to left.

simultaneous stimulation are reviewed in the works of Bigler, 1984; Lezak, 1983; and Kolb & Whishaw, 1985.) Vision also may be affected, since visual projection fibers course through the posterior aspect of the temporal lobe, and damage along this projection tract produces a contralateral quadrantanopia in the superior visual field (see Figure 4.3). The mesial temporal cortex is the terminus for olfactory projections, but other than testing for anosmia (via olfactory stimulation using aromatic compounds), no specific behavioral measures of olfactory cortex functioning have been developed. It should be noted, however, that an olfactory sensation may be produced during seizure ictus, and this may be a clinical finding implicating temporal lobe disturbance.

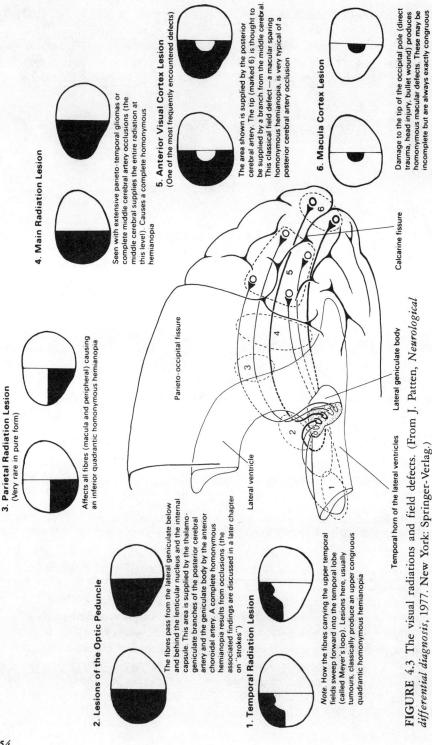

3. Parietal Radiation Lesion
(Very rare in pure form)

Affects all fibres (macula and peripheral) causing an inferior quadrantic homonymous hemianopia

2. Lesions of the Optic Peduncle

The fibres pass from the lateral geniculate below and behind the lenticular nucleus and the internal capsule. This area is supplied by the thalamo-geniculate branches of the posterior cerebral artery and the geniculate body by the anterior choroidal artery. A complete homonymous hemianopia results from occlusions (the associated findings are discussed in a later chapter on "strokes")

1. Temporal Radiation Lesion

Note. How the fibres carrying the upper temporal fields sweep forward into the temporal lobe (called Meyer's loop). Lesions here, usually tumours, classically produce an upper congruous quadrantic homonymous hemianopia

4. Main Radiation Lesion

Seen with extensive parieto-temporal gliomas or complete middle cerebral artery occlusions (the middle cerebral supplies the entire radiation at this level). Causes a complete homonymous hemianopia

5. Anterior Visual Cortex Lesion
(One of the most frequently encountered defects)

The area shown is supplied by the posterior cerebral artery. The tip (marked 6) is thought to be supplied by a branch from the middle cerebral. This classical field defect — a macular sparing homonymous hemianopia, is very typical of a posterior cerebral artery occlusion

6. Macula Cortex Lesion

Damage to the tip of the occipital pole (direct trauma, head injury, bullet wound) produces homonymous macular defects. These may be incomplete but are always exactly congruous

Parieto-occipital fissure

Lateral ventricle

Temporal horn of the lateral ventricles

Lateral geniculate body

Calcarine fissure

FIGURE 4.3 The visual radiations and field defects. (From J. Patten, *Neurological differential diagnosis*, 1977. New York: Springer-Verlag.)

Language

When examining language deficits, it is best first to distinguish between fluent and nonfluent disorders. As discussed in the frontal lobe section, nonfluent speech disorders typically are associated with frontal damage. Fluent aphasic disorders are associated with damage/dysfunction posterior to the Rolandic and Sylvian fissures, implicating temporal or parietal areas. In fluent aphasia, speech quality, while being fluent, is contaminated with paraphasic errors. Paraphasic errors may be either literal or phonemic—transposition of sounds or syllables (e.g., stool for pool), or lexical or semantic—entire world substitutions (e.g., chair for table). Sometimes the paraphasic word is a nonsense, newly created word (e.g., "my *clak* is broken"). This is termed neologistic paraphasia. The major aphasic disorders associated with temporal lobe damage, typically in the lateral superior association cortex regions, are presented below (this outline is based on the work of Albert et al., 1982; Benson, 1979; and Goodglass & Kaplan, 1972):

Wernicke's aphasia: Fluent but paraphasic speech, associated with impaired comprehension, naming, reading, and writing.

Anomic aphasia: Fluent speech, but with impaired naming and word-finding difficulty. Comprehension may be relatively intact in comparison to naming deficits. Reading and writing may or may not be affected, but both are severely impaired with large posterior temporal-parietal lesions.

Conduction aphasia: Phonemic paraphasia, fluent speech associated with frequent blocking are commonplace, particularly evident during attempts at repetition, dyslexia, and dysgraphia. The areas of damage responsible for this syndrome are on the peri-Sylvian region, usually including damage to the arcuate fasciculis.

Transcortical sensory aphasia: Repetition is remarkably preserved in the patient, but otherwise grossly paraphasic speech is present, associated with poor comprehension, anomia, alexia, and agraphia. Damage to the area surrounding, but not including, Wernicke's area is responsible for this syndrome.

The language disorders outlined above arise from damage to the dominant cerebral hemisphere. Correspondingly, nondominant hemispheric damage usually does not interfere with language functions per se, but may affect the receptive awareness of affective quality of speech (e.g., a receptive dysprosodia, see Ross & Rush, 1981). Also, nondominant temporal lobe damage may affect the patient's appreciation of rhythm in musical processing.

Tests. With temporal and parietal lobe lesions affecting language areas, there should be an examination based on comprehensive assessment of verbal abilities, as previously outlined in the frontal lobe section. Briefly, clinical examination, sometimes at bedside, should always assess the patient's articulation, reading, comprehension, writing, repetition, and copying abilities. Several excellent comprehensive language batteries have been developed and were previously discussed in the frontal lobe section.

Memory

Verbal memory, particularly immediate or recent recall, is affected by medial and ventral lesions of the dominant temporal lobe; correspondingly, visual memory is affected by damage to similar areas of the nondominant temporal lobe. With bilateral hippocampal damage, amnestic syndromes may develop in which a rather complete loss of short-term memory is present, with remote memory remaining relatively intact. The most notable syndrome with these features is Korsakoff's disease, which is secondary to alcoholism. In Korsakoff's syndrome, in addition to hippocampal damage, there is involvement of the dorsomedial nucleus of the thalamus and surrounding diencephalic and upper midbrain structures. Memory disturbance is also commonplace with a variety of generalized disorders (e.g., Alzheimer's disease), but it is frequently impossible to determine whether the memory disturbance is due to direct temporal lobe involvement or is secondary to generalized cerebral failure.

Tests. Clinical interview of the patient frequently can outline the major aspects of disturbed memory, but for specific documentation of affected memory more detailed assessment is necessary. On direct clinical interview, the examiner should first establish whether the patient is oriented to time, place, and person, since disorientation and confusion can mimic memory disturbance. Next, the examiner should ask about current news events. This permits an assessment of recent memory. At the beginning of the interview, the patient should be requested to learn and recite four words—"brown, honesty, tulip, and eyedropper" (see Strub and Black, 1977). The normal individual should have little difficulty in recalling these words, and any patient who requires three or four trials to learn them may have a short-term verbal retention deficit or deficit in new learning. Without notifying the patient, approximately five minutes after the first presentation, the patient should be asked to recall the four words again. The intact individual should have little difficulty in recalling all four words at a five minute interval or at later intervals. This should then be repeated in about 30 minutes. A good technique for interim interview, so as not to interfere with or contaminate the word-list recall, is to discuss current news or sports events. This also permits the assessment of the patient's processing of incidental information. Assessing visual memory (see Figure 4.4) is also a good technique during this intervening period, because it does not interfere with or contaminate verbal memory/learning. Remote memory (e.g., date of birth, vocational history, family history, and historical facts—e.g., "name four presidents of the United States since 1900, when was WWII?") should also be assessed. Another rather straightforward clinical

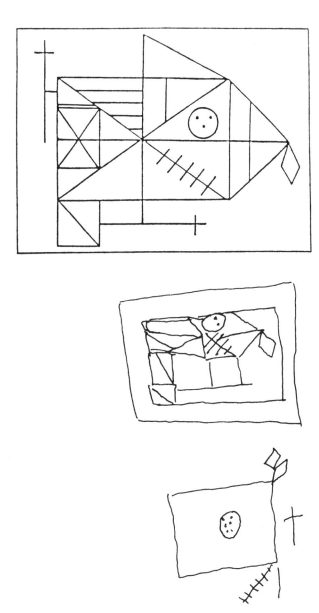

FIGURE 4.4 *Top*: Rey-Osterrieth Complex Figure design as presented to the patient. *Middle*: Patient's attempt at copying. Note the size distortion, the displacement of the figure toward the right and neglecting the left, as well as the dyspraxic quality of the drawing. The patient was a 52-year-old male who had suffered a right-parietal cerebro-vascular accident. *Bottom*: Patient's attempts at recalling the figure after three minutes, thereby indicating prominent deficits in visual memory recall. Thus, the Rey-Osterrieth figure can be used to not only assess visual-praxic abilities, but also visual-memory.

interview measure of short-term verbal retention is a short-form associate learning task. Strub and Black (1977) suggest the following list: "weather–bad; high–low; house–income; book–page." Note that two of the word pairs are easily related associations and two are not. The normal individual should have little difficulty in learning this list within two trials and should likewise have little difficulty in recalling all word pairs immediately postacquisition or after a 10 to 15 minute interval.

More detailed studies of memory functioning can be achieved by use of the following tests: Benton Visual Retention Test (Benton, 1974), Rey Auditory Verbal Learning Test (Rey, 1964), Rey–Osterrieth Complex Figure Design (Osterrieth, 1944), Selective Reminding Test (Buschke & Fuld, 1974), Wechsler Memory Scale (Wechsler, 1945), Denman Memory Battery (Denman, 1984).

Personality

There is no one personality syndrome associated with temporal lobe damage. However, since the temporal lobes house the major nuclei of the limbic system, temporal lobe damage, particularly that which is ventral and mesial, may affect a wide spectrum of emotional behaviors. Depression is more associated with dominant-hemispheric lesions, whereas nondominant temporal damage may result in indifference. Where temporal lobe involvement also acts as a focus for seizure activity, this may be associated with a variety of symptoms, including impulsiveness, aggressiveness, hypo or hypersexuality, increased emotionality, anger, irritability, and impulsive behaviors (Strub & Black, 1981). The so-called Kluver-Bucy syndrome is seen with bilateral temporal lobe damage, with the patient displaying hypersexuality, hyperorality, visual agnosia, and amnesia (Cummings & Duchen, 1981).

Parietal Lobe

Motor

The area around the post-central gyrus is not a pure tactile sensory area, since numerous motor fibers co-exist within this primary sensory region. Also, since it is rare to have precisely focal vascular or traumatic damage to the post-central area exclusively, such damage to the peri-central area normally results in both motor and sensory loss. Thus, even with anterior parietal lesions, there usually will be some motor involvement in addition to disturbance in tactile perception. However, with parietal lobe damage the sensory loss typically will be greater than the motor involvement, and noting the relationship between motor and tactile sensory dysfunction enables one to implicate greater frontal or parietal involvement. Parietal lesions may also produce apraxic deficits, as have been outlined. This further underscores the observation that praxic deficits, while a pathologic sign, are a sign of nonlocalization.

Sensory

The primary function of the post-central gyral region is touch perception; direct damage to this gyrus results in loss of touch, which obviously then affects all other kindred aspects of tactile perception. If the post-central gyrus is spared or minimally involved, then the tactile-processing deficits will involve more complex aspects of tactile functioning. Such lesions may interfere with finger recognition, hand/finger graphesthesic perception, and stereognosis. Also, an imperception may develop contralateral to the lesion site when simultaneous tactile stimulation is applied to both hands or both sides of the face. This is the so-called extinction phenomenon (Bender, 1952) in which the patient does not perceive stimulation on the contralateral (to the lesion sight) hand or face when simultaneous stimulation is applied, but can perceive the stimulation following unilateral application. Thus the presence of tactile extinction on one hand implicates contralateral parietal lobe dysfunction. Because of the overlap between such high-order tactile functions and language, patients with fluent dysphasic deficits secondary to parietal lobe involvement frequently have contralateral tactile extinction, finger dysgnosia, dysgraphesthesia, or dysstereognosis. Sensory examination of the patient with parietal lobe involvement also requires visual field studies. One-half of the thalamic visual projections course through the posterior parietal area on their way to the visual cortex. Damage in this projection area will produce an inferior contralateral quadrant anopia (see Figure 4.3).

Tests. Benton, de Hamsher, Varney, & Spreen (1983) have developed a variety of sensory-perceptual tests that can be used to examine the major aspects of parietal lobe functioning. Also, the sensory-perceptual examination outlined by Reitan and Klove (see Reitan, 1984) is an excellent screening battery that covers assessment of stereognosis, graphesthesia, finger gnosis, and tactile extinction.

Language

Damage to the dominant parietal lobe may result in dysphasia. The posterior and inferior regions of the parietal region are involved in a variety of functions critical to reading, writing, calculation, naming, and higher-order language processing. Dominant-hemisphere parietal lesions may affect any or all of these functions. The major aphasic syndromes have been reviewed earlier under temporal lobe language function, and that outline applies here as well. Typically, the patient with aphasia secondary to dominant parietal lobe involvement will have greater tactile-perception deficits and/or motor disturbance than the aphasic patient with just temporal lobe damage, and this enables clinical differentiation. One language-sensory syndrome does need further mention here and typically is associated with dominant–parietal lobe damage. Gerstmann's syndrome (see Strub & Geschwind, 1983) is comprised of the following clinical findings: right–left disorientation, finger agnosia, acalculia, and agraphesthesia. The observation of these findings in relative isolation of any other major neurocognitive deficit implies dominant-hemisphere parietal damage.

Memory Functioning

With lesions limited to the parietal lobe, memory functioning may be relatively spared or only mildly affected, and there are no specific parietal lobe memory syndromes. However, memory functioning may be affected secondary to dysphasic deficits associated with dominant–parietal lobe involvement and visual-spatial deficits with nondominant parietal damage. Accordingly, these deficits in memory may not be true memory disorders, but rather deficits in sensory processing and encoding information. From the assessment standpoint, the memory tests that were reviewed in the temporal lobe section would also apply here.

Visual-Spatial

This area has not been fully discussed until now, because it is in large part a lateralized, nondominant hemisphere (and a relatively specific function) of the parietal lobe (see Figures 4.2 and 4.4).

Dominant-hemisphere parietal damage may affect visual-spatial and manipulo-spatial abilities to some degree, typically in the form of diminished attention to detail and oversimplification when copying geometric forms. With nondominant parietal damage the full spectrum of visual-spatial/manipulo-spatial deficts can be seen. Figure 4.1 depicts severe constructional apraxia in a patient with right parietal lobe lesion who is not aphasic and does not have any type of specific motor involvement, but cannot carry out the visual praxic copying task. With large parietal lesions, the patient may develop a contralateral hemispatial neglect (see Figure 4.4). In some cases the severity of the neglect reaches a point where the patient may deny a contralateral paralysis and/or sensory loss. Such patients may only shave one side of the face or comb one side of the head or dress on just the nonaffected side and feel quite confident that they have completed their task.

Tests. Probably the most straightforward tests are the pencil and paper tests utilizing simple geometric form copying (see Figure 4.2). These can be made up at bedside (e.g., "copy a square, flower," etc.), or more formalized testing can be obtained with the Bender Visual-Motor Gestalt Test (Bender, 1938) or the Beery–Buktenica Visual Motor Integration Test (1967). Also, the Block Design subtest on the WAIS is an excellent measure of constructional praxic abilities that does not require drawing skill. A major contributing factor to the overall performance IQ (PIQ) score on the WAIS is also based, to a large extent, on the patient's manipulo-spatial abilities, and therefore the PIQ score is something of an index of visual-spatial-motor abilities. A PIQ score that is substantially below VIQ (i.e., greater than one standard deviation—15 scaled score points) may have implications for impaired abilities on nondominant hemispheric functioning.

Personality

With nondominant hemispheric lesions that involve the parietal lobe, the patient may develop a neglect syndrome, as described above, which may be mistaken for a change in personality. These patients usually demonstrate a lack of concern over the deficits present and an apparent unwillingness to accept the loss. However, this is just part of the neglect syndrome and probably relates to impaired complex sensory and spatial processing due to the parietal lobe damage. There is no specific personality change associated with dominant-hemispheric lesions that has been documented in the literature, although there has been some indication that dominant temporal-parietal lesions may be associated more with depression and the corresponding nondominant analog with indifference (Ross & Rush, 1981).

Occipital Lobe

Of the four different lobes, the occipital lobe is the one most dedicated to a single specific function, that being visual-perceptual abilities.

Sensory

Focal damage to visual cortical areas always produces some deficit in visual processing or cortical blindness. Because of the continuity between temporal-occipital and parietal-occipital regions, there is frequently overlap of dysphasic and visual deficits (contralateral hemi- or quadrantanopia) with posterior dominant lesions, and of visual-spatial deficits with posterior nondominant hemisphere lesions (see Figure 4.2). Dominant-hemispheric occipital damage that includes the splenium of the corpus callosum (and may involve posterior temporal and parietal areas) produces a condition of alexia without agraphia and contralateral hemianopia. The corresponding analog with nondominant-hemispheric damage of the occipital lobe is a contralateral hemispatial neglect, as well as hemianopia. Regardless of whether occipital involvement is in the dominant or nondominant hemisphere, where damage is incomplete and the patient still has some visual-perceptual abilities in the affected visual field, there frequently will be inattention to double simultaneous visual stimulation contralateral to the affected occipital lobe. With bilateral occipital damage that is not of sufficient magnitude to produce a complete cortical blindness, the patient's ability to perceive and discriminate objects (agnosia) and faces (prosopagnosia—see Damasio, Damasio, & Van Hoesen, 1982) may be affected.

Tests. Satisfactory visual-field assessment can be achieved with standard visual-field confrontation techniques (see Bigler, 1984). For more objective visual-field studies, formal perimetry techniques are recommended. Visual agnosia can be informally tested by having the patient name objects visually presented, given that the patient is not dysphasic or demented. Formal assessment of facial recognition and visuospatial judgment can be obtained through the use of tests developed by Benton and colleagues (1983). Double simultaneous visual stimulation techniques employ simultaneous movement in both visual fields, usually accomplished by brief finger movements (see Bigler, 1984).

Language Functioning

As discussed above, there may be posterior temporal and/or parietal damage in association with occipital damage because of the overlap in vascular supply by the posterior (to ventral temporal and occipital lobe) and middle (to posterior lateral surface of temporal lobe, lateral surface of the parietal and the border zone parietal-occipital region) cerebral arteries as well as the physical proximity. Deep parietal and, particularly, parietal-temporal lobe lesions also may isolate the occipital area, sometimes producing a visual-field defect even though the occipital area may not be focally damaged. This in effect disconnects the occipital lobe, producing a contralateral hemianopia. Accordingly, involvement of the posterior parietal and/or temporal area frequently will produce some dysphasia as well as visual-field defect, either a homonymous hemianopia or quadrantanopia.

ASSESSMENT BY PRESENTING PROBLEM

In the preceding sections brain functioning and its assessment have been outlined by examining functions lobe-by-lobe. In this last section, an outline is provided that overviews brain pathology by presenting symptom. In this section the presenting problems of motor disturbance, language disturbance, memory loss, sensory, personality, and intellectual change are all reviewed in terms of the area(s) of possible cerebral involvement. Tests to determine the presence or absence of cerebral pathology and certain clinical considerations will also be reviewed.

Fluent Speech Without Articulation Disturbance but Impaired Content

Lesions of the dominant hemisphere posterior to the central sulcus usually produce this type of dysphasia. The presence of a visual field defect may specify greater focal involvement of the temporal (superior quadrantanopia) or parietal (inferior quadrantanopia) lobe. If repetition is intact, this suggests sparing of Wernicke's area, with damage in the surrounding peri-Sylvian region. The presence of pure word deafness suggests bitemporal lobe involvement.

Clinical Considerations

Comprehensive batteries examining language function were discussed in the frontal, temporal, and parietal lobe sections. Any evaluation of language function needs to examine articulation, naming, reading, spelling, repetition, calculations, handwriting, and comprehension. Praxic abilities should also be examined.

Nonfluent, Dysarthric Speech That Is Agrammatic and Telegraphic

Lesions of the dominant hemisphere anterior to the central sulcus usually produce this type of dysphasia. Additionally, the nonfluent dysphasic (Broca's aphasia) patient is typically hemiparetic/hemiplegic, and this permits further delineation to the involvement of the frontal region. If repetition is intact and dysarthria is minimal or absent, then this implies sparing of Broca's region but with surrounding frontal damage.

Clinical Considerations and Tests

Speech articulation can be informally evaluated during clinical interview and observations. Formal testing can be accomplished with the language tests previously recommended. Associated with such frontal lesions may be a buccofacial apraxia; accordingly, praxic movements of the face, lips, and tongue should be examined. Since the nonfluent aphasic patient typically has some motor involvement, the motor tests previously outlined should also be administered and observation should be focused on whether there is indication for any behavioral features of a frontal lobe syndrome. Naming may also be affected with frontal lobe lesions and should be examined. Useful tests are the Western Aphasia Battery (Kertesz, 1982); Boston Diagnostic Aphasia Examination (Goodglass & Kaplan, 1972); Reitan-Indiana Aphasia Screening Test (Reitan, 1984); and Porch Index of Communicative Ability (Porch, 1967).

Memory Loss

Damage to frontal and/or temporal areas, either unilateral or bilateral, or diffuse cerebral dysfunction, may affect memory. The delineation of the locus of damage/dysfunction depends upon the presence of focal (i.e., frontal or temporal) as opposed to bilateral or nonspecific findings. For example, the patient with a specific amnestic syndrome, but otherwise normal examination, is suspect for focal temporal lobe (hippocampus) involvement, whereas global memory loss associated with a variety of frontal lobe behavior symptoms suggests a more nonspecific process, such as that seen with degenerative disease. In Wernicke-Korsakoff syndrome there is marked short-term memory loss, but relatively preserved long-term memory. Bilateral hippocampal involvement is implicated in this disorder, as well as a variety of other subcortical lesion sites. If memory deficts are predominantly affected, while verbal retention and visual-spatial memory are unaffected, then this suggests dominant-hemisphere temporal lobe involvement. The opposite of this, intact verbal memory but impaired visual-spatial memory, implicates nondominant temporal-parietal involvement.

Clinical Considerations and Tests

The various tests of memory function were outlined in the frontal and temporal lobe sections. One should always attempt to assess short- as well as long-term memory for both verbal and visual-spatial abilities. Since memory disorder is commonplace following head injury, in such patients one needs to differentiate whether the memory disturbance is due to focal frontal-temporal effects or general disruption of cerebral functioning. Drug and alcohol history needs to be taken into consideration because of the association between substance abuse and memory disorders. Vascular insufficiency in the basilar artery–posterior cerebral arteries may produce global amnesia that is temporary and transient. Likewise, transient ischemic attacks involving the distribution middle cerebral artery may produce disrupted memory function that may also be temporary and potentially treatable (e.g., carotid endarterectomy). Useful tests are the Wechsler Memory Scale (Wechsler, 1945); Denman Memory Battery (Denman, 1984); Selective Reminding Test (Buschke and Fuld, 1984); Benton Visual Retention Test (Benton, 1974); and Rey Auditory Verbal Learning Test (Rey, 1964).

Tactile Change

The primary cortical-processing area for tactile perception is in the parietal lobe. If there is a complete loss of simple touch, provided peripheral and spinal cord function is normal, this implicates damage involving the post-central gyrus. If simple touch is intact, but finger gnosis, graphesthesia, and stereognosis are impaired, this implicates more posterior parietal involvement, particularly if motor findings are minimal or absent.

Clinical Considerations and Tests

Since higher-order tactile perception (i.e., stereognosis) is dependent on the integrity of brain regions in the parietal lobe that also subserve language function in the absence of motor findings but in the presence of tactile perceptual deficits, along with receptive dysphasic disturbance, parietal lobe involvement is implicated. Also, parietal lobe lesions may damage visual projection fibers, producing an inferior quadrantanopia. With nondominant parietal lesions, tactile perception may be affected and associated with visual-spatial and/or visuopraxic deficits. Dominant lesions may also produce the so-called Gerstmann's syndrome (right–left confusion, acalculia, finger agnosia, and agraphia). Useful tests are the Double Simultaneous Tactile Stimulation (Bender, 1952); Reitan-Kløve Sensory Perceptual Examination (Reitan, 1984); Finger Localization (Benton et al., 1983); and Tactile Form Perception (Benton et al., 1983).

Hearing (Audition) Change

The superior temporal gyrus houses the cortical terminations of the auditory projection system. Damage to this area, when bilateral, produces pure word deafness. Typically, damage is not just restricted to the superior temporal gyrus and involves much of the peri-Sylvian region of the temporal lobe. This does not necessarily affect hearing per se, but does impair auditory perception of language.

Clinical Considerations and Tests

Damage to the VIII cranial nerve does produce unilateral hearing loss, but no dysphasia. Invariably when the superior and posterior aspects of the dominant temporal lobe are involved, there is some type of dysphasia. In such cases, the patients do not display a deficit in hearing (e.g., audiogram will be negative), but they will have substantial deficits in perception of language. Useful tests are the Double Simultaneous Auditory Stimulation (Bender, 1952) and Reitan-Kløve Sensory Perceptual Examination (Reitan, 1984).

Vision/Visual-Perceptual Change

The visual system projects the entire length of the brain; accordingly, damage to any lobe may affect visual functioning. Frontal injury or a space-occupying lesion may be associated with optic nerve damage, which will produce optic nerve dysfunction or blindness. Occipital or temporoparietal damage may produce a contralateral hemianopia. Focal temporal damage disrupting the visual projection fibers coursing back to visual cortex will produce a superior quadrantanopia. Similarly, focal parietal damage may produce an inferior quadrantanopia. Bilateral visual cortex damage may produce cortical blindness or visual agnosia. Prosopagnosia (facial agnosia) usually implicates bilateral occipital damage.

Clinical Considerations and Tests

Careful visual-field examination is invaluable in examining for focal cerebral damage, since either directly or indirectly the visual system is associated with each lobe. Since quadrantanopias are associated with parietal or temporal involvement, language and spatial-perceptual functions should always be assessed when quadrantanopia is found on examination. Partial unilateral occipital damage may not produce an actual visual field cut, but the patient may display visual inattention to double simultaneous stimulation, and such testing should be a part of every examination. Useful tests are the Reitan–Kløve Sensory Perceptual Examination (Reitan, 1984); Facial Recognition Test (Benton et al., 1983); and Visual Form Discrimination (Benton et al., 1983).

Olfaction Change

The location of the olfactory nerve and bulb make them vulnerable to compression by space-occupying lesions and cerebral edema, as well as to contusion effects with trauma. Accordingly, the loss of smell is frequently considered to be an indication of possible ventral-frontal lobe damage. The actual termination of the olfactory projection system is in the mesial temporal lobe, and temporal damage at this level may also affect smell, although damage to the olfactory nerve and bulb is considerably more common than anosmia secondary to temporal lobe damage.

Clinical Considerations and Tests

Testing for anosmia is not formalized and consists of a simple discrimination task (i.e., the patient can or cannot smell the substance presented). Each nostril is tested separately with an aromatic compound (e.g., coffee grounds, peppermint extract) as to whether smell is present or absent. The presence of anosmia in association with other frontal and/or temporal lobe signs aids in lesion localization.

Personality Change

Damage to frontal and/or temporal regions may be associated with change in personality as well as disorders that affect the entire cerebrum. Patients with parietal and/or occipital damage infrequently show significant changes in personality functioning, although nondominant parietal-occipital damage may produce an indifference that is mistaken for a change in personality.

Clinical Considerations and Tests

There are no formal psychometric test batteries for personality change associated with an organic brain syndrome. Probably the best approach here is the correlation of cortical function studies with documented history of change in personality as corroborated by spouse, other family members, minister, or employer. In cases of possible dementia, pseudodementia may mimic basic personality change and impaired cognition, but on formal testing neuropsychological studies will usually be negative and tests such as the Minnesota Multiphasic Personality Inventory (Hathaway & McKinley, 1951) will frequently demonstrate presence of depression and related psychiatric symptomatology. A useful test is the Minnesota Multiphasic Personality Inventory (Hathaway & McKinley, 1951).

Intellectual Change

Changes in intellect typically involve either diffuse cerebral dysfunction or damage/dysfunction in frontal and/or temporal lobes.

Clinical Considerations and Tests

In examining for intellectual change, one needs to determine an estimate of probable premorbid level of functioning. Typically, this can be gained by historical facts such as education, employment, and socioeconomic status, as well as from family input. The WAIS is the most standardized measure of intelligence, but is too dependent on overlearned material and therefore may not necessarily demonstrate reduction in IQ. The comparison of WAIS scores with level of performance on tasks more dependent on new learning (e.g., Raven's Category Test, Wisconsin Card Sorting) can, however, assist in determining if there is in fact cognitive decline. Useful tests are the Wechsler Adult Intelligence Scale (Wechsler, 1981); Raven Coloured Progressive Matrices (Raven, 1962); Wisconsin Card Sorting Test (Berg, 1948); and Halstead Category Test (Reitan & Davison, 1974).

Motor Disturbance

If a spastic hemiplegia is present, this suggests pre-central gyrus or pyramidal tract involvement contralateral to the side of paralysis. If motor exam is normal for power and strength, but integrative movements are impaired, this suggests damage anterior to the pre-central gyrus. If the patient is apraxic, then this needs to be correlated with language evaluation since apraxic movement disorder may result from frontal, parietal, or temporal lesions. Apraxic disorders also may arise from diffuse nonspecific cerebral dysfunction.

Clinical Considerations and Tests

The frontal lobe section gives a more complete description of tests. Although paralysis is obvious on clinical examination, more subtle motor deficits may only be elucidated by careful motor examination. Handgrips should be tested bilaterally and should be generally equal, with possibly slightly greater strength noted in the dominant hand. Finger movements should be examined bilaterally, as well as integrative and alternating hand movements; with extensive frontal lobe involvement, primitive reflexes may be elicited. Also, with extensive frontal lobe damage in addition to motor involvement, the patient may develop a frontal lobe behavioral syndrome (inability to maintain a series of directed associations or to function efficiently during interference, inability to make conceptual shifts, apathy, or motivational disturbance, impaired judgment, and/or diminished social awareness). The presence of such behavioral findings in association with motor disturbance suggests extensive frontal lobe involvement. Useful tests are the Luria–Christensen Motor Exam (Christensen, 1979) and Finger Oscillation Test (Reitan & Davison, 1974).

REFERENCES

Albert, M. L., Goodglass, H., Helm, N. A., Rubens, A. B., & Alexander, M. P. (1981). *Disorders of human communication: Vol. 2. Clinical aspects of dysphasia*. New York: Springer-Verlag.

Beery, K. E., & Buktenica, N. A. (1967). *Developmental test of visual-motor integration*. Cleveland, OH: Modern Curriculum Press.

Bender, L. (1938). *A visual motor Gestalt test and its clinical use* (Research Monograph No. 3). New York: American Orthopsychiatric Association.

Bender, M. B. (1952). *Disorders in perception*. Springfield, IL: C. C. Thomas.

Benson, D. F. (1979). *Aphasia, alexia and agraphia*. New York: Churchill Livingstone.

Benson, D. F., & Blumer, D. (1975, 1982). *Psychiatric aspects of neurologic disease I & II*. New York: Grune & Stratton.

Benton, A. L. (1974). *The revised visual retention test* (4th ed.). New York: Psychological Corporation.

Benton, A. L., de Hamsher, K., Varney, N. R., & Spreen, O. (1983). *Contributions to neuropsychological assessment: A clinical manual.* New York: Oxford University Press.

Berg, E. A. (1948). A simple objective test for measuring flexibility in thinking. *Journal of General Psychology, 39,* 15-22.

Bigler, E. D. (1984). *Diagnostic clinical neuropsychology.* Austin, TX: University of Texas Press.

Blumer, D., & Benson, D. F. (1975). Personality changes with frontal and temporal lobe lesions. In D. F. Benson & D. Blumer (Eds.), *Psychiatric aspects of neurologic disease* (pp. 151-170). New York: Grune & Stratton.

Brodal, A. (1981). *Neurological anatomy.* New York: Oxford University Press.

Buschke, H., & Fuld, P. A. (1974). Evaluating storage, retention and retrieval in disordered memory and learning. *Neurology, II,* 1019-1025.

Christensen, A. L. (1979). *Luria's neuropsychological investigation.* Copenhagen, Denmark: Munksgaard.

Cummings, J. L., & Duchen, L. W. (1981). The Kluver-Bucy syndrome in Pick's disease. *Neurology, 31,* 82.

Damasio, A. R. (1985). The frontal lobes. In K. M. Heilman & E. Valenstein (Eds.), *Clinical Neuropsychology* (2nd ed., pp. 339-375). New York: Oxford University Press.

Damasio, A. R., Damasio, H., & Van Hoesen, G. W. (1982). Prosopagnosia: Anatomic basis and behavioral mechanisms. *Neurology, 32,* 331-341.

Denman, S. B. (1984). *Denman neuropsychology memory scale.* Charleston, SC: Privately published.

Freemon, F. R. (1981). *Organic mental disease.* Jamaica, NY: Spectrum Publications.

Goodglass, H., & Kaplan, E. (1972). *Assessment of aphasia and related disorders.* Philadelphia: Lea & Febiger.

Hathaway, S. R., & McKinley, J. C. (1951). *The Minnesota Multiphasic Personality Inventory manual* (rev.). New York: Psychological Corporation.

Heilman, K. M., Rothi, L., & Kertesz, A. (1983). Localization of apraxia-producing lesions. In A. Kertesz, *Localization in neuropsychology* (pp. 35-76). New York: Academic Press.

Kertesz, A. (1982). *The Western Aphasia Battery.* New York: Grune & Stratton.

Kolb, B., & Whishaw, I. Q. (1985). *Fundamentals of human neuropsychology* (2nd ed.). New York: W. H. Freeman.

Lezak, M. D. (1978). Living with the characterologically altered brain injured patient. *Journal of Clinical Psychiatry, 39,* 592-598.

Lezak, M. D. (1983). *Neuropsychological assessment* (2nd ed.). New York: Oxford University Press.

Luria, A. R. (1966). *Higher cortical functions in man.* New York: Macmillan.

Osterrieth, P. A. (1944). Le test de copie d'une figure complex. *Archives de Psychologie, 30,* 206-356.

Porch, B. E. (1967). *Porch Index of Communicative Ability.* Palo Alto, CA: Consulting Psychologists Press.

Raven, J. C. (1962). *Coloured Progressive Matrices.* London, England: E. T. Heron & Co.

Reitan, R. M. (1984). *Aphasia and sensory-perceptual deficits in adults.* Tucson, AZ: Reitan Neuropsychology Laboratories.

Reitan, R. M., & Davison, L. A. (1974). *Clinical neuropsychology: Current status and applications.* Washington, DC: Winston.

Rey, A. (1964). *L'examen clinique en psychologie*. Paris, France: Presses Universitaires de France.

Ross, E. D., & Rush, A. J. (1981). Diagnosis and neuroanatomical correlates of depression in brain-damaged patients. *Archives of General Psychiatry, 38*, 1344–1354.

Russell, E. W. (1979). Three patterns of brain damage on the WAIS. *Journal of Clinical Psychology, 35*, 611–620.

Squire, L. R., & Butters, N. (1984). *Neuropsychology of memory*. New York: Guilford Press.

Stroop, J. R. (1935). Studies of interference in serial verbal reactions. *Journal of Experimental Psychology, 18*, 643–662.

Strub, R. L., & Black, F. W. (1977). *The mental status examination in neurology*. Philadelphia: F. A. Davis.

Strub, R. L., & Black, F. W. (1981). *Organic brain syndromes*. Philadelphia: F. A. Davis.

Strub, R. L., & Geschwind, N. (1983). Localization in Gerstmann syndrome. In A. Kertesz (Ed.), *Localization in neuropsychology* (pp. 345–372). New York: Academic Press.

Stuss, D. T., & Benson, D. F. (1983). Frontal lobe lesions and behavior. In A. Kertesz (Ed.), *Localization in neuropsychology* (pp. 429–454). New York: Academic Press.

Wechsler, D. A. (1945). A standardized memory scale for clinical use. *Journal of Psychology, 19*, 87–95.

Wechsler, D. (1958). *The measurement and appraisal of adult intelligence*. Baltimore: Williams and Wilkins.

Wechsler, D. (1981). *The Wechsler Adult Intelligence Scale—revised administration manual*. New York: The Psychological Corporation.

5

The Neuropsychological Examination

David C. Osmon

The multifaceted nature of higher cortical function necessitates a test battery approach to neuropsychological evaluation. All of the widely accepted techniques, including Arthur Benton's battery (Benton, de Hamsher, Varney, & Spreen, 1983), Charles Golden's battery (Golden, Hammeke, & Purisch, 1980), Muriel Lezak's battery (Lezak, 1983), and Ralph Reitan's battery (Reitan, 1969), consist of several tests and subtests that attempt to survey comprehensively, more or less, all behavioral manifestations of higher cortical functions. It is difficult to agree upon the most satisfactory categorization of the different aspects of higher cortical function, although all of the following should be represented in any scheme: orientation, attention/concentration, information-processing speed, sensory-perceptual function, motor/psychomotor function, language, memory, verbal and nonverbal concept formulation, and behavioral programming.

While all of the above batteries may be roughly equivalent in terms of their efficacy and comprehensiveness, they represent fundamentally different methodological approaches to the evaluation of higher cortical functions. One important methodological distinction is the *actuarial versus the process* approach to identifying and defining neuropsychological deficits. The actuarial method detects dysfunction by quantifying how much of a performance decrement exists, while the process method attempts to demonstrate the cognitive process that underlies the dysfunctional performance (Kaplan, 1983). A theoretically derived test battery that evaluates the fundamental elements of brain function that combine to make up the higher cortical abilities weds the actuarial and process methods of interpretation (Osmon, 1983). The theory upon which a test battery rests specifies the cognitive processes underlying the major categories of higher cortical function and allows a quantitative measurement of each fundamental element underlying any particular ability. A neuropsychodynamic analysis of the various fundamental elements of brain function can demonstrate which part of the process is dysfunctional, as well as identify how much of a performance decrement is present.

At present, only two test batteries qualify as theoretically derived, and both are derived from the theory of A. R. Luria. The first battery, developed by Anne-Lise Christensen (1975), most closely conforms to Luria's (1980) approach to neuropsychological evaluation. This approach is a flexible examination wherein pathognomonic findings dictate the course of the evaluation, much in the style of the neurological exam. Each evaluation is tailored to the unique situation that every patient represents because of his/her differing deficits and clinical presentation. The second battery, Luria–Nebraska (LNNB) developed by Charles J. Golden and associates, standardizes and quantifies the various items developed by Luria and adapted by Christensen.

While this instrument necessitates a rigid battery format wherein each patient receives the same test items, the process approach to interpretation is still possible. Because the battery comprehensively and systematically surveys the fundamental elements of higher cortical function, one can determine the underlying deficits that make up the neuropsychological deterioration. The LNNB is chosen as the subject of this chapter since it helps wed the actuarial psychometric tradition with the theoretically more powerful process method. While the LNNB has received theoretical criticism, it has yet to suffer empirical criticism. For a complete account of the test battery and its empirical foundation, see Moses, Golden, Ariel, and Gustavson (1983).

The use of an actuarial versus a process method of evaluation tends to promote different styles of examination. Those using the process method typically have a large repertoire of instruments that are used flexibly, depending upon the idiosyncrasies of the individual evaluation. The actuarial method, on the other hand, demands that the same items be administered rigidly to each patient so that a standardized examination is provided. Again a combination of these two examination styles seems most advantageous (Golden, 1981). Written under the assumption that a rigid battery (such as the LNNB) should be administered and supplemented with other instruments in order to compensate for the weaknesses of that battery, this chapter will focus on certain key deficits that amplify the process method of interpretation.

What follows is a brief discussion of the advantages and disadvantages of the neuropsychological evaluation over the neurological evaluation, a discussion of the LNNB procedure, and supplemental instruments for each scale of the LNNB.

ADVANTAGES AND DISADVANTAGES OF
THE NEUROPSYCHOLOGICAL EXAM

Perhaps the greatest improvement over the neurological evaluation is the use of standardized instruments where reference norms allow the quantification of dysfunction. A rigid test battery format takes advantage of the uniform procedure of administration by developing a research base. Reference norms that define normal and abnormal performance for various patient groups are easily developed from this research base and provide for a widely applicable and comprehensive assessment of brain function. Such an evaluation is not as dependent upon the presence of pathognomonic signs as is the neurological evaluation. In fact, the test battery is constructed in order to detect degrees of quantitative performance deficit; and while pathognomonic signs (e.g., motoric perseveration, loss of categorical structure of number, verbal paraphasia, unilateral spatial neglect, etc.) are thus apparent, they are not as necessary for detecting brain dysfunction with the test battery.

By design, the neuropsychological battery is particularly suited to three clinical tasks in the neurological/rehabilitation situation. The first task, *quantification of neuropsychological performance*, allows the specific delineation of brain-related deficits, serving both diagnostic and treatment purposes. For example, while neurological exams can detect the pathognomonic signs of degenerative dementia (such as primitive reflexes, akinetic-abulic syndrome, etc.), a quantitative neuropsychological exam can detect earlier signs, such as memory and cognitive dysfunction, that typically occur long before the more severe pathognomonic indicators. More specific delineation of the deficits is also important in designing a remediation program to rehabilitate the neuropsychological sequelae of brain injury. Forensic applications are a direct by-product of the ability to quantify brain dysfunction. The determination of brain dysfunction following head trauma, competency and commitment determinations, and the iatrogenic effects of medical procedures are all examples of forensic applications.

The second clinical task is the diagnostic function of *detecting subtle deficits*. Unlike the neurological exam, detecting abnormal performance does not rely so heavily on qualitatively different (pathognomonic) productions. Since performance is expressed as a continuous variable, degrees of performance can be detected and compared to the reference norms. Subtle deficits that do not necessarily occur concomitantly with pathognomonic signs can be identified because of their quantitative difference from the reference norms. Subtle deficit detection is important in most neurological situations; and while a complete delineation is beyond the scope of this chapter, a few examples are in order. Postconcussional syndrome associated with apparent neurological recovery can be an insidious process that requires careful and sensitive examination in order to verify the patient's complaints of memory and information-processing speed difficulties. Transient ischemic attack is another condition in which the neurological sequelae are difficult to detect and to differentiate from other cerebrovascular problems. Well-timed neuropsychological evaluations are often able to verify subtle deficit associated with the functions of the arterial distribution in question versus the more focal and severe dysfunction associated with occlusion.

The third clinical task for which the neuropsychological evaluation is specifically suited is the *baseline examination*. A baseline examination with follow-up testing may be of use for diagnostic, prognostic, and treatment considerations. Perhaps one of the more important diagnostic examples of repeated neurological evaluation occurs in Alzheimer's-type dementia. Since a definitive diagnosis of this dementia is not possible short of brain biopsy, repeat examination in which degeneration in function can be demonstrated over testings provides a conservative method of making the diagnosis while the disease is still in its earlier stages. Prognostic functions of the examination include such things as making patient disposition statements (as in the case of independent living capability in dementia), helping to determine pre- to postsurgical changes, and identifying the end of the spontaneous recovery of function period. Finally, the neuropsychological evaluation plays a role in the treatment of brain dysfunction by providing a baseline examination that can assist in designing a cognitive rehabilitation program. Follow-up examinations determine the appropriateness and success of the rehabilitation program.

In these times of health care cost containment, when auxiliary consultation is deemphasized, the neuropsychological examination is not without its disadvantages. The cost of neuropsychological services is relatively high due to the length of comprehensive testing. The disadvantage inherent in the cost of the original diagnostic service is partially offset by later savings, which tend to accrue because of the efficiency of the service. For example, making the diagnosis of degenerative dementia after two neuropsychological evaluations may avert the process of "doctor-hopping" that sometimes occurs when, after numerous CT scans and other diagnostic tests, the family doctor, the neurologist, the psychiatrist, and others are unable to provide satisfaction to the patient and family. Nevertheless, the original diagnostic outlay is expensive, and a prudent referral process and a cost-effective examination are necessities. Hence the current practice of a comprehensive, rigid screening battery, supplemented sparsely by selected tests that complete the process analysis, is recommended.

NEUROPSYCHOLOGICAL SCREEN AND SUPPLEMENTAL TESTS

The LNNB is, at the time of this writing, the second most widely used neuropsychological battery after the Halstead–Reitan Battery. It consists of

269 independent items organized into 11 subscales: Motor, Rhythm, Tactile, Visual, Receptive Speech, Expressive Speech, Writing, Reading, Arithmetic, Memory, and Intellectual Processes. Other derived scales are commonly used both in research and clinical interpretation, and these scales number over 50, including Pathognomonic, Right Hemisphere (2 scales), Left Hemisphere (2 scales), Localization scales (8 scales), and Factor scales (30 scales). The LNNB appears to be a reliable instrument, with split-half coefficients of .89–.95 and a test–retest coefficient of .88. Validity studies have demonstrated clinically acceptable hit-rates (75–90%) in lateralizing, localizing, and differentiating schizophrenic from brain-damaged subjects. Studies of both clinical judgment and actuarial prediction have found the LNNB and Halstead–Reitan batteries to be comparable in making clinical discriminations in brain-damaged populations. Because of the wide use of the LNNB, a more thorough review of the research will not be undertaken here; for a comprehensive psychometric treatment of the LNNB, refer to Moses and associates (1983).

The 11 subtests of the LNNB, listed above, serve as a useful outline in discussing the various aspects of the neuropsychological screening method. In order to facilitate a process approach to interpretation, in which a neurodynamic analysis of brain deficits is to occur, a more detailed breakdown of neuropsychological abilities according to a theory of brain function is needed. This breakdown, as shown in the Appendix, is derived by the present author from Luria (1980), from Christensen (1975), and from the factor scales found by Golden and associates (see Moses et al., 1983). Because the items of each subtest are rationally divided according to the predominant elemental brain function evaluated by each item, they facilitate a neurodynamic analysis of the test performance.

What follows is a consideration of the LNNB items and appropriate tests to supplement the examination according to this breakdown of brain function. Test items are discussed conceptually, and some familiarity with the LNNB is assumed. For a detailed explanation of the individual test items, see the LNNB manual (Golden, Hammeke, & Purisch, 1980).

Motor Functions Scale

Various aspects of psychomotor abilities are evaluated on the 51 items of this scale, from simple movements to more difficult gestural imitations to verbally regulated motoric programmes. Elemental aspects of motor function are broken down into tasks relating to pyramidal function (Motor Speed and Coordination), parietal contributions (Kinesthetically Based Movement), visuomotor integration (Optic-Spatial Imitation and Construction Dyspraxia), prefrontal regulation (Bilateral Rapid Alternating Movement), and verbal regulation (Dyspraxia and Motor Selectivity). Evaluating such various aspects of motor function allows the localization of deficit on this scale to numerous brain functional systems (e.g., pyramidal tract, parietal, temporal, lateral prefrontal, medial prefrontal areas).

Motor Speed and Coordination

Four items include unilateral finger-thumb sequential touching and unilateral hand clenching, scored for number completed in 10 seconds. These items are more complicated than the Halstead–Reitan Finger Oscillation Test (see Golden et al., 1980) and represent a less pure measure of motor speed because of confounding with coordination. The Finger Oscillation Test may be supplemented when a more pure and more sustained (repeated trials) measure of pyramidal function is desired, with the added advantage that a more reliable measure of lateralized speed decrement will be obtained.

Extrapyramidal function is not systematically examined on the LNNB; a quantitative evaluation of tremor and other aspects of involuntary regulation of movement requires supplemental tests from the Wisconsin Motor Steadiness Battery (Beardsley, Matthews, Cleeland, & Harley, 1978). An electrical apparatus is used to measure the number and duration of touches with a stylus that occur along the edges of various test boards (e.g., maze, straight line groove, gauge, etc.). An electric finger tapper and a foot tapper are also included to allow a relative comparison of upper and lower extremities. While normative data is scarce, these instruments can be qualitatively useful in rounding out the motor functions examination. Limb-kinetic dyspraxia may also be an important factor to consider if extreme clumsiness is apparent (see Heilman & Rothi, 1985).

Kinesthetically Based Movement

Four items evaluate the sensory basis of movement by having the patient move according to cutaneous prompting. Ideally these items clarify the elemental deficit operating in body schema problems such as finger dysgnosia. Coupled with items from the tactile, visual, and language scales, a neurodynamic analysis tries to discover whether the finger dysgnosia deficit is derived from tactile perceptual, sensory-motor integration, spatial orientation, or language understanding/expression problems. No other supplemental tests are usually required for this section.

Optic-Spatial Imitation

Likewise, visual-motor integration is an important functional system to evaluate, and this is done by demonstrating certain body positions that the patient must imitate. These 12 items evaluate the patient's ability to translate visual cues into motor movements through the use of simple static positions as well as more complex static, oppositional positions, for example, where the right hand crosses over to the left body side. Right–left confusion is easily elicited by these items. Perseverative mirror-imaging is often demonstrated when the patient repeatedly raises the wrong arm because of a failure to appreciate the relative juxtaposition of the examiner's face-to-face position (echopraxia related to frontal dysfunction). These items demonstrate the visual-motor integrity that is necessary before an evaluation for dyspraxia can proceed. That is to say, dyspraxia cannot be reliably diagnosed unless sufficient visual-motor integrity is present to perform these items. Typically, no supplemental tests are required.

Bilateral Rapid Alternating Movements

Whereas unilateral rapid alternating movements (RAMs) serve to evaluate extrapyramidal (especially cerebellar) contributions to movement, bilateral and simultaneous RAMs help to evaluate the higher cortical aspects of motor programming. These four items test the patient's ability to establish, maintain, and switch flexibly between motor stereotypes. The contributions of the orbital and lateral prefrontal as well as the premotor areas are examined. The inability to establish a simple motor stereotype, such as simultaneously opening and closing alternate hands, may be a rough indication of lateral prefrontal lobe dysfunction in which the various elements are unable to be integrated into an overall motor program. Likewise, a poorly maintained motor stereotype may be a rough indication of orbital prefrontal lobe dysfunction in which active programs lose their strength and selectivity. Premotor area dysfunction may be indicated by the lack of smooth, simultaneous alternation between the two hands. Supplemental tests are not usually required, although in evaluating simultaneous bilateral movements care should be taken to rule out cerebellar contributions as well as unilateral hypokinesia associated with basal ganglia dysfunction, which can impair motor programming independent of higher cortical involvement.

Dyspraxia

Both ideomotor and ideational dyspraxia of the buccofacial and hand/arm variety are addressed in these 11 items. The ideomotor items, which including such single near-automatisms as demonstrating the use of scissors and chewing, relate more to posterior brain lesions; while the ideational items, which involve programming several such discrete movements as showing how to pour and stir tea, tend to be associated with prefrontal lesions. Both types of dyspraxia, however, can be associated with both lesions sites. Reliably quantifying dyspraxia is difficult, and the limited number of items in the section makes the chance for false negatives great. Supplemental items are often necessary in order both to increase reliability and to make a specific effort to include items that evaluate nondominant hand/arm, limb-kinetic, disconnection, and dissociation dyspraxia (see Heilman & Rothi, 1985; Kimura & Archibald, 1974).

Construction Dyspraxia

These 12 items evaluate both speed and accuracy of the drawings of simple geometric shapes. Only gross deficits are identified by this section, and supplemental tests such as drawing a Greek cross or a Necker's cube and constructing three-dimensional objects (see Benton, 1973) are often necessary. The Rey-Osterrieth Complex Figure Test (Rey, 1941) is also an excellent supplemental test, especially when differentially diagnosing construction dyspraxia due to visual orientation deficits secondary to parietal-occipital dysfunction, versus that due to visual reasoning/problem-solving deficits associated with frontal lobe dysfunction. The use of these more complex construction praxis tests is mandatory when evaluating a more intelligent and/or more educated patient.

Motor Selectivity

These four items make use of oppositional instructions to test the strength and selectivity of the motor trace. The patient with a weak motor trace will be seduced by the stimulus to a more preferred or automatic response. The required, but less preferred, responses give way to motoric echopraxia. For example, if the examiner knocks once on the table, then the patient must knock twice and vice versa. The patient may demonstrate conceptual or linguistic difficulty in not being able to establish the stereotype or may show the poor selectivity of trace deficit typical of orbital frontal dysfunction by not maintaining the stereotype. These tasks do not require supplemental tests, although re-administration of the same task, at some later time, is often useful in verifying the deficit. A true deficit is typically robust to positive transfer effects.

Rhythm Scale

This scale attempts to evaluate nonverbal auditory gnostic functions according to three elemental aspects of brain function: Nonverbal Auditory Perception and Expression, Tracking nonverbal auditory signals, and Motor Imitation of rhythms. Performance on this scale is easily disrupted by peripheral hearing problems, and all attempts to work around hearing problems should be made to insure valid testing. While this scale appears to be a relatively pure measure of auditory gnosis and auditory-motor integration, performance on this scale is greatly affected by attentional problems. Likewise, serious language comprehension difficulties may preclude an accurate evaluation (i.e., gestural, nonverbal communication); prior to proceeding, demonstration by example should be used to determine that the patient understands the purpose of each item. While rhythm skills are generally thought to relate more to the right hemisphere, clinical experience suggests that difficulties on this scale occur with lesions in either hemisphere, especially when the damage is more anterior in the brain (Osmon, Sweet, & Golden, 1978).

Nonverbal Auditory Perception and Expression

These six items test the patient's ability to discern simple pitch differences as well as more complex tonal patterns. The patient is asked to hum tonal patterns as well as to generate melodies. This subscale represents a cursory screening of rhythm perception, which probably achieves a clinically useful hit-rate only when moderately severe deficits are present. The Halstead–Reitan Rhythm Test should be used when more subtle deficits are to be detected. Although the Halstead–Reitan test surveys nonverbal auditory perceptual functions, it is even more susceptible to attentional problems that can only be differentiated from actual perceptual deficits by clinical judgment.

Expressive rhythm skills are evaluated according to the simple vocal reproduction of two-tone and three-tone relationships and the ability to sing. This distinction is made in an attempt to differentiate between deficits due simply to poor auditory-motor integration versus deficits due to problems with extemporaneous generation of the appropriate behavioral program. While the simple reproduction task appears to be adequate, the singing tasks are difficult to score, and their scoring is a clinical rating rather than an objective quantification. Differentiation of reproduction versus generation deficits is therefore tenuous, and alternate, supplemental tests are not available. Likewise, no provision for the evaluation of auditory sound dysgnosia is made, although formal psychometric instruments are limited (see Albert, Sparks, von Stockert, & Sax, 1972; Spreen, Benton, & Fincham, 1965).

Tracking

These four tasks consist of the ability to encode a sequence of monotonic tones as well as sequences of nonmonotonic tones and to report how many tones were heard. These tasks evaluate short duration and focal attention, as well as auditory perception. Supplemental tasks are not required; however, testing-the-limits procedures are often quite useful. Asking the patient vocally to reproduce the test stimulus is sometimes helpful to work around mental control or behavior verification deficits that are independent of attentional or auditory gnosis problems. Simply repeating the items is sometimes necessary to overcome confoundment of results due to "warm-up" effects, comprehension difficulties, or temporary inefficiencies on the part of the patient. Examiner experience and ability is often crucial in obtaining the most useful assessment of the elemental deficit operating in this subscale.

Motor Imitation

These two items assess the ability of the patient to reproduce a rhythm sequence in a motoric manner that is either heard by cassette tape or verbally represented (for example, the subject is asked to make a series of two taps). While these items assess auditory gnosis to the extent that the patient must understand the rhythm, these items appear to be more associated with motor programming ability similar to the skills assessed in the Bilateral RAMs section on the Motor Scale. No supplemental tests are required.

Tactile Scale

The evaluation of cutaneous and proprioceptive sensation follows closely the neurological examination, with the exception that a strict standardized procedure with accompanying quantitative norms is provided. Impairment on this scale may represent dysfunction extending from sense organ to the cortical sensorimotor analyzer and posterior parietal secondary areas of the cortex. Therefore, while performance on this scale may be helpful in localizing damage, interpretation of deficits associated with this scale alone are not a prudent practice. For further discussion of this type of examination procedure see Chapter 4. A final cautionary note involves the normative data for this scale. Normal older patients may perform in the borderline and even impaired range, especially on the first subscale, simply as a result of age. Careful test administration procedures may circumvent this problem by insuring adequate strength of stimulation, although impairment in tactile perceptual functions without appropriate accompanying cognitive defects should be conservatively interpreted. Four subscales comprise this scale: Simple Cutaneous Sensation, Graphesthesia, Proprioception, and Stereognosis.

Simple Cutaneous Sensation

Ten items evaluate the bilateral aspects of cutaneous localization, discrimination of sharp versus dull pressure, discrimination of stimulus intensity, two-point discrimination, and directionality of cutaneous stimulation. Task performance varies with impairment in peripheral, spinal, brainstem, and cortical sensory systems, as well as varying with age. This scale suffers from a lack of strong age-related normative data, and accurate interpretation must allow for increased variability of performance in older patients. It is also important to develop a reliable reporting system for the patient (especially for the cutaneous localization items) to insure that tactile perception, and not language difficulties or left–right confusion, is assessed by this item.

This scale is meant to evaluate higher-level sensory deficits and, as such, does not try to reproduce the homologous aspects of the neurological examination. Deficits that occur on this subscale in the absence of deficits on the other tactile subscales, or on other subscales that relate to parietal function, may need to be further evaluated. A thorough neurological examination by an experienced neurologist may be essential to help rule out peripheral, spinal, or brainstem impairment. Also, the double simultaneous stimulation procedures from the Sensory-Perceptual Exam of the Halstead–Reitan Battery are strong measures of parietal lobe dysfunction in tactile information processing and probably would serve well as a routine supplement to this subscale.

Graphesthesia

Six items evaluate the patient's ability to identify both verbal and nonverbal symbols written on the back of the right and left wrists. These items also suffer from a lack of adequate age-related norms, as well as lacking the most advantageous administration procedure. Clinical experience suggests that before the item begins, it is useful to demonstrate the symbols for the patient (especially the older patient). This procedure may help to differentiate between the performance errors occurring because of the unpreparedness of the patient and those occurring because of a deficit in tactile integration (simultanagnosia). While supplemental tests are not usually necessary, it is sometimes advisable to increase the number of items on this subscale to insure an adequate sampling of behavior.

Proprioception

Two items attempt to determine the patient's ability to identify given arm positions and to match those positions with the opposite arm without visual cues. These items are difficult to score, and it is unclear whether the items actually measure proprioception. First, the laterality of the deficit is confounded by whether the problem is in identifying the original position or in matching it with the other arm. Second, because the subject must move his arm into position, proprioception is not the only skill involved. It is probably more useful to position the arm and then give the subject a multiple choice of different positions of the same arm, placed by the examiner.

Given the problems within this subscale, any deficit should be followed up with the neurological tests for vibratory sense loss (pallesthesia) and position sense loss (see Van Allen & Rodnitzky, 1981). If position sense loss occurs in the absence of pallesthesia, then deficits on this subscale more than likely relate to cortical dysfunction (especially parietal dysfunction).

Stereognosis

These four items examine the patient's ability to identify common objects by palpation with the right and left hands. Caution should be taken that errors are not due to verbal inabilities in generating the name of the object. Gestural indications of the use of the object are acceptable responses.

This subscale is essentially a standardization of the analogous task of the neurological exam. Errors in identification are the strongest sign of the test, although standardization of the item allows differences in identification speed to be noted. Slowed identification speed in the absence of errors makes for a tenuous diagnostic decision; however, lateralized speed deficits, especially in the presence of other parietal signs, may be a useful hint of subtle dysfunction.

Visual Scale

As Luria notes, there is no clear distinction between elementary (noncortical) and higher cortical visual impairment (Luria, 1966). This fact emphasizes the importance of establishing the integrity of visual acuity and the absence of the visual-field loss or unilateral spatial neglect prior to the administration of this scale. One final preparation recommended by Luria includes a procedure that evaluates eye movement controlled by the cortical optic analyzer in the occipital lobes by moving an object in the visual fields that must be fixated by the patient. Complex, psychomotor eye movements are tested by having the patient move his eyes according to verbal command, both with and without distractors. A distractor is created by placing an object in the field opposite to where the eye movement is to occur. Patients with dysfunction of the frontal eye fields or prefrontal lobes will find it difficult to overcome the controlling influence of the distractor, yet reflex movement will be intact.

Having established the integrity of elementary visual function and evaluated eye movement, the neuropsychological assessment can commence, making use of three subscales: Visual Perception, Orientation, and Spatial Reasoning.

Visual Perception

Six items are designed to evaluate visual and simultaneous dysgnosia through the use of common objects, photographs of objects, blurred and silhouetted representations of objects, and superimposed line drawings of objects. Impairment on these items results from peripheral visual dysfunction, cortical blindness, apperceptive dysgnosia, or visual/simultaneous dysgnosia (see DeRenzi, 1982; Luria, 1980). Discrimination between these various deficits is often not possible without further testing, although clinical decisions rarely require such fine distinctions. Since pure states of associative visual dysgnosia are rare, usually the important information is whether deficits on these items represent cortical dysfunction, not whether associative, apperceptive, or simultaneous dysgnosia is present.

Supplemental tests should begin with the neurologist's examination of the eyes to rule out visual-field cuts and visual tracking problems. Assuming the absence of dysphasic confoundment (e.g., optic aphasia), the viability of attributing deficits to occipital dysfunction can be corroborated by evaluating for prosopagnosia and central achromatopsia (see Damasio, 1981; Damasio, Damasio, & Van Hoesen, 1982). The test of Facial Recognition, while not actually a test for prosopagnosia (Benton & Van Allen, 1973), and a battery of tests to evaluate different aspects of color perception (DeRenzi & Spinnler, 1967) are appropriate supplements.

The items included in this subscale are easy and may miss subtle deficits, especially in patients with above average education and/or intelligence. Likewise, the normative data may be inadequate for interpretation with older patients. The Mooney Test of Face Closure (Mooney, 1957) can provide useful qualitative information to improve sensitivity when used impressionistically, although it lacks adequate normative data as well.

Visual Orientation

These five items largely test the ability to discern alignment in two-dimensional space by having the patient complete a complex design, match several spatially similar alternatives, read and draw clock faces, and identify direction on a compass. Impairment on this subscale rests with the demonstration of right–left confusion or spatial reversals (e.g., reading ten o'clock as two o'clock on the clock face). These items are confounded with educational and intellectual status, especially at the lower levels of attainment. Impairment on these items in the absence of spatial reversals must be interpreted cautiously. Comparison with evidence for higher premorbid levels of function or disproportionate performance on other parts of the battery helps in deciding whether poor performance is related to brain dysfunction. Supplemental items are usually not required; however, subtle deficits may be missed in patients with high intelligence or educational levels. In these cases, the Line Orientation Test (Benton, de Hamsher, Varney, & Spreen, 1983) may be helpful to rule out visual orientation deficits.

Spatial Reasoning

Three items test two aspects of nonverbal reasoning: mental rotation of visual configurations and spatial problem solving. These tasks require a great deal of conceptual skill and may be impaired due to low general intellectual level independent of visual-spatial deficits. For example, degenerative dementia patients or aphasic patients with language comprehension problems are typically unable to do the mental rotation task (#99; throughout the remainder of this chapter, such numbers refer to items in the Appendix) because they are unable to understand the instructions. The visual-spatial requirements of the item cannot be evaluated if the patient cannot understand the task well enough to demonstrate the presence of such skill. Qualitative interpretation of performance problems on these items must determine the process that underlies poor performance.

Deficits in spatial reasoning that are brain related, and not artifacts of educational or intellectual variables, may sometimes be differentiated into perceptual difficulties related to posterior brain dysfunction (especially in the right hemisphere). While impairment on items #97 and #98, in the absence of significant difficulties with item #99 and the other two Visual subscales, may often indicate anterior brain dysfunction, this deficit complex is not always present. A more reliable method is to determine through process analysis that the impairment on this subscale is related to poor problem-solving strategy. A successful strategy on the block-counting items (#97 and #98) consists of the realization that the stack is made up of rows of blocks, each with the same number of blocks in them (see Figure 5.1). A qualitative analysis of the process used in solving this item may, therefore, help in differentiating anterior from posterior brain dysfunction.

Receptive Speech Scale

This scale, along with the other language (i.e., Expressive Speech, Writing, and Reading) scales, has been sharply criticized because of the confoundment of impressive and expressive functions on any given item. In fact, the entire test has been criticized as being so heavily dependent upon verbal ability as to penalize the aphasic patient with verbal response requirements even on tests of nonverbal abilities. With the moderately to severely impaired aphasic patient, these criticisms are largely valid, and every attempt should be made on the nonlanguage scales to work around the verbal problems. The quantitative measures on the LNNB (Form I and II) are not capable of differentiating types of aphasia according to current typologies; nor was the battery designed to do so. The competent examiner should be able to make such differentiations through qualitative analysis of the test results and familiarity with the patient. The original normative data of the test, however, lacked appropriate aphasic patient groups to develop quantitative measures to separate the types of aphasic diagnostic groups. In fact, the scoring procedures that tend to confound different language functions may make such measures impossible to develop.

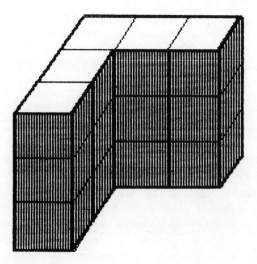

FIGURE 5.1 Three-dimensional block counting item (#97 in the Appendix.)

Any patient with apparent aphasia, demonstrable on clinical presentation, should receive a specialized test for aphasia (such as the Porch Index of Communicative Ability, Boston Diagnostic Aphasia Exam, etc.) as a supplement to the LNNB and as a substitute for the Receptive, Expressive, Writing, and Reading scales. For all but the moderately-to-severely impaired aphasic patient, however, the LNNB language scales provide an adequate screening of language comprehension and speech output.

Auditory Perception

Eight items test the ability to perceive and reproduce (vocally and graphically) individual phonemes when auditorily presented one at a time, in pairs or triplets, and when presented as part of a nonsense word. The patient's ability to establish a motor stereotype, which is regulated by an auditory signal, is also tested in one item (#106). Performance on this subscale is significantly hampered by peripheral hearing problems and by motoric difficulties that preclude graphic or vocal reproduction. These problems should be excluded before phonemic hearing difficulties or audiographic problems are diagnosed. In cases where motoric difficulties interfere, a matching-to-sample procedure can be substituted, wherein the patient points or otherwise indicates which phoneme was heard from among various alternatives. The Speech Sounds Perception Test (SSPT) of the Halstead–Reitan Battery also evaluates phonemic perception without requiring complex motor skills (only an underlining response is required). The most unique contribution of the SSPT is a better sample of behavior (60 items). It may be, however, that the sound combinations (e.g., theet) on the SSPT are a more sensitive measure of auditory dysgnosia than the individual phoneme tasks of this subscale.

Simple Commands

Nine items test low-level comprehension by having the patient carry out simple commands through pointing responses, verbal explanations, and gestural demonstrations. Errors on this subscale are rare, except in a moderately-to-severely impaired aphasic population. One exception to this rule is item #109 where the patient is to point sequentially to his eye, nose, ear, eye, nose. Errors on this item are common and appear to indicate many problems, such as comprehension difficulties, memory overload, concentration difficulties, dyspraxia, and deficits in the verbal regulation of behavior. Where errors occur only on items #110, 113, and 116 in the Appendix, visual dysgnosia should be ruled out as a cause of the impairment by referring to the performance on the Visual Perception subscale.

Logical-Grammatical Relationships

These 16 items further evaluate comprehension by testing the patient's ability to decode meaning in spatial-verbal relationships, oppositional instructions, complex prepositional phrases, and phrases with unusual word order. More subtle comprehension problems are evaluated on this subscale, although deficits associated with poor performance on this subscale can also occur in problems unrelated to aphasia. For example, right anterior hemisphere injury commonly impairs performance, probably for similar reasons that Picture Arrangement (see, below, Thematic Pictures subscale) performance is impaired. That is, both types of tasks require a simultaneous, spatial alignment of information that is sequentially presented. In the task "who is lightest, if Mary is lighter than Kate but darker than Jane?", this simultaneous, spatial synthesis is necessary in order to bring some juxtaposed order to the verbal chaos.

Because of the complexity of the items in this subscale, general intellectual deficits must be ruled out as the cause of impairment. Assuming an aphasic cause, two elemental deficits must be discriminated. Both the agrammatism associated with the anterior, nonfluent aphasias and the tertiary deficits associated with the supramarginal and angular gyri syndromes can be responsible for the impaired scores on this subscale. Attendant deficits of finger dysgnosia, dysgraphesthesia, dysstereognosis, dyscalculia, right–left confusion, and possibly visual dysgnosia and mild construction dyspraxia help to locate the damage more posteriorly. Likewise, concomitant motor impairment and behavioral programming problems help locate the damage anteriorly.

Supplemental tests may be desirable to evaluate comprehension level independent of the logical-grammatical relationship component. The Token Test (Boller & Vignolo, 1966; for a shortened version, see Spellacy & Spreen, 1969) is one of the best all-around measures of auditory language comprehension, and adequate performance on this measure is essential for the validity of the LNNB administration. Another short test that serves to measure lexical comprehension in relation to the relative skill level of grammatical ability is the Sentence Order Test (von Stockert & Bader, 1976). This instrument has the patient make a sentence by ordering three cards that can be arranged according to word order or grammatical order. Anterior, nonfluent aphasics tend to use word order because of their impairments in grammatical skill, while posterior, fluent aphasics use grammatical order because of lexical deficits. Verbal conceptual abilities may also need to be evaluated independent of the confounding factors associated with spatial and syntactical aspects of logical-grammatical relationships. A series of matching tasks where a conceptual association serves to mediate two words (e.g., white mediates the word pair swan–snowman) fulfills this purpose (Kelter, Cohen, Engel, List, & Strohnor, 1976).

Expressive Speech Scale

This scale represents the output of language functions; and, while the Receptive and Expressive Speech scales can generally be interpreted along traditional anterior versus posterior aphasia lines, this distinction is often misleading because of the functional-system aspect of brain function. Most traditional aspects of anterior, nonfluent aphasia deficits are evaluated, including verbal praxis; repetition of words, phrases, and sentences; automatic speech; generative and spontaneous language; and confrontation naming. Other aspects are evaluated from performance on other subscales, including prosody, inferred from performance on the Rhythm subscales and grammatical ability, tested on the Logical-Grammatical subscale.

The functional-system theory necessitates that a neurodynamic analysis of all performance problems by made in order to discern the underlying deficit responsible for the impairment. Anterior aphasia syndromes are not the only disorders to cause impairment on this scale; hence, elevations on this scale do not automatically imply deficits associated with such disorders. For example, some mental control problems associated with subclinical confusional states often cause impairment on the Automatic Series Repetition subscale, despite the lack of any nonfluent aphasia deficits. This finding exists because of the participation of the skills associated with this subscale in various functional systems, besides the functional system of speech fluency. It becomes important, then, to analyze dynamically the performance problems on the scale (and, indeed, all scales) in light of the quantitative and qualitative performance patterns seen throughout the test battery.

Repetition

Ten items test repetition of single phonemes, consonant combinations, single- and multiple-syllable words, and phrases. Educational confoundment is common on this subscale, interfering with the distinction between verbal dyspraxia, learning disability, and simple lack of educational experience. Educational deficiencies are typically distinguished by relatively poorer performance on the rarer multisyllable words that are outside patients' academic experience. Language-related learning disabilities demonstrate problems with the consonant combinations more often than other diagnostic groups. Verbal dyspraxia is most evident on the items where word pairs and triplets (e.g., #135, see-seen, tree-trick; #141, hat-sun-bell, hat-bell-sun) must be serially repeated. The classic repetition deficits associated with arcuate fasciculus damage are less specific to the type of material being repeated, showing up across the range of tasks on this subscale. Supplemental tasks are not required.

Pronunciation

These 11 items are almost the identical items from the previous subscale, with the addition of one word-triplet item (i.e., #146, cat-dog-man). The task here, however, is to generate the spoken form of the item from a visual stimulus without benefit of hearing the item. Both educational deficiencies and verbal dyspraxia are especially prominent on these items. Educational deficiency is more commonly the problem when impairment on this subscale follows flawless performance on the previous subscale. Verbal dyspraxia shows up more often on this subscale as problems chaining together the sounds of multisyllable words into a smoothly pronounced unit. Supplemental tasks are not required.

Sentence Repetition

These three items simply test the patient's ability to repeat simple and compound sentences. This subscale is poorly constructed to evaluate repetition because of the length of the material to be repeated. The items are so long that verbal information overload, rather than repetition, is tested. In theory, the items are designed to evaluate impaired word order secondary to deficits in sequential programming of syntax due to premotor region damage. Were it not for the inordinate length of the items, this purpose would be served. As it stands, however, the subscale best detects anxiety and memory-span dysfunction. The supplemental test mentioned in the Logical-Grammatical subscale, the Sentence Order Test, and another word order task by Scholes (1982) in which agrammatic aphasics revert to the more natural "subject-object-verb" sentence order are appropriate tasks to substitute in order to serve the intended purpose of this subscale.

Confrontation Naming

Three tasks have the patient name an object from either a picture or a verbal description of the object. The first two items use a visual stimulus so that visual dysgnosia must be ruled out before dysnomia can be accurately diagnosed. The third and fourth objects of item #157 should be ignored since they are often missed by normal, non–brain-damaged patients because the form of the object is not easily discerned. Otherwise, impairment on this subscale, as well as on the first item of the Visual Perception subscale, can be a sensitive indication of dysnomia. Since dysnomia is such a common concomitant of dysphasia, a supplemental test (such as the Picture Naming subtest of the Boston Diagnostic Aphasia Exam or the Visual Naming subtest of the Multilingual Aphasia Exam) may be desired when dysnomia is suspected but does not show up on the LNNB.

Automatic Series Repetition

Four items test the forward and backward repetition of automatic or stock verbal stereotypes (counting from 1 to 20 and saying the days of the week). The original purpose of the subscale is twofold: (1) to detect premotor damage via the nonfluid repetition of the stereotypes and (2) to detect prefrontal damage via the inability to overcome the saliency of the stereotypes in repeating the series backwards. While this purpose can be achieved in principle, the objective scoring of the item fails to capitalize upon the important factor of fluidity, which is instrumental in detecting the effects of premotor damage. In addition to the objective scoring of the item, it is desirable to rate nonfluidity as defined by hesitant or unevenly spaced repetition of the elements of the item.

Clinical experience suggests that another important diagnostic distinction is associated with poor backward (as opposed to forward) repetition. Poor backward repetition, especially where errors of omission are made, seems to be either a subtle sign of mental control problems associated with incipient confusional states or a localized dysfunction of the medial limbic system structures. Medial prefrontal lobe damage, as well as dysfunction to the ascending reticular activating system, can be responsible for deficits in the ability to manipulate mentally a system of associations. These deficits cause impairment of backward repetition for reasons that are different from the impairment associated with prefrontal lobe damage to the lateral convexity. Whereas lateral prefrontal lobe dysfunction can lead to pathological inertia even to the point of inertly repeating the series in a forward manner, medial dysfunction causes errors of omission and dysfluencies of repetition because the patient has trouble keeping track of his place in the sequence (discontinuous mental stream).

In general, supplemental tests are not required. In patients with above average premorbid education/intellectual attainments, however, it is advisable to make the task more difficult by using longer and less overlearned stereotypes, such as the months of the year. Corroboration for mental control deficiency can be sought by comparison with performance on the mental arithmetic and the serial arithmetic items on the Numeric Control subscale.

Spontaneous/Generative Speech

Eleven items investigate the predicative aspects of narrative speech. In the first of three different aspects of this subscale, referred to as reproductive narrative speech, the patient is asked to narrate by reiterating either what was seen on a picture or heard in a story. Since quantitative evaluation of performance is limited (response latency and production quantity), qualitative notice of fluency, spontaneity, relevancy, and whether language production is characterized only by nominative description ("telegraphic" speech) serves for the fundamental detection of nongenerative narration. Noting performance differences between the picture and the story items gives some indication of whether there is a dissociated deficit in the visuomotor and audiomotor language systems.

The second aspect, productive narrative speech, has the patient extemporaneously generate language on a chosen subject. While the previous items evaluated the mechanical or motoric and syntactic aspects of narration, this item is used to evaluate the higher cortical, executive aspects of formulating ideas and translating those ideas into relevant, fully informative narration. The quantification of such a skill is a difficult task, and the LNNB scores for response-latency and number-of-words-spoken are certainly inadequate to capture the richness of productive narration. Qualitative evaluation of actual patient productions is necessary in order to evaluate this skill adequately.

The third aspect, complex grammatical expressions, includes both missing-link and word-arrangement tasks. In missing-link tasks the patient must fill in the correct word to complete a sentence in which the missing word is a stereotype (e.g., winter is *cold*) or is a word that is not automatic and requires an immediate adaptive response that synthesizes the two parts of the sentence (e.g., the airplane came down *although* its engine was working properly). The word-arrangement tasks require the patient to make a sentence from words given auditorily or presented in printed form. Both types of tasks in this subscale are designed to evaluate the syntactical deficits associated with anterior, nonfluent aphasia; however, it is recognized that sensory, posterior aphasia deficits may preclude this evaluation because of severe comprehension problems and paraphasic expression.

Supplemental tests include, as mentioned above, a traditional aphasia battery whenever evaluating a moderate-to-severe aphasic. Even when evaluating a mildly aphasic or nonaphasic patient, however, the productive narrative task may need to be substituted with a task like the Cookie Theft Picture from the Boston Diagnostic Aphasia Exam (BDAE). While the scoring procedures from the BDAE may be applied to the LNNB task in a successful manner, clinical experience suggests that the LNNB task lacks the richness and detail of the BDAE task. Other qualitative tasks that may be considered in order to evaluate fluidity of expression include the rapid repetition of *pu-te-ka* (motoric fluidity) and the number of words that can be generated beginning with a *B* or the Controlled Oral Word Association Test from the Benton battery (ideational fluidity).

Writing Scale

The lack of the dynamic character of a rigid test battery is perhaps most damaging to the assessment in this scale, and indeed in the whole of the educational triad of the LNNB (Writing, Reading, and Arithmetic scales). Not being able to vary the examination procedure, as Luria himself did, makes the assessment of these functions sometimes inaccurate because of the patients' varying levels of educational experience. It is crucial in the educational scales to determine how automatic a process (e.g., writing, reading, or calculation) has become in order to judge whether or not a deficit is present. For example, someone unfamiliar with the word *astrocytoma* may appear verbally dyspraxic when pronouncing the word for the first time. On the other hand, someone highly familiar with the word or well practiced in pronouncing complex words may mask their verbal dyspraxia because the task is an overlearned skill for them. Without changing the task to meet the patient's skill level, an accurate assessment is difficult; and considerable qualitative analysis of patient performance is necessary on this subtest in order to detect compensation for a deficit.

This scale is divided into four somewhat arbitrary subscales: Phonetic Analysis, Copying, Dictation, and Generative Writing. The phonetic analysis and phonetic synthesis (in the Reading scale) subscales were arbitrarily divided between the Writing and Reading scales. The order of the remaining subscales is somewhat progressive in that patients with gross motor disorders are identified early in the Copying subscale so that alternate assessment methods may be made available. Luria (1966) recommends that these subjects be assessed using a cut-out alphabet with which to form the words rather than having to write them out. The Dictation subscale is used to evaluate spatially based writing problems (optic dysgraphia), while the Generative Writing subscale evaluates for higher cortical dysfunction as it affects graphic skills.

Phonetic Analysis

Two items evaluate the ability to discern the component letters in a word, by having the patient either name the number of letters in a word or name the letter that fits a specific question about a word (e.g., "what is the first letter in *cat?*"). These items were originally designed to test for acoustico-articulatory analysis, which requires individual phonetic discrimination capability. Educationally related spelling dyspraxia is one confound that must be eliminated before this evaluation is successfully accomplished. Supplemental tasks (see below) may be necessary in order to rule out this type of spelling problem.

The evaluation of phonetic analysis rests heavily upon the qualitative assessment of how easily the patient analyzes each word. That is, an attempt is made to discern whether the patient "hears/sees" (i.e., audio-visual analysis) or "feels" (i.e., kinesthetic-articulatory analysis) the individual component elements of the word. It is practically impossible to discriminate acoustic versus visual analysis; however, articulatory analysis can be impeded by having the patient do the tasks either with the mouth open or with the tongue clenched between the teeth (Luria, 1966). Discriminating acoustic/visual from articulatory strategies of phonetic analysis not only indicates developmental sophistication (the acoustic/visual strategy being more advanced), but may also provide a clue about the origin of a dysgraphia—whether it is secondary to an acoustico-amnestic dysphasia or an afferent-motor dysphasia.

Supplemental tasks are typically unnecessary except in cases of educational advantage or disadvantage where the academic level of the tasks is inappropriate for the patient. Where educational deficiency leads to spelling difficulty, other tasks, such as the first six items from the Reitan–Indiana Aphasia

Screening Test or other items from the LNNB (#183, #185, #186), may be used to judge spelling skill. In cases where spelling skill is quite low, the items that include words with elided consonants (e.g., hedge, bridge) should be ignored and more simplistic words may be added to these tasks in order to judge acoustic analysis more accurately. Where educational advantage leads to overly automatic acoustic analysis, more sophisticated, less familiar words need to be utilized in order to provide an accurate assessment.

Copying

Four items evaluate the mechanistic visual and motor aspects of writing by having the patient copy letters, syllables, and words from both visual stimuli and from memory. An attempt is made to capture errors in the visuomotoric formation of the graphemes, such as perseverative errors of commission (e.g., *pa* is written as *paa*), mirror-image reversals of letters (e.g., *b* is written as *d*), and motor dysfluencies. The patient is also asked to write his/her name to obtain an overlearned graphic stereotype with which to evaluate automatic motor programming. As an overlearned automatism, the signature is alternately a snapshot of premorbid graphic fluency or a singular depiction of decreased graphic control due to premotor area damage. In its extreme, the lack of fluency is characterized by discrete and isolated production of the elements of the signature rather than the smooth, concatenated movement that produces the signature as a well-orchestrated unit. The memory item is included not as a test of memory per se, but rather to provide a facilitory environment for the production of graphic errors secondary to the instability of the trace. For example, perseverative errors were elicited in one case (Osmon, 1984) due to the relative unfamiliarity of the words and the similarity of their endings (e.g., *match, district, antarctic* were reproduced as *maatich atritch district*).

Use of supplemental tasks and qualitative analysis, as well as correlation with results from other subscales, is often a necessary aspect of the interpretation of the results of this subscale. One important supplemental task, mentioned by Luria (1966), is useful when visual-spatial dysgraphia is suspected. That task uses letters printed in different typefaces (e.g., B, B, B, B) in order to determine whether or not the patient is able to discern and reproduce the varying form characteristics of the letters. Qualitative observations of motor behavior are also necessary and include noting tremor, difficulty handling the writing implement, and dysfluent or nonautomatic qualities in the motoric execution of writing. These observations should be correlated with results from the Motor scale.

Dictation

Four items consisting of orally dictated sounds, words, and phrases, which must be written, make up this subscale (note that while the fourth item, #185, is actually a dictated item it may fit better with the Generative Writing subscale from a localization of dysfunction perspective). Again, auditory-acoustic analysis plays an important role in the successful negotiation of these tasks and is revealed by careful qualitative analysis of the ease with which the patient decodes the sounds and translates them into graphemes. The added complication of this subscale posed by the auditory nature of the stimuli, however, adds another interpretative dimension. Without the support of visual stimulation, optic dysgraphia is much more likely to be manifest. Difficulties in constructing the grapheme from auditory stimulation may be overcome through the use of articulatory support. Qualitative observation of vocalizations or subvocalizations for the purpose of enlisting parietal support in constructing graphemes can be diagnostic. These observations are especially productive with elided (or silent) consonants (e.g., wren). Other common mistakes on this subscale are the misordering of letters secondary to acoustic-articulatory problems, the repetition of letters or syllables, and perseverative additions to some individual letters (commonly *m*, *n*, etc.) due to pathological inertia secondary to posterior frontal dysfunction. One additional difficulty, which comes from writing word series and phrases, involves the ability to retain word order while handling the extra processing required to translate the material into graphic production. This difficulty stems from frontal and frontotemporal dysfunction.

Perhaps the greatest criticism of this subscale is the sparsity of writing samples and the particular words that make up the tasks. Supplementary tasks are generally needed in order to increase the writing samples or make them more educationally/intellectually appropriate for the patient. Many people are unfamiliar with the words *wren, physiology* and *probabilistic* and score poorly on these items because of poor education rather than because of brain dysfunction.

Generative Writing

These two items (three if #185 is included) compose an extemporaneously generated writing sample of the patient's own ideas about bringing up children. While all of the above aspects of writing problems may be manifest in this subscale, the unique contribution of the assessment lies with the generative programming aspects of prefrontal lobe function. The purpose of this subscale is to bring to light difficulties with executive functions (Lezak, 1983) in the form of sparsity of ideation and decreased immediate adaptive abilities. Qualitative observation of these kinds of deficits reveals both a general lack of substantive and relevant ideation, as well as a profound difficulty in planning a response to such a complex and open-ended task. Often, the patient with these problems will balk at the prospect of having to attempt such an ambiguous task and will give no response or a limited and poor one. Those patients who ask for clarification and guidance or otherwise attempt some stalling or deflective technique are more often incompetent secondary to anxiety rather than frontal dysfunction. Lesser organic deficits are manifested as poorly formulated narrative, which is less than fully informative or even irrelevant. While spelling dyspraxia and verbal and literal paraphasias are apparent in this subscale, such signs are generally taken from other subscales. Likewise, indications of educational attainment can be gleaned from performance on this subscale, although its primary purpose remains the assessment of prefrontal deficits as they impair writing. Syntactical problems, however, may be apparent on this subscale alone.

Supplemental tests of generative writing may be required for the purpose of obtaining a more extensive sample of behavior (in order to bring to light paraphasia, etc.) or for further exploring more severe deficits in immediate adaptive behavior. More extensive samples are best obtained by having the patient write spontaneously on other topics. Higher- or lower-level topics can be selected according to what is more appropriate to the subject's level of function. In cases where extemporaneous writing is severely impaired, written answers to concrete questions (which tax generative abilities less) can be substituted.

Reading Scale

This scale is noted as one of the most important parts of the assessment of brain dysfunction, especially for localization (Luria, 1966). Unfortunately, the LNNB version has neglected to examine this function adequately because of both the type of items selected from Luria's sample and the focus of scoring for those items. This shortcoming is being partially rectified in the LNNB III version; however, the primary component of the reading functional system according to Luria's theory is still given short shrift. Apart from educational considerations, visual perception is the most important aspect of reading skill because of the neurodynamic structure of its functional system.

The functional system for reading is essentially the opposite of that for writing: (1) visual perception of the grapheme is the first step; (2) recoding the grapheme into its phonetic structure then occurs; (3) comprehension of the meaning of the written text that is read can then take place. Because of this functional system, the ability to read relies first upon sequential processing of graphic text according to auditory and articulatory schemes. Those initial auditory/articulatory forms of processing lend verbal meaning to the graphic structures so that later processing can take the quicker form of verbal ideographic recognition. This later processing relies upon quick visual recognition of entire syllables and words so that each phonetic element of a word does not need to be processed in order to understand the meaning of the text. Understanding reading problems in terms of the various types of brain dysfunction necessitates the assessment of both sequential, auditory/articulatory aspects, as well as the simultaneous, visual aspects of reading. Differential performance in these two aspects of reading is diagnostic of parieto-occipital (simultaneous) versus temporo-occipital (sequential) dysfunction.

Luria (1966) notes four different aspects of reading skill that require assessment. The first part is a preliminary examination of peripheral function, including tests that insure the adequacy of visual "acuity, range, and movement." The neuropsychological investigation of reading follows this preliminary examination and includes: (1) visual perception of letters, (2) reading syllables and words, and (3) reading text. These areas are investigated by having the patient read aloud, except in cases where speech problems prohibit doing so. Reading the material silently will suffice in such cases, and the patient indicates his/her answer by pointing to a pictorial representation (the requisite pictures are not furnished in the LNNB version). Luria also notes that the difficulty of the assessment can be varied, as required for any particular patient, by varying the exposure time and complexity of the material or by changing various obstacles for the patient to overcome (e.g., hatch lines over letters to be read). The LNNB attempts to cover this assessment in thirteen items, which can be divided into three subscales: *Phonetic Synthesis*, *Confrontation Reading*, and *Generative Reading*.

Phonetic Synthesis

Two items consist of letter series that the patient hears and pronounces as a word. This is a sequential-processing task that assesses the patient's ability mentally to manipulate phonetic material using the auditory/articulatory mechanism. This type of task is the most sensitive item on the Reading scale to brain dysfunction in general because it has a significant simultaneous-processing component. In order to complete the items successfully, the letter sequence must be processed as a gestalt. This skill is especially prominent on the second item (#189), where the letter sequence is longer and harder to put together piece-by-piece. Careful qualitative analysis of patient performance is required in order to determine if hesitant, articulatory-supported pronunciation reveals a reliance on sequential processing because of a deficit in simultaneous processing.

Supplemental tasks are often required in order to differentiate simultaneous- and sequential-processing deficits. Additional tasks suggested by Luria include visual stimuli that require the patient to read misprinted words (e.g., *jiuce*) in order to see if the patient misses minor errors because of a global, simultaneous-processing style that neglects phonetic detail. This type of test, however, is best accomplished via a psychometric method, since many normal errors would occur due to inattention and temporary inefficiency. No such instrument, however, is yet available. Also, supplemental efforts may profitably increase the number of words to be decoded. The four words that make up this subscale do not survey the broad range of educational experience that a typical patient population brings to bear on the assessment.

Confrontation Reading

Nine items include tasks of reading individual letters, familiar letter series, syllables, and words from visual stimuli. The difficulty of the task is varied by reading overlearned graphic structures, such as single letters and familiar letter series (e.g., *USA*); by reading familiar and simple words versus words with complex structures (e.g., *insubordination*); by reading nonsense syllables; and by reading completely unfamiliar words (e.g., *astrocytoma*).

Careful qualitative analysis of the pronunciation of these varied words can yield important information about the patient's ability to recode the grapheme into phonetic structure. One pathognomonic sign occurs when the patient recodes a nonsense syllable into a more familiar verbal structure (e.g., *prot* becomes *port*) because of a problem with the auditory or sensory/motor afferent analyzer. That is, the patient is unable to "hear" or to "feel" the sounds in their correct order and substitutes more familiar structures in the absence of the ability to sound out the syllable. Hesitancies in pronunciation become important observations because they indicate difficulties in the sequential, auditory/articulatory processing of the verbal material.

Supplemental tasks again emphasize the simultaneous processing of the verbal structures into whole perceptions. Luria recommends several tasks, which are not incorporated into the LNNB, that evaluate the global perception of verbal material. For example, two tasks assess directly the visual perception of letters, syllables, and words either by having the patient match the material to corresponding material in different typefaces or by superimposing cross-hatching or wavy lines over the material. These tasks tax the parieto-occipital simultaneous processor in order to assess the degree of difficulty the patient has in ideographic recognition of words as wholes. One pathognomonic sign (literal visual agnosia) is apparent when letter series that intermix the same letter in different typefaces are rapidly presented. When hesitations occur in recognizing the same letter in different typefaces, literal visual agnosia may be present. This sign may sometimes be seen on LNNB item #192 (and #178), where the patient, because of an inability to perceive the whole stimulus at once, runs together the various elements of the items (e.g., *pan* instead of *pa-an* on #178). Item #191 (which letter—*B, J,* or *S*—stands for *John?*) is designed to be a test of visual perception of single letters; however, on the LNNB it does not appear to be measuring this function. When the item is wrong, it appears merely to be an indication that the patient did not understand the instructions. The task is better given with a demonstration and more letters for the patient to perceive. The letters should be accompanied by visual perceptual obstacles such as different orientations (e.g., mirror image), unusual typefaces, or visual interference in order to tax the simultaneous processor.

Generative Reading

Four items test the patient's reading of sentences and text with several lines. Items #197 and 198 may be placed in either this subscale or the previous one; although they seem to fit better in the generative category, since more than one verbal unit is read at one time. It is with these items that the visual-perceptual aspects of reading often become more evident, since visual tracking along and between lines is necessary. Problems with this type of task often involve poor integration of the sequential- and simultaneous-processing aspects or reading, such that the patient is unable to develop a complete understanding of a phrase or sentence. What Luria calls "guesswork" reading usually occurs, characterized by impulsive integration of the meaning based upon isolated details of the phrase or sentence (Luria, 1966).

Careful qualitative observation of the performance reveals either that important aspects of the material are ignored or that visual-tracking problems cause the patient to lose his/her place in the item. Two sentences in #198 contain subtle inconsistencies (e.g., "the sun rises in the west") in an attempt to catch "guesswork" reading where important details are ignored. Visual-tracking problems are often more difficult to recognize unless severe perceptual problems, such as unilateral spatial neglect, are present. It is, again, important to watch for slight hesitancies and superfluous eye movements, which suggest that the patient is having difficulty maintaining his/her visual place along and between lines of text. The instructions to read quickly but carefully are designed to encourage the patient to read fluently so that difficulties become manifest at the reading of discrete, isolated words rather than a syntactically connected unit of meaning.

Supplemental tasks become necessary because of the limited sample of reading obtained from this subscale. The use of items such as #198, where subtle inconsistencies try to catch "guesswork" reading, is limited by the small sample of patient behavior. When "guesswork" reading secondary to deficits in sequential processing is suspected, many more items are usually required in order to judge whether a true deficit exists. Ideally, normative data should be available for actuarial interpretation, although such a psychometric instrument does not yet exist. Likewise, samples of reading text must be increased (if not in number, then at least in length of the text) when various types of dyslexia are suggested in order to distinguish between dyslexia secondary to sequential, verbal difficulties and to simultaneous, visual-perceptual difficulties.

Arithmetic Scale

Luria's theory that arithmetical processes are based upon visual-spatial skills (Luria, 1966) guides the construction of this scale, making it a useful localizing tool. While primary acalculia localizes to the angular gyrus area, it does so because of a primary deficit in the understanding of the categorical structure of number. Difficulties with the arithmetic tasks making up this scale may arise from a variety of lesion locations, depending upon the primary underlying deficit. This scale is constructed so as to sort out that underlying deficit, whether it consists of problems with spatial analysis, verbal-logical ability, or programming facility.

Luria calls upon our understanding of the developmental aspects of how arithmetic skills are learned in order to appreciate the spatial nature of the task. Upon first acquiring arithmetic concepts, the idea of number is appreciated only as a spatial arrangement of concrete objects in space. The next step in arithmetical understanding occurs when visual and motor actions materialize ideas either in external space or mentally as a numerical idea. From there, actual arithmetic calculation can take place. Such calculation begins as an active, accumulative mental process but with experience becomes an automatic, mnestic activity. The more arithmetically sophisticated the patient, the more difficult it is actually to test that person's arithmetic skill because more and more complicated calculations are performed automatically.

In order to test all aspects of arithmetic ability this scale is divided into five subscales: Number Writing/Reading, Spatial Numerics, Numeric Operations, Numeric Reasoning, and Numeric Control.

Number Writing/Reading

This subscale consists of eight items that require the patient either to write numbers that are dictated or to read numbers from a card. Both Roman and Arabic numerals are utilized, and difficulties in visual recognition are brought to light through the use of spatially similar numbers. For example, complementary pairs, such as *17 and 71* or *IV and VI*, are written and read. Interpretation of this subscale centers around errors in writing and reading numbers due to phonemic paraphasia, dysgraphia, and optic alexia.

Outside of educationally related errors on the Roman numerals, errors on this subscale are rare. The most frequent error occurs when the patient has lost appreciation for the categorical structure of number. That is, the spatial juxtaposition of tens, hundreds, and thousands is not appreciated, and the patient has difficulty writing (less often reading) four-digit numbers. Commonly, the numbers *1023* and *9845* (and in severe cases, the number *109*) are miswritten (e.g., *100023* or *900845*). Assuming that the person had at one time learned this skill, the presence of this error represents a pathognomonic sign, usually indicating parieto-occipital (angular gyrus region) pathology. Other common errors are number substitutions or transpositions secondary to literal paraphasia or poorly constructed, spatially inaccurate numbers due to visual-perception problems. No supplemental tasks are required.

Spatial Numerics

Three items on this subscale evaluate more closely the spatial aspects of the categorical structure of number. Three- and four-digit numbers are arranged vertically and are to be read as a single number. The other tasks require the patient to identify which of two numbers is larger. Understanding the categorical structure of these numbers is specifically tested by the vertical arrangement of the numbers in the one case and by the fact that the larger number is composed of smaller numbers, on the whole, in the other case (e.g., *189* versus *301*). The purpose of these tasks is sometimes thwarted, especially in item #209, by the complexity of the instructions. Care must be taken to insure that the patient understands the requirements of the items.

Supplemental items are sometimes required either to increase the sampling of behavior or to establish a level of complexity that more suits the patient's estimated premorbid capability. An increased sample of items is especially important when the patient has not understood the instructions and the first item serves as a demonstration item. It also may become necessary to utilize larger numbers (six- and seven-digit numbers) in order to notice categorical structure of number deficits in more highly educated or more intelligent patients.

Numeric Operations

Six items evaluate simple calculation skills that are relatively free of mnestic requirements. On all but the last two items, the patient is allowed to use pencil and paper so as to minimize errors that might occur because of attention/concentration or memory problems. While the last two items are solved mentally, they do not require switching between different systems of associations and, therefore, also do not tax mnestic operations.

The purpose of this subscale is to identify primary acalculia, in which only the ability to do arithmetic operations is affected. The items occur in sequential order of difficulty, with memorized multiplication problems, where little to no active calculating is necessary, coming first. Single-digit addition and subtraction comes next and also represents a fairly automatic system of associations for all but the most educationally disadvantaged patients. Where acalculia is typically manifest is in the next set of problems, where the spatial requirements of calculation become necessary. These items require carrying and borrowing between columns of numbers (e.g., $44 + 57$) and, therefore, require both additional steps and a spatial element in the mental operations of calculating beyond the number 10. Errors in this set of items typically represent directional misjudgments that occur because of the spatial deficit that underlies primary acalculia. For example, in the problem "$31 - 7$" the patient may give the answer "26." After subtracting 1 from both 31 and from 7 to simplify the problem, the acalculiac patient goes the wrong direction from 25

in subtracting 6 from 30. Finally, the last two items retain the spatial requirements of calculating beyond the number 10 but take away the stabilizing
influence of the external supports of paper and pencil. More subtle manifestations of acalculia are brought out with this added complexity. Again, however,
care must be taken to insure that conceptual obstacles inherent in item #217 do
not account for error. In this item, 18 is to be subtracted from 24; however, the
18 is placed above the 24 on the stimulus card. This added spatial complexity
(with a lack of traditional vertical cues) confuses many patients into thinking
that the problem is impossible. In that case, an error is not reflective of
acalculia.

Again, supplemental tasks may be necessary to increase the sample of
behavior and to find tasks that more appropriately conform to the patient's
premorbid intellectual level. Other tasks that further tax the spatial abilities
associated with calculation may be included. For example, mental arithmetic
tasks of two- or three-digit numbers, in which single-file vertical alignment
further stresses the patient's spatial skills, may be used. Also, misaligned
problems may be used for the same purpose.

Numeric Reasoning

Two items test the patient's understanding of the conceptual roots of arithmetic operations. One item has the person fill in the missing sign while the
other item has the person fill in the number in a arithmetical expression
[respectively, $10 ( )2 = 20; 12 - ( ) = 8$]. These items require a conscious
reasoning process rather than just the rote tabular calculation needed for
traditionally presented problems ($10 \times 2 = ?$). Dissociation is said to occur
when practical, traditionally presented problems are able to be completed
successfully, while equally easy items on this subscale are poorly performed.
Again, however, patients with higher intellectual/educational attainments,
having been exposed to such problems in the past, may require more complex
versions of this type of task.

Supplemental tasks are, therefore, necessary with higher functioning patients. Rather than making the calculations more difficult, however, it is best to
make the supplemental tasks more symbolic. For example, using nonnumeric
symbols such as letters [$Y \times ( ) = YX; Y + ( ) = 2Y$] better suits the purpose of these tasks as tests of conceptual ability rather than arithmetic operations.

Numeric Control

Three tasks evaluate mental control in selectively and flexibly manipulating a
system of associations. Mental arithmetic with three two-digit numbers and
two three-digit numbers and serial 7's and 13's make up this subscale. Assuming the patient does not have primary acalculia, the major component in these

tasks involves frontal-limbic processes. The trace currently active in the patient's awareness loses its stability, making it difficult for the person to maintain a steady stream of thought. Also, earlier traces lose their selectivity and fail to control behavior. For example, in serial arithmetic the previous calculation must be kept on "hold" while other calculations are performed. The trace on "hold" must be selective enough to allow the person to come back to their place in the calculation. If the trace is not selective, other traces interfere and confuse the patient or lead to a wrong conclusion. For example, having attained the answer to $100 - 7$, the patient then must hold in mind the answer while the original purpose of the task (to subtract 7) is recalled. Coming back to the first answer (93), the patient with poor selectivity may subtract 7 from 97. The current trace (7) contaminates the first answer (93).

Supplemental tasks may be required in order to work around an acalculia. Counting backward by fives or twos usually serves this purpose, although in particularly dense acalculia counting forward by fives or twos may be a necessity. Making the task more difficult for higher-functioning patients is rarely required; although, since serial arithmetic is a popular mental status exam task, the mental control aspect can be circumvented by a patient with extensive prior experience who has memorized the answers. Finally, anxiety and depression must be considered as etiologic factors in difficulties with the subscale and must be ruled out by clinical impression and psychometric evaluation.

Memory Scale

No single test currently available is capable of comprehensively evaluating memory in its clinically relevant dimensions: immediate, recent, and remote. Most instruments (Benton Visual Retention Test, Memory-for-Designs, Wechsler Memory Scale, etc.) focus on immediate or near-immediate (intervals less than 24 hours) memory, and there are severe limitations in most clinical situations to doing otherwise. Unfortunately, this scale is limited to immediate memory items and is a rather curtailed evaluation consisting of only 13 items. The scale does, however, benefit from Luria's (1976) promising theory of memory functions.

A central tenet of this theory is the notion that immediate short-term memory is equivalent to the gnostic processes of the modality in which the remembered material is analyzed. Storing a memory is a process of assigning an "address" to this gnostic analysis, which is done by the medial temporal (at least in the case of auditory memory) and midline limbic structures. The retrieval of memories is a varied process depending upon which type of memory (immediate, recent, remote) is being recalled. Retrieving immediate memories does not require much of an active search process, so it is simply a read-out of the short-term register. The retrieval of recent memories, on the other hand, is a reintegrative process that involves the active search of contextually related cues in order to reconstruct or recapture the original reminiscence. This process is carried out by the strategizing and problem-solving functions of the prefrontal areas and the cortical tone regulatory and trace selectivity functions of the medio-basal frontal regions. Lastly, retrieving remote memories is a poorly understood process, but one that seems to be relatively automatic; as such, it is independent of active recall processes. Remote memories are like semantic memory in that they are not ephemeral reminiscences that are dependent upon contextual cues in order to be reconstructed. Instead, they are lifeless facts that have been overlearned. We do not need the emotionally laden cues of the original context in order to find the memory address. It is found automatically because it is overlearned.

The memory scale evaluates the gnostic, short-term, "read-out" functions in four modalities (verbal and nonverbal auditory, visual, and kinesthetic) on the Span/Learning Curve subscale. Retrieval of remote memories is not evaluated, although recent memory retrieval is perhaps approximated by the items on the Interference subscale. Finally, prefrontal lobe contributions are evaluated by the learning curve items on the first subscale, and by the ability to "chunk" information through semantic strategies as evaluated on the Semantic Organization subscale.

Span/Learning Curve

Eight items evaluate the short-term register capacity for verbal and nonverbal auditory, visual, and kinesthetic modalities, as well as evaluating for a learning curve. One of the two visual items (#226) is designed to be an interference item; however, its ability to function in this capacity is questionable. The item is easily encoded through verbal means and a simple "yes" or "no" answer is required, making it difficult to determine whether the patient's response is correct or a lucky guess. It is best to rely on the other item (#227, where the patient must reproduce five geometric forms) as a measure of visual span. The kinesthetic item (#229) consists of only three hand positions, because of the relatively unpracticed nature of this kind of skill and the relatively great amount of gnostic processing required to encode this information. One error on this item is common even in non–brain-damaged samples, and its importance should be minimized. The error typically occurs when the last three fingers are fanned instead of tightly closed on the final hand position.

Younger patients should remember six or seven words on the first trial (#223), while older patients will only remember five or six words. The second verbal-span item (#230) serves as a check on item #223. The span on the other modalities conforms to the norms represented by the scaled scores of the individual items. The visual, nonverbal auditory, and kinesthetic items (#226 to 229) generally represent right-hemispheric function, and differential performance between these items and the verbal ones is often a good lateralizing sign.

Interpretations of the learning curve information involve more than the analysis of scores on items #224 and 225. Item #224 is designed to evaluate verification deficits associated with deficient problem-solving skills of the prefrontal lobes. This item has occasional utility when it reveals perseverative judgments (i.e., predicting the same number of words across trials).

This pathognomonic sign, however, is not oftentimes recognized in the scoring because the "frontal" patient ends up with a flat learning curve that makes his/her perseverative predictions correct! Personality factors and test anxiety also seem to affect the patient's predictions adversely, thus confounding the interpretation of the results. More important aspects to evaluate involve the active character of the memorization process. If a flat learning curve occurs, then it must be decided whether it represents a limitation in auditory span or a problem with the memorization strategy. With intact prefrontal lobe abilities, a problem-solving strategy can be utilized in order to compensate or improve upon memory-span limitations, except in cases of anxiety, attentional problems, language difficulties, and the slowed processing speed associated with Korsakoff-type amnesia. To demonstrate active memorizing strategies, it is necessary to order the words recalled by placing numbers on the grid in the scoring sheet. The numbers reveal the active strategies by showing that different words in a different order are recalled each time. The "frontal" patient usually recalls the same words in the same order each time.

Supplemental tasks are often needed because of the limited samples of behavior that occur in this subscale. Oftentimes, in superior patients, the seven words on item #223 do not represent a supraspan list. In order properly to evaluate both auditory span and verbal learning curve, eight to ten words must be utilized. It is sometimes useful, in brain-damaged samples, to give eight to ten trials of a supraspan list in order to evaluate the stability of the memory trace. Finally, the samples of visual and spatial forms of memory are not only limited but are confounded to a large extent with verbal encoding strategies. While the nonverbal memory items may show differential performance decrement in right-hemisphere lesions, this decrement does not always occur and cannot be relied upon to diagnose lateralized dysfunction consistently. The Benton Visual Retention Test [or the Visual Reproduction subscale from the Wechsler Memory Scale, using delayed recall as suggested by Russell (1981) if a shorter test is desired] is an excellent supplement when memory problems associated with the right hemisphere must be ruled out.

Interference

Three items assess the vulnerability of verbal material, in the form of individual words or sentences, to the effects of interference between presentation and recall. Interpolated activity, in the form of both heterogeneous or homogeneous information, serves to tax the stability and retrievability of the trace. While the etiology of difficulties with interference tasks is not clearly understood, it often involves dysfunction of the medial temporal and medial frontal areas. A common error is perseverative contamination and involves mixing words between different items. This error typically occurs when item #231 or 232 is contaminated by the list of seven words in item #223. Perseverative contamination may also involve intra-item contaminations, especially in items #232 and 233. Another common finding involves retroactive and proactive inhibition, where either the first stimulus set or the second stimulus set in items #232 and 233 is inhibited by the other stimulus set.

Supplemental tasks are generally not required because these items are rather sensitive to memory impairment of all sorts. However, interpretation of poor performance as being indicative of organic memory impairment should be made with care. Depression, anxiety, and temporary inefficiencies may easily disrupt performance even in the absence of brain dysfunction. Testing-the-limits may be useful, especially with the first two items (#231 and 232). The item may simply be repeated, or, with higher-functioning patients, different words may need to be used. True brain-based memory disorders tend to lead to impairment even on a second repeat trial. Exceptions, of course, include subtle memory disorders such as occur with recovered post concussional syndrome patients who have only mild and subjective residual neurological effects, yet who show subtle memory and information-processing speed deficits on neuropsychological testing.

Semantic Organization

Two items evaluate the ability to utilize verbal strategies to organize information for improvement of short-term capacity. One item involves a supraspan story heard by the patient, which is to be reiterated as best as possible immediately after presentation. The other item consists of word–picture pairs to which the patient forms an association so that when shown the picture the word will be recalled associatively. This subscale, like the learning-curve item, evaluates the frontal skills of active memorization. An active system of associations must link the bits of information together, whether it be a theme that ties together the various elements of the anecdote or a series of connections between the individual word–picture pairs. In either case, the system of associations that are actively formed serves as entry into the address of the information to be remembered.

Supplemental tasks are generally not required, with one major exception— for patients who have language disturbances. This subscale (and to a large extent the entire LNNB) is overdependent upon our linguistic ability, which stems from Luria's insistence that language, as the second signal system, is the basis of thought or association. Whether this theory is correct or not, visual processes seem able to provide associations that facilitate memory retrieval. A useful supplemental test for aphasic patients would be one in which nonsense visual forms that are spatially complementary serve as associational pairs (no such instruments are currently available). Active memorization ability could then be demonstrated without relying upon linguistic material.

Intellectual Processes Scale

Intellectual ability is approached not from the standpoint of determining the limits of a person's innate and acquired skills, but from the standpoint of insuring the intactness of all underlying elemental aspects of general immediate adaptiveness. The purpose of this scale is to create problem situations for which the person has no ready-made solution. A solution must be conjured up from the relevant bits of the problem, according to an overriding strategy that regulates the person's behavior. This characterization of intellectual ability follows other notions, such as fluid intelligence (Cattell, 1963) and executive functions (Lezak, 1983). Such extemporaneous adaptivity obviously calls upon the integrity of the entire brain, although certain specialized elementary functions of the anterior frontal lobes play a major role. These functions are summarized by Luria (1966) as disturbances of "preliminary investigative activity" and "selective logical operations."

Patients with dysfunction of the medial frontal area or the lateral convexity of the prefrontal regions are impaired in immediate adaptive ability because an overriding plan does not regulate behavior. Disturbances in preliminary investigative activity associated with the lateral prefrontal region preclude the ability to form a relevant overall plan with which to guide intellectual activity. The person does not thoroughly investigate all the relevant aspects of the problem space. Instead, salient aspects of the problem prompt an impulsive response. For example, given the problem "Mary has four apples and Betty has two more than Mary, altogether they have?", the patient answers "six." Here, the "frontal" patient who is seduced to the obvious aspects of the problem fails to integrate the subtler information into a complete solution. By contrast, disturbances in selective logical operations associated with the medial frontal area do not so much preclude the formation of a general plan as they impair the regulation of behavior according to the plan. The system of associations conjured up by the plan is not selective, and irrelevant associations are not differentiated from more appropriate ones. For example, when shown the comical picture of a man in bed throwing alarm clocks out of the window, the patient may mention the correct answer but be distracted by other associations. The correct observation that the man does not like to get up in the morning may be bypassed in favor of an incorrect judgment that is suggested by some single aspect of the picture. For example, from the pile of clocks outside the window, the patient may conclude that the person in the picture collects alarm clocks.

While the divisions of this scale (Thematic Pictures, Abstraction, and Problem Solving) conform generally to Luria's, the quantitative scoring on the LNNB does not easily lend itself to identifying signs associated with frontal lobe dysfunction. In order to differentiate these signs from other sources of variation, such as anxiety/depression, motivational problems, thought disorder, and normal variation in intellectual ability, it is important to utilize procedures that test the limits and promote a process analysis of patient performance. Likewise, the complexity of intellectual processes makes them suspectible to disruption by all varieties of neuropsychological dysfunction. In order to identify frontal lobe dysfunction it is necessary to rule out contributions of deficits from all other parts of the examination.

Thematic Pictures

Eight items evaluate the discursive reasoning of visual themes. Single pictures with an underlying theme, picture series that must be arranged into a specific order, and picture series with a comical theme to be discerned make up the tasks on this subscale. Generally, these tasks relate to frontal lobe problem-solving skills, especially the simultaneous-processing strategy of the right anterior hemisphere. The relevant aspects of the problem space must be simultaneously put together in order to comprehend the underlying theme of the material. This theme may, of course, be discerned by a sequential, accumulative strategy accomplished in the left hemisphere, although such a process is more time consuming and laborious. Either method, however, provides an overriding plan that guides the completion of the task (e.g., ordering the picture sequence).

The first two items (#236 and 237) turn out to be relatively poor "frontal" items because a simple description of the obvious elements of the picture without inferential integration is sufficient to score well. The single pictures lack the necessary detail that lends itself to multiple interpretations of the theme. Ideally, several themes should suggest themselves by different discrete aspects of the picture. The correct theme, however, would be discernible only through integration of all the relevant details in the picture. This ideal is better accomplished in the picture series items (#238–243) where the gist of all pictures must crystallize into a unified theme.

A process analysis of the items on this subscale, then, makes extensive use of testing-the-limits procedures that attempt to expose the patient's thought process. First, does the preliminary investigation make note of all relevant aspects of the picture(s)? Second, are those facts manipulated selectively and logically into an overriding theme that regulates completion of the task? Such a process analysis is accomplished by having the patient verbalize his/her thoughts and by asking strategic questions whose answers betray his/her understanding of the theme of the material.

Supplemental tasks are sometimes necessary in order to get a better sample of behavior. The Picture Arrangement subtest from the Wechsler intelligence tests is the best alternative to mimic the skills associated with this subscale; these skills are probably related to the right anterior hemisphere (especially the right anterior and basal temporal lobe) and are best evaluated by the backward portion of the Digit Span subtest of the Wechsler intelligence tests.

Abstraction

Fourteen items evaluate two aspects of abstraction that are identified by Luria as metaphorical understanding and concept formation (Luria, 1966). Metaphorical understanding, as evaluated by proverbs and passages with morals, represents an intermediate task between thematic picture interpretation and abstraction. These tasks are placed in this subscale because they tend to be more related to left-hemispheric function. Likewise, concept formation tasks tend to be associated with left-hemispheric function because they are best evaluated through the verbal modality. Types of tasks that make up this part of the subscale are suggested by Luria (1966) and include word definitions, comparison and differentiation of ideas, and logical relationships.

The purpose of this subscale is to determine whether the patient is able to maintain an abstract attitude and can apply it in a variety of situations in an immediately adaptive fashion. Again, the complexity of these tasks makes it necessary to insure that the contribution of other neuropsychological deficits is understood. Otherwise, the underlying frontal lobe functions that make up general intellectual processes cannot be accurately evaluated. Simple definition of words helps to establish (in the absence of aphasic disorder) that an abstract attitude can be maintained toward a given stimulus. If a patient can place a given word into a more general system of associations that both broadens its semantic utility and endows it with differentiated characteristics (e.g., "an island is a body of land surrounded by water"), then we know that he can make general use of ideas in an immediately adaptive fashion. Furthermore, the ability to solve problems or to put together several ideas into an overall plan requires a selective system of associations. This skill is partially evaluated by a series of categorization tasks wherein the patient is required to move back and forth between specific and general elements, or between whole and part relationships, to find opposites, to analyze analogies, and to determine which item in a series does not fit with the others.

Supplemental tasks to take the place of these items are generally not required, although some tests help add extra information to the assessment of immediately adaptive abstract ability. The first supplement one often needs is some measure of formal or crystallized intelligence in order to provide an estimate of premorbid attainment. This estimate is necessary in order to know what level of abstract ability to expect from the patient and may be obtained by using the VIQ (or just the Vocabulary subtest) from the Wechsler intelligence tests. Secondly, the Stroop Color-Word Test (Golden, 1976), as another measure of cognitive selectivity and flexibility, is an excellent measure of the pathological inertia that prevents the regulation of behavior by an overall plan.

Problem Solving

Twelve items evaluate the ability to solve arithmetic story problems. The first two problems (#258–261) are so easy that they have little use other than as an orientation to the subscale. The remaining problems, however, test the patient's ability to survey the problem space in order to sift out the relevant information and put it together into an appropriate strategy for finding a solution (refer to the Mary–Betty example above, in the introduction to the Intellectual Processes scale). Various types of problem situations are included in the final four story problems. The "farmer" problem (#264 and 265 reads: "A farmer had 10 acres of land. From each acre he harvested 6 tons of grain. He sold 1/3 to the government. How much did he have left?") taxes the ability to put together a strategy made up of many subroutines. A great deal of information must be held in mind while all the individual parts of the problem are completed. On the other hand, the "books" problem (#266 and 267 reads: "There were 18 books on 2 shelves. There were twice as many on one shelf as on the other. How many books were there on each shelf?") requires that a single, difficult concept (that the 18 books must be divided into thirds) be recognized. The remaining calculation is rather automatic and does not tax the person's mental manipulative abilities. This item may also be improved by rewording it to read: "There were 18 books divided between 2 shelves . . ." Finally, the "pedestrian" problem (#268 and 269 reads: "A pedestrian walks to the station in 15 minutes, and a cyclist rides there 5 times faster. How long does the cyclist take to get to the station?") is couched in oppositional language so that incorrect strategies are suggested unless the underlying arithmetical concept is understood. For example, the "cyclist rides there five times faster" suggests to multiply the 15 minutes it takes the pedestrian to walk by 5 and obtain the answer 75. Those who understand the underlying concept, however, are not seduced to the more obvious aspects of the problem and they divide 15 by 5 and come up with the correct answer.

   Supplemental tasks may be desired to lend a richer interpretation to this subscale, which more closely approaches the complexity of the executive functions of the frontal lobes. Luria suggests another type of story problem as the most complex problem-solving situation. It requires the patient to create his own intermediate steps of the strategy. Luria uses the example: if a son is 5 years old and the father will be 3 times as old in 15 years, then how old is the father now? In this example, the steps of the problem are not immediately obvious from the words in the story, but must be garnered from the meaning of the story by devising an appropriate sequence of steps. Further tests may be taken from outside sources, especially when patients of above average premorbid attainment are examined. The Tactual Performance Test of the Halstead-Reitan Battery represents such an instrument. Since it relies much less on verbal mediation and more on the less practiced tactile and spatial mediation, it is a task which better evaluates immediate adaptive skills. Certain problems are associated with its interpretation, in that psychological factors such as frustration may work against the successful completion of the test.

CONCLUSIONS

This chapter is an attempt to present a neuropsychological screening technique that can be developed into a complete and comprehensive examination that serves a wide range of general purpose needs. While any specific clinical situation requires specific assessment devices (see Chapters 6 through 10), most prudent neuropsychologists begin with an assessment instrument which briefly surveys the range of higher cortical functions. The Luria–Nebraska Battery, as a bridge between the psychometrically sound quantitative approach and the clinically powerful qualitative approach, serves the purpose well. While the research literature tends to focus on the quantitative aspects of the LNNB, this chapter attempts to present the more qualitative, process-oriented aspect of the battery and to present supplemental tasks that broaden the applicability of the LNNB to most clinical situations.

REFERENCES

Albert, M. L., Sparks, R., von Stockert, T., & Sax, D. (1972). A case study of auditory agnosia: Linguistic and non-linguistic processing. *Cortex, 8*, 427–433.

Beardsley, J. V., Matthews, C. G., Cleeland, C. S., & Harley, J. P. (1978). *Experimental T-score norms for CA 34- on the Wisconsin neuropsychological test battery.* Privately published at Neuropsychology Laboratory, Department of Neurology, University of Wisconsin Center for the Health Sciences.

Benton, A. L. (1973). Visuoconstructive disability in patients with cerebral disease: its relationship to side of lesion and aphasic disorder. *Documenta Ophthamologica, 34,* 67–76.

Benton, A. L., deS. Hampsher, K., Varney, N. R., & Spreen, O. (1983). *Contributions to neuropsychological assessment.* New York: Oxford University Press.

Benton, A. L., & Van Allen, M. W. (1973). Impairment in facial recognition in patients with cerebral disease. *Cortex, 4,* 344–358.

Boller, F., & Vignolo, L. A. (1966). Latent sensory aphasia in hemisphere damaged patients: An experimental study with the Token test. *Brain, 89,* 815–831.

Cattell, R. B. (1963). The theory of fluid and crystallized intelligence: A critical experiment. *Journal of Educational Psychology, 54,* 1–22.

Christensen, A. L. (1975). *Luria's neuropsychological investigation: Manual.* New York: Spectrum.

Damasio, A. R. (1981). Central achromatopsia. *Neurology, 31,* 920-921.

Damasio, A., Damasio, H., & Van Hoesen, G. W. (1982). Prosopagnosia: Anatomic basis and behavioral mechanisms. *Neurology, 32,* 331-341.

Damasio, A., Yamada, T., Damasio, H., Corbett, J., & McKee, J. (1980). Central achromatopsia: Behavioral, anatomic, and physiologic aspects. *Neurology, 30,* 1064-1071.

DeRenzi, E. (1982). *Disorders of space exploration and cognition.* New York: Wiley.

DeRenzi, E., & Spinnler, H. (1967). Impaired performance on color tasks in patients with hemisphere damage. *Cortex, 3,* 194-217.

Golden, C. J. (1976). Identification of brain disorders by the Stroop Color-Word Test. *Journal of Clinical Psychology, 32,* 621.

Golden, C. J. (1981). *Diagnosis and rehabilitation in clinical neuropsychology.* Springfield, IL: Charles Thomas.

Golden, C. J., Hammeke, T. A., & Purisch, A. D. (1980). *The Luria-Nebraska Neuropsychological Battery: Manual.* Los Angeles: Western Psychological Services.

Heilman, K. M., & Rothi, L. J. (1985). Apraxia. In K. M. Heilman & E. Valenstein (Eds.), *Clinical neuropsychology* (2nd ed.). New York: Oxford.

Kaplan, E. (1983). Achievement and process revisited. In S. Wapner & B. Kaplan (Eds.), *Toward a holistic developmental psychology* (pp. 123-157). Hillsdale, NJ: Erlbaum Associates

Kelter, S., Cohen, R., Engel, D., List, G., & Strohnor, H. (1976). Aphasic disorder in matching tasks involving conceptual analysis and covert naming. *Cortex, 12,* 383-394.

Kimura, D., & Archibald, Y. (1974). Motor functions of the left hemisphere. *Brain, 97,* 337-350.

Lezak, M. D. (1983). *Neuropsychological assessment* (2nd ed.). New York: Oxford University Press.

Luria, A. R. (1966). *Higher cortical functions in man.* New York: Basic Books.

Luria, A. R. (1976). *The neuropsychology of memory.* Washington, DC: V. H. Winston.

Luria, A. R. (1980). *Higher cortical functions in man* (2nd ed.). New York: Basic Books.

Mooney, C. M. (1957). Ager in the development of closure ability in children. *Canadian Journal of Psychology, 2,* 219-226.

Moses, J. A., Jr., Golden, C. J., Ariel, R., & Gustavson, J. L. (1983). *Interpretation of the Luria-Nebraska Battery* (Vol. 1). New York: Grune & Stratton.

Osmon, D. C. (1983). The use of test batteries in clinical neuropsychology. In C. J. Golden & P. Vicente (Eds.), *Foundations of clinical neuropsychology* (pp. 113-141). New York: Plenum Publishing.

Osmon, D. C. (1984). Luria-Nebraska Neuropsychological Battery case study: A mild drug-related confusional state. *International Journal of Clinical Neuropsychology, 6,* 251-255.

Osmon, D. C., Sweet, J., & Golden, C. J. (1978). Neuropsychological implication of rhythm and aphasia deficits in unilateral left hemisphere injuries. *International Journal of Neuroscience, 8,* 78-82.

Reitan, R. (1969). *Manual for the administration of neuropsychological test batteries for adults and children.* Indianapolis: Author.

Rey, A. (1941). L'examen psychologique dans les cas d'encephalopathie traumatique. *Archives de Psychologie, 28,* 286-340.

Russell, E. W. (1981). The pathology and clinical examination of memory. In S. B. Filskov & T. Boll (Eds.), *Handbook of clinical neuropsychology* (pp. 287-319). New York: Wiley.

Scholes, R. J. (1982). The verb-right strategy in agrammatic aphasia. *Neuropsychologia, 20,* 361–363.

Spellacy, F. J., & Spreen, O. (1969). A short form of the Token test. *Cortex, 5,* 390–397.

Spreen, O., Benton, A. L., & Fincham, R. (1965). Auditory agnosia without aphasia. *Archives of Neurology, 13,* 84–92.

Van Allen, M. W., & Rodnitzky, R. L. (1981). *Pictorial manual of neurologic tests* (2nd ed.). Chicago: Yearbook Medical Publishers.

von Stockert, T. R., & Bader, L. (1976). Some relations of grammar and lexicon in aphasia. *Cortex, 12,* 49–60.

Appendix

Name: _____ Age: ____ Educ: _____ Date: _____ R L
Occupation: _____ Examiner: _____
Place: _____ MRI #: _____ Physician: _____

MOTOR FUNCTIONS SCALE
Speed/Coordination

1.) 0 1 2   2.) 0 1 2   3.) 0 1 2   4.) 0 1 2

#_____   #_____   #_____   #_____

Qualitative: _____ Following directions
_____ Peripheral impairment (arthritis, etc.)
_____ Awkwardness
_____ Motivation problems

Kinesthetically Based Movement

5.) 0 2   6.) 0 2   7.) 0 2   8.) 0 2

Qualitative: _____ If incorrect, which finger touched
_____ Perseveration of instruction set

Optic-Spatial Imitation

9.) 0   2   10.) 0   2   11.) 0   2   12.) 0   2   13.) 0   2
14.) 0   2   15.) 0   2   16.) 0   2   17.) 0   2   18.) 0   2
19.) 0   2   20.) 0   2

Qualitative: _____ Mirror-imaging
_____ Number of corrections for wrong hand
_____ Right–left confusion
_____ Poor voluntary control of movements

Bilateral RAMs

21.) 0 1 2   22.) 0 1 2   23.) 0 1 2   24.) 0   2

#_____   #_____   #_____   #_____

Qualitative: _____ Establish stereotype poorly
_____ Maintain stereotype poorly
_____ Slow to train to task
_____ Perseveration of instruction set
_____ Perseveration of movement

Dyspraxia

25.) 0   2   26.) 0   2   27.) 0   2   28.) 0   2   29.) 0   2
30.) 0   2   31.) 0   2   32.) 0   2   33.) 0 1 2   34.) 0   2
35.) 0   2   #_____

Qualitative: _____ Motor impersistence (#29)
_____ Body-part-as-object
_____ Incomplete sequence (dropped pot, etc.)

Construction Dyspraxia

36.) 0 1 2   37.) 0 1 2   38.) 0 1 2   39.) 0 1 2   40.) 0 1 2
                    t_____   t_____
41.) 0 1 2   42.) 0 1 2   43.) 0 1 2   44.) 0 1 2   45.) 0 1 2
t_____   t_____   t_____
46.) 0 1 2   47.) 0 1 2
                    t_____

Qualitative: _____ Impulsive/careless
_____ Greek cross
_____ Didn't know triangle

Motor Selectivity

48.) 0 1 2   49.) 0 1 2   50.) 0 1 2   51.) 0 1 2

E_____   E_____   E_____   E_____

Qualitative: _____ Echopraxia
_____ Lost program (1–2 correct then erred)
_____ Slow to train
_____ Perseveration of instruction set
_____ Perseverative contamination

Total _____

RHYTHM SCALE
Nonverbal Auditory Perception and Expression

52.) 0 1 2   53.) 0 1 2   54.) 0 1 2   55.) 0 1 2   56.) 0   2

E_____   E_____   E_____   E_____   57.) 0   2

Qualitative: _____ Slow to learn
_____ Attention
_____ Motivation

Tracking

58.) 0 1 2   59.) 0 1 2   60.) 0 1 2   61.) 0 1 2

E_____   E_____   E_____   E_____

Qualitative: _____ Attention

Motor Imitation

62.) 0 1 2   63.) 0 1 2

E_____   E_____

Qualitative: _____ Slow to learn
_____ Motor perseveration
_____ Perseveration of instruction set
_____ Perseverative contamination

Total _____

TACTILE SCALE
Simple Cutaneous Sensation

64.) 0 1 2   65.) 0 1 2   R: 1 F 3 5 P 2 S 4
                             L: P 2 3 S 5 4 F 1
66.) 0 1 2   67.) 0 1 2   R: P H P P H
                             L: H P P H H
68.) 0 1 2   69.) 0 1 2   R: S H H S
                             L: H S H S
70.) 0 1 2   71.) 0 1 2   R: 5 10 15
                             L: 5 10 15
72.) 0 1 2   73.) 0 1 2   R: Up   Down

Qualitative: _____ suppressions
_____ peripheral px

Graphesthesia

74.) 0 1 2   R: Circle   Cross Triangle
75.) 0 1 2   L: Triangle Cross Circle
76.) 0   2   77.) 0   2   R: 3   L: 3
78.) 0   2   79.) 0   2   R: S   L: S

Qualitative: _____ Warm-up effect

Proprioception

80.) 0 2   81.) 0 2   Error in degrees: 10° > 10°   Drift: R L Both

Stereognosis

82.) 0 1 2   83.) 0 1 2   84.) 0 1 2   85.) 0 1 2

  RE___   RT Q___ K___   LE___   LT E___ PC___   **Total** _____

       E___ PC___   K___ Q___

VISUAL SCALE

Visual Perception

86.) 0 1 2	87.) 0 1 2	88.) 0 1 2	89.) 0 1 2	90.) 0 1 2
E_____	Handbag	Book: 1 2	Telephone	Pail
91.) 0 1 2	Nutcracker	Glasses: 1 2 3	Profile	Scissors
Teapot	Test Tube			Rake
Fork Bottle	Camera	Qualitative: ___ Dysnomia		Brush
Glass Bowl	Egg Carton			Ax

Visual Orientation

92.) 0 1 2   94.) 0 1 2   95.) 0 1 2   96.) 0 1 2
  E___   7:53___ 5:09___   12:50___ 4:35___   N___ E___ W___

93.) 0 1 2   1:25___ 10:35___   11:10___
  T___

Spatial Reasoning

97.) 0 1 2   98.) 0 1 2   99.) 0 1 2

  15:___   t: ___   E:___

  18:___   t: ___   t: ___   Qualitative: ___ Slow to learn

  15:___   t: ___   ___ Performs slowly

  10:___   t: ___   **Total** _____

RECEPTIVE SPEECH SCALE

Auditory Perception

100.) 0 1 2   101.) 0 1 2   102.) 0 1 2
B___ P___ M___   B___ P___ M___   M-P___ P-S___
                                        B-P___ D-T___
                                        K-G___ R-L___

103.) 0 1 2
MP___PS___
BP___DT___
KG___RL___

104.) 0 1 2
sos___usi___
MSD___BPB___
DTD___bibabo___

105.) 0 1 2
sos___usi___
MSD___RPB___
DTD___bibabo___biboba___

106.) 0 1 2
b(R)___p(L)___
p(L)___b(R)___

107.) 0 2
b-p___b-r___

Qualitative: ___ Peripheral hearing loss

Simple Commands

108.) 0 1 2
I___N___E___

109.) 0 2
I___N___E___I___N___

110.) 0 1 2
E_____

111.) 0 1 2
E_____

112.) 0 1 2
cat_____
bat_____
pat_____

113.) 0 1 2
E_____

114.) 0 2
E_____

115.) 0 2
E_____

116.) 0 2
_____

Logical–Grammatical Relationships

117.) 0 2
E_____

118.) 0 2
E_____

119.) 0 2
E_____

120.) 0 2
E_____

121.) 0 2

122.) 0 2

123.) 0 2
E_____

124.) 0 2

125.) 0 2

126.) 0 2

127.) 0 1 2
E_____

128.) 0 2
E_____

129.) 0 2

132.) 0 1 2
E_____

130.) 0 2

131.) 0 2

Total _____

EXPRESSIVE SPEECH SCALE

Repetition

133.) 0 1 2
A___I___M___
B___SH___

134.) 0 1 2
SP___TH___PL___
STR___AWK___

135.) 0 1 2
see-seen_____
tree-trick_____

136.) 0 1 2
house_____
table_____
apple_____

137.) 0 1 2
hairbrush_____
screwdriver_____
laborious_____

138.) 0 1 2
rhinocerous
surveillance
hierarchy

139.) 0 2
cat-hat-bat

140.) 0 2
streptomycin
Mass, Episcopal

141.) 0   2
hat–sun–bell
hat–bell–sun

142.) 0 1 2
house–ball–chair
ball–chair–house

Qualitative: _____ Slow to learn (syllables, etc.)

Pronunciation

143.) 0 1 2
a___i___m___
b___sh___

144.) 0 1 2
sp___th___
pl___str___
awk_____

145.) 0   2
see-seen___
tree-trick___

146.) 0 1 2
cat___dog___
man_____

147.) 0 1 2
house_____
table_____
apple_____

148.) 0 1 2
hairbrush
screwdriver
laborious

149.) 0 1 2
rhinoceros
surveillance
hierarchy

150.) 0   2
cat-hat-bat

151.) 0   2
streptomycin
Mass, Episcopal

152.) 0   2
hat-sun-bell

153.) 0   2
house-ball-chair

Qualitative: _____ Education
              _____ Phonetic skills

Sentence Repetition

154.) 0   2
Weather-fine
Sun-shines-sky

155.) 0 1 2
Apple-grew-garden-fence
Edge-forest-hunter-wolf

156.) 0 1 2
house-fire
moon-shining
broom-sweeping

Confrontation Naming

157.) 0 1 2
guitar___table_____
c.opener___candle___
stapler_____

158.) 0 1 2
foot_____
arm_____
finger_____

159.) 0 1 2
comb_____
watch_____
umbrella___

Automatic Series Repetition

160.) 0   2
1--20

161.) 0   2
20--1

162.) 0   2
MTWRFSS

163.) 0   2
SSFRWTM

Qualitative: _____ Perseveration of instruction set
              _____ Ommission/comission errors

Spontaneous/Generative Speech

164.) 0 1 2   165.) 0 1 2   166.) 0 1 2   167.) 0 1 2

  T____   #____   T____   #____

168.) 0 1 2   169.) 0 1 2   170.) 0 1 2   171.) 0 1 2   172.) 0   2

  T____   #____   E____   T____   _____

                                             ____E__

173.) 0   2   174.) 0   2

  #____   T____

Qualitative: ____ Sparse ideation

             ____ Labored expression

                 Total _____

WRITING SCALE
Phonetic Analysis   ### Copying

175.) 0 1 2   176.) 0 1 2   177.) 0 1 2   178.) 0 1 2   179.) 0   2

cat__trap__   a__m__   B__L__   F__T__   match__

banana_____   d__p__   L__D__   H__L__   district__

hedge_____   d__   B__   antarctic__

                       180.) 0 1 2   181.) 0 1 2

                         E_____   F__T__

                                 H__L__

Dictation

182.) 0 1 2   183.) 0 1 2   184.) 0 1 2   Qualitative: ____ tremor

ba__da__   wren____   physiology

back__pack__   knife____   probabilistic   ____ education

Generative Wording

185.) 0 1 2   186.) 0 1 2   187.) 0 1 2

hatsundog_____   grammar__

allofasudden_____   spelling__

lastyearbeforeChristmas__   content__

                                         Total _____

READING SCALE
Phonetic Synthesis

188.) 0 1 2   189.) 0 1 2

G-R-O___P-L-Y___   S-T-O-N-E___K-N-I-G-H-T___

Confrontation Reading

190.) 0 1 2	191.) 1 2	192.) 0 1 2	193.) 0 1 2
KSWRT_____	BJS	po___cor___	juice_____
		cra___spro___	bread_____
		prot_____	bonfire___
cloakroom___	194.) 0 1 2	195.) 0 1 2	196.) 0 1 2
fertilizer_____	UN___USA___	insub._____	astro._____
	USSR_____	indist._____	hemop.___
197.) 0 1 2	198.) 0 1 2		

197.) 0 1 2   198.) 0 1 2

_____   _____

_____   _____

Generative Reading

199.) 0 1 2   200.) 0 1 2

   #_____   t_____   **Total _____**

ARITHMETIC SCALE
Number Writing/Reading

201.) 0 1 2	202.) 0 1 2	203.) 0 1 2	204.) 0 1 2	205.) 0 1 2
206.) 0 1 2	207.) 0 1 2	208.) 0 1 2	Qualitative: ___ attention	
793_____	IV___VI___	27___34___	___ phobia	
357_____	IX___XI___	158_____		
	17___71___	396_____		
	69___96___	9845_____		

Spatial Numerics

209.) 0 1 2   210.) 0 1 2   211.) 0 1 2

158___396___1023___   17/68___23/56___189/201___   _____ ___

Numeric Operations

212.) 0 1 2   213.) 0 1 2   214.) 0 1 2

3×3___ 5×4___ 7×8___ $3 + 4$___ $6 + 7$___ $7 - 4$___ $8 - 5$___

215.) 0 1 2   216.) 0 1 2   217.) 0   2

$27 + 8$___
$31 - 7$___
$44 + 57$___
$44 - 14$___

Numeric Reasoning   Numeric Control

218.) 0 1 2   219.) 0 1 2   220.) 0   2   221.) 0 1 2   222.) 0 1 2

$10(\times)2 = 20$___ $12 - (4) = 8$___   75_____   _____   _____

$10(+)2 = 12$___ $12 + (7) = 19$___   554_____   _____   _____

$10(-)2 = 8$___

$10(/)2 = 5$___

Total _____

MEMORY SCALE
Span/Learning Curve

PREDICTION	ACTUAL	HOUSE	FOREST	CAT	NIGHT	TABLE	NEEDLE	PIE
_____	_____	_____	_____	____	_____	_____	_____	___
_____	_____	_____	_____	____	_____	_____	_____	___
_____	_____	_____	_____	____	_____	_____	_____	___
_____	_____	_____	_____	____	_____	_____	_____	___
_____	_____	_____	_____	____	_____	_____	_____	___

223.) 0 1 2   224.) 0 1 2   225.) 0 1 2   226.) 0   2   227.) 0 1 2

#____   #____   Y N   C I   E____

228.) 0   2   229.) 0 1 2   230.) 0 1 2

LLSSLLSS   E____   house moon street boy water

Interference

231.) 0 1 2
house tree cat
____ ____ ___

232.) 0 1 2
man hat door
____ ____ ____

light stove cake
____ ____ ____

233.) 0 1 2
The sun rises in the east
_____

In May the apple trees blossom
_____

Semantic Organization

234.) 0 1 2

A crow heard/that doves had plenty to eat./He colored himself white/and flew to the dove cote./The doves thought/he was one of them/and took him in./However, he could not help cawing/like a crow./The doves then realized that he was a crow/and threw him out./He went back to rejoin the crows,/but they did not recognize him/and would not accept him./

235.) 0 1 2

M10 (energy)_____   M14 (family)_____

M11 (employment)_____   M15 (project)_____

M12 (party)_____   M16 (pollution)_____

M13 (happy)_____   **Total** _____

INTELLECTUAL PROCESSES

Thematic Pictures

236.) 0 1 2	237.) 0 1 2	238.) 0 1 2	239.) 0 1 2
_____	_____	_____	t____
_____	_____	240.) 0 1 2	241.) 0 1 2
_____	_____	_____	t____
242.) 0 2	243.) 0 2		
_____	_____		
_____	_____		

Abstraction

244.) 0 1 2	245.) 0 1 2	246.) 0 1 2	247.) 0 1 2	248.) 0 1 2
_____	_____	_____	E____	_____
_____	_____	_____		_____
_____	_____	_____		_____
249.) 0 1 2	250.) 0 1 2	251.) 0 2	252.) 0 2	253.) 0 2
_____	_____	E____	_____	_____
_____	_____	_____	_____	_____
_____	_____	_____	_____	_____
254.) 0 1 2	255.) 0 2	256.) 0 1 2	257.) 0 2	
E____	E____	E____	E____	
_____	_____	_____	_____	

Problem-Solving

258.) 0   2   259.) 0 1 2   260.) 0   2   261.) 0 1 2

_____   t_____   _____   t_____

262.) 0   2   263.) 0 1 2   264.) 0   2   265.) 0 1 2

_____   t_____   _____   t_____

266.) 0   2   267.) 0 1 2   268.) 0   2   269.) 0 1 2

_____   t_____   _____   t_____

Qualitative: ____ operations OK but strategies wrong

____ confused by verbiage

____ nervous

____ attention

____ correct with guidance

Total _____

6

Brief and Extended Neuropsychological Assessment of Learning Disabilities

Greta N. Wilkening

SCREENING FOR LEARNING DISABILITIES

Several months ago I spoke with a local physician. He had received a call that day from a family he knew well. Their seven-year-old daughter, who was performing adequately in first grade, had been screened for learning problems by a local provider of developmental therapy while at her day-care center. The family then received a report noting questionable difficulties in several areas and recommending an in-depth evaluation. This conscientious, caring family was concerned as to what they should do. They consulted their equally concerned physician, who was not certain how to advise the family.

This vignette raises a number of issues regarding screening and more in-depth assessment of learning disorders in children. One issue concerning this physician was whether the screening instrument used was valid and how much emphasis he should place on these initial results. His second concern was what further evaluation should be considered if the child truly needed referral on the basis of the screening. Finally, he wanted to know what evaluation he could complete within his office so as to make informed decisions. In this chapter some of the conceptual issues regarding developmental screening will be discussed. Screening instruments and tasks with known predictive and concurrent validity will be described. Finally, a description of several batteries, based upon neuropsychological theories regarding the presentation and underlying deficits seen in learning-disordered children, will be discussed. Before dealing with these issues, some initial information regarding definition and prevalence is required.

DEFINITION AND PREVALENCE
OF LEARNING DISABILITIES

Research and clinical work in the area of learning disabilities has been complicated by the multiplicity of names and definitions attached to the disorder. The legislative definition, which was required by the passage of Public Law 94-142 insuring appropriate education for handicapped children, defines a learning-disabled child as one who is failing to make adequate academic progress despite adequate intelligence. Failure to learn in learning-disabled children cannot be secondary to a major sensory handicap, emotional disturbance, or cultural deprivation. Failure to learn is presumed to be secondary to a central processing failure. The stimuli are registered and available to the child; failure occurs at the level of integration or interpretation of data, or reflects difficulty with organized expression of a response. In practice, "failure to achieve academically" is generally defined by describing some necessary discrepancy between current and expected level of academic achievement on the basis of measured level of intelligence. Establishing that a specified level of discrepancy exists is required for placement in publicly supported programs for treatment of learning disabilities.

Though this practical definition of a learning disability is required for bureaucratic decisions, it is a problematic definition from a theoretical and practical point of view when one is attempting to develop protocols allowing one to identify learning-disabled children. Theoretically, learning-disabled children are considered to be those with specific deficits in higher cortical functions. This is presumed to be secondary to central nervous system immaturity or dysfunction. It is the presence of an underlying deficit in processing, organizing, and retaining input and output that is significant. Consequently, at a theoretical level it is the integrity or the maturity of the central nervous system that is of significance, not the discrepancy in performance. The legislative definition, by requiring failure to acquire skills at an adequate rate, demands that the child fail to learn for a substantial period of time before that child can be labeled as learning-disabled. The more theoretical description focuses on those processes essential for adequate learning. Though for most purposes the definitions are congruent, statements of prevalence and identification strategies may differ on the basis of which definition is utilized.

The description of learning disorders as a "low severity, high prevalence" condition (Levin, Meltzer, Busch, Palfrey, & Sullivan, 1983) is a useful reminder of the prominence of learning disorders in the school-aged population.

Prevalence estimates vary both as a consequence of definitional criteria and identification strategies. The prevalence of learning disabilities not attributable to major handicapping conditions has reported to be from 4–20% of the school-aged population (Levine, Brooks, & Shonkoff, 1980). Many experts feel prevalence estimates in the 10–16% range to be the most accurate (Hynd & Cohen, 1983), and school districts assume that about 10% of their students will require special services. School difficulties are thought to be one of the fastest growing areas of morbidity in the pediatric population; consequently, they are an area of concern for medical practitioners.

CONCURRENT AND PREDICTIVE VALIDITY

Screening children for learning difficulties can take two different forms, each demanding different developmental methodology. One group of screening tests is that which has been developed to identify a disability that exists at the same time the screening is completed. The other type of instrument is that which has been developed to predict whether a child will encounter difficulty in the future.

The thrust of most screening tools is the identification of children who are experiencing learning difficulties at the time they are screened. The purpose of such identification is to make appropriate referrals for more intensive evaluation, to encourage an appropriate response from the school, and to provide consultation to the family. Such screening tools demand methodology insuring concurrent validity. That is, the screening device must be able to predict current group status (in this case, learning-disabled versus normal achievement) as defined by some external criteria (in this case, grades, achievement test data, etc.).

Since the primary goal of these screening tests is to see that children who require more intensive evaluation receive it, a necessary criteria for judging the success of such instruments is their efficient determination of the current status of the child. The perfect screening tool would identify every child who, upon a more intensive and expensive follow-up evaluation, is shown to have learning difficulties. Additionally, no children would be identified as being at risk who, on more intense evaluation, are found to be normal. Clearly, no screening tool is this accurate. As the number of false positive (those children identified as abnormal by the screening test, but not by the complete evaluation) decreases, the number of false negatives (those children identified as normal during screening, but who do indeed have problems) increases. The determination of acceptable levels of accuracy is a matter of public policy (Gorell, 1981), as the cost of detailed evaluation is weighed against the cost of not identifying those truly requiring intervention.

Predictive Tests are rare

Those screening tests designed expressly for prediction are rarer. Conceptually and practically they may be of far more importance, since they allow for early, and perhaps more successful, intervention (Satz, Taylor, Friel, & Fletcher, 1978). Screening tests with good predictive validity are designed to identify preschool-aged children who are at high risk for developing later learning problems. Performance on the screening tasks must be able to predict later performance on relevant variables (in this case, academic achievement). Such screening devices require longitudinal studies, since they identify children who do not, at the time of identification, necessarily demonstrate any achievement deficits. Development of screening tests with good predictive validity requires that the tests demonstrate statistically acceptable levels of accuracy in predicting group status at a later date. The level of accuracy required is, again, a matter of social policy. If we assume the children who are identified as at high risk to have learning problems will receive immediate intervention, the number of false positives (the children identified as at risk to have problems when ultimately they will not) and false negatives (those children not identified as at risk who ultimately encounter learning problems) that are tolerated depends upon the value society places on preventing academic failure and the amount of resources it is willing to commit to that end.

SCREENING TOOLS WITH CONCURRENT VALIDITY

Several formats have been developed to identify children currently evidencing learning problems. The simplest and least time-consuming, in the terms of staff time, are those that utilize a parent checklist format. Several screening tools identifying children with academic and/or psychological difficulties are available.

Parent Checklist Tools

The Missouri Children's Behavioral Checklist (Sines, Pauker, Sines, & Owen, 1969) was designed to identify those dimensions of children's behavior important in making diagnostic decisions about the need for and type of psychological intervention. It is composed of 78 items, with the parent required to respond to the presence and frequency of behavior. Seven scales are derived (Aggression, Inhibition, Activity Level, Sleep Disturbance, Somatization, Sociability, and Sex). Though the Missouri Children's Behavioral Checklist was developed to further examine epidemiologic aspects of psychopathology in children, its use in identifying children who have learning difficulties suggests that some useful discriminations can be made (Thompson, Curry, Sturner, Greene, & Funk, 1982; Curry & Thompson, 1982). Parental descriptions of preschool-age children found to be performing at abnormal levels (over one standard deviation below the mean on the McCarthy Scales of Children's Abilities) demonstrated that these children were significantly different from children previously identified as developmentally disabled, as well as from children whose performance on the McCarthy Scales was within normal limits (Thompson et al., 1982). Differences between the abnormal and normal children emerged on scales assessing both externalizing and internalizing behavior. Though at a statistical level the checklist can make relevant distinctions, no cutoffs are available. It would be difficult for the practitioner to know which children ought to be referred for which type of further evaluation on the basis of the Missouri Children's Behavior Checklist.

The Personality Inventory for Children (Wirt, Lachar, Klinedinst, & Soat, 1977) is another parent-completed assessment device. The short form of the Personality Inventory for Children requires the child's mother to complete 280 true-false questions describing the child's behavior. Unlike the Missouri Children's Behavior Checklist, the Personality Inventory for Children includes questions specifically designed to assess achievement, intellectual processes, and development within the context of assessing overall psychological adjustment. The achievement scale was specifically designed to assist in the identification of those children whose academic achievement is below what one would anticipate upon the basis of intellectual ability. Concurrent validity based upon performance on the Peabody Individual Achievement Test demonstrates that the scale is most successful in identifying children with reading deficits and least successful in identifying children with arithmetic difficulties (Wirt et al., 1977).

Though the Intellectual Screening Scale of the Personality Inventory for Children does not substitute for an individual intellectual assessment, use of the specified cutoff accurately identified 83% of the children whose Full-Scale IQ's on various psychometric tests were over one standard deviation below the mean in a sample other than the construction sample. Only three (7%) of the children whose intellectual performance was within one standard deviation of the mean were misidentified as having intellectual deficits. However, four of 12 children who had IQ's of less than 80 (33%) were not identified as having intellectual deficits on the basis of scale performance, and presumably would not have been referred for further evaluation.

Clearly, the Personality Inventory for Children offers useful diagnostic information regarding the developmental and achievement status of children. Drawbacks for use within a primary-care facility include time necessary for scoring (around 20 minutes, though a computer program is available) and the degree of sophistication and training necessary for accurate and useful interpretation. Additional concerns in clinical usage are parental resistance to the length of the instrument.

Greater commitment of resources is necessary for those screening tests that involve direct contact with the child. Though in most cases the examiner can be a trained paraprofessional, some level of training (so that reliable and valid results can be obtained) is required. Ongoing supervision of the tester is necessary, and direct patient contact time is increased. The following screening tools entail direct evaluation of the child.

The North Carolina Psychoeducational Screening Test (PET) was specifically designed as one component of a statewide screening procedure for evaluating pre-kindergarten–aged children (Gorrell, 1981). The PET was designed by selecting from a variety of other standardized tests those tasks completed successfully by four-year-old children. The PET is composed of seven scales: Gross Motor, Visual Memory, Auditory Perception, Auditory Memory, Visual and Motor Performance, Concept Development, and Language Development. Each scale can be scored as delayed, average, or advanced on the basis of points received for success. The PET's ability to identify children who, when seen for a more detailed evaluation, were found to be experiencing developmental deficits was 100%. However, of the remaining children, 26% were identified as requiring further evaluation without subsequent confirmation. Very good ability to identify children requiring further assessment was achieved by overidentifying children (i.e., too many false positives). Though the PET is highly sensitive, it is not specific. Clinicians wishing to utilize this screening tool must weigh the consequences of overlooking children who need further assessment against the financial and emotional cost of referring many children who will subsequently prove to be normal.

A screening program for identification of children with psychological and learning deficits has been developed by the Permanente Medical Group in San Francisco (Allen, Metz, & Shinefield, 1971). This program, which can be administered by a trained paraprofessional, involves parental report in addition to direct child assessment. A parental inventory, requiring the parents to sort cards, which are then machine scored to identify high-risk factors, asks about the child's visual motor development, learning and communication skills, personal–social development, and symptomatic behavior. The child completes the Rutger's Drawing Test and three tests of conceptual ability (a shortened Peabody Picture Vocabulary Test, a shortened version of the Columbia Mental Maturity Scale, and a Human Figure Drawing). Older children (seven-to-eight-year-olds) are asked to complete the reading section of the Wide Range Achievement Test.

All test results can be converted into statistically meaningful standard scores or percentiles. A report to the physician indicating areas in which the child performs at less than the fifth percentile can be generated in one-to-three minutes, according to the authors. The entire assessment, including examiner and child time, is estimated to be 35 minutes.

Validity studies using this set of screening tools have investigated the relationship between an overall risk index and professionally diagnosed psychosocial problems. Though 12% of the sample had independently diagnosed deficits, only 5% of the sample were identified. Two percent of the sample were misidentified as having deficits when they did not. Unlike the PET, the

Kaiser Permanente exam has too many false negatives rather than too many false positives. Comparison of screening test results with classroom, teacher-identified learning problems indicates that only 55% of the children with difficulties identified by teachers were identified by screening, when performance below the 10th percentile was the requirement for an abnormal label. However, by identifying children below the 20th percentile as abnormal, 77% of the children having classroom difficulties were identified. This was with little increase in number of false positives.

The use of neuromaturational or extended neurologic exams for identification of children with learning difficulties has been suggested (Peats, Romine, and Dykman, 1975; Shaywitz, Shaywitz, McGraw, & Groll, 1984). Such evaluations may be integrated into routine neurologic exams. There have been a number of attempts to standardize the administration of such exams to help physicians less experienced in observing children make adequate observations of subtle findings and to evaluate empirically the utility of such exams in identifying learning-disabled children. *Neuromaturational exams*

Peats and associates (1975) present a series of 80 items encompassing the evaluation of fine- and gross-motor skills, impersistence, laterality, extraocular movements, oral movements, speech and language skills, graphesthesia, writing, and finger agnosia. They found that 44 items discriminated normal from learning-disabled children at least at the P < .05 level. They suggest a series of 21 items as those best identifying abnormal children. Interestingly, performance on several of these 21 items was not significantly different between the groups.

Recently, Shaywitz and associates (1984) investigated the ability of a standardized neuromaturational exam (NME) comprised of 103 items to discriminate gifted, normal, and learning-disabled children. Of note is that the items best discriminating learning-disabled children from normal and gifted children did not include items typically used in screening tests. In particular, gross-motor tasks, sinistrality, mixed dominance, and the presence of choreiform movements were unrelated to academic success. The items were grouped into scales on the basis of whether the items were basic unlearned skills, acquired academic skills, or a mixture of basic and specifically taught skills (i.e., three groups: basic, acquired, and mixed). The tasks were also grouped on the basis of content (laterality, fine-motor proficiency, short-term memory, synkinesis, and language). The learning-disabled boys performed more poorly than the normals or the gifted boys on all but fine-motor speech and short-term memory (whereas the gifted children's performance was significantly better than that of both the learning-disabled and the normal children's performances). When IQ was used as a covariate, significant differences were demonstrable only for the mixed skills, short-term memory, synkinesis, and fine-motor proficiency. Learning-disabled children differed from normals only on the fine-motor proficiency and synkinesis scales. Interestingly, the gifted boys

[handwritten notes at top: Neuromaturational status may be related to overall IQ then no learning disab.]

[handwritten notes in left margin]

also demonstrated more synkinesis than normals. Short-term memory and mixed skills discriminated gifted children, since they had superior performance when compared to both normal and learning-disabled children. The authors suggest it may be that neuromaturational status is related to overall intelligence rather than to learning disabilities per se.

Of interest was Shaywitz and associates' (1984) attempt to develop a limited series of tasks that could reliably discriminant learning-disabled from normal children. Seventeen tasks of the 103 items were chosen. These items demonstrated significant differences between the two groups (P < .01) when scored dichotomously in a Chi-square analysis. Discriminate function analysis demonstrated classification accuracy of 93.1% and 100% for normal and learning-disabled children, respectively. No cross-validation is reported. One would anticipate accuracy to decrease in another sample. Despite what one would consider to be quite good results on the discriminate function analysis, Shaywitz and associates did not feel the results supported neurodevelopmental evaluation as an adequate screening for learning disabilities.

Levine and associates (1983) have developed the Pediatric Early Elementary Examination (PEEX), which includes, among other things, a neuromaturational exam to facilitate screening for early identification of learning-disabled children, to establish whether children require subspecialty evaluation, to uncover areas of concern not previously identified, and to assist pediatricians in contributing to the care of learning-disabled children. Administration of the PEEX takes about 45 minutes, independent of interview time. It is to be used with children from seven to nine years of age.

The PEEX allows for qualitative evaluation of the child's approach to the task, including patterns of attention and concentration, efficiency of responding, and type of errors committed, as well as allowing for measurement of correctness and speed of response. The exam includes assessment of minor neurologic indicators, temporal-sequential and visual-spatial orientation, auditory-language function, fine- and gross-motor skills, and memory. Cutoff levels suggesting the need for concern about a child's performance are provided.

An initial validation was completed using a mixed sample of normal and learning-impaired children. All normal children were given the Wechsler Intelligence Scale for Children–Revised (WISC-R) and the California Achievement Test (CAT). Performance on the achievement and IQ measures were inversely related to the number of areas of concern identified on the PEEX for normal children. These relationships are impressive, since the prevalence of academic difficulties and the standard deviation within the group were quite small. Those children who were receiving special services within the school had more areas of concern identified on the PEEX than normal children receiving no special services. Only 55% of the group of children currently receiving services were identified as having at least one area of concern on the PEEX.

SCREENING TOOLS WITH PREDICTIVE VALIDITY

Screening tests designed to identify preschool-aged children who are likely to have later school difficulties require difficult-to-complete longitudinal studies. Difficulties include definitional criteria, statistical analysis, establishment of an appropriate sample, and control for attrition. The Florida Kindergarten Screening Battery (Satz & Fletcher, 1982; Satz, Friel, & Rudegeair, 1979) was developed specifically to detect high-risk children prior to the time they begin overtly demonstrating deficits. A group of all male children was initially evaluated in kindergarten, with academic achievement evaluated during grade 2 and grade 5. The screening test has been cross-validated in a number of populations, including Australian schools (White, Batini, Satz, & Friel, 1979). The battery, as it is commercially available, is comprised of five tests: Alphabet Recitation, the Peabody Picture Vocabulary Test, Recognition–Discrimination, the Finger Localization Test, and the Beery Test of Visual Motor Integration. The test requires about 20 minutes to administer.

Analytical factor studies of the battery (completed on an expanded set of tests) have consistently demonstrated that the tasks group into three more basic measures: a general sensorimotor perceptual factor, a verbal-conceptual factor, and a verbal factor (Satz, Taylor, Friel, & Fletcher, 1978).

Discriminant function analysis was completed at the end of grade 2 and during grade 5 in order to assess the predictive validity of the screening battery. Outcome criteria to assess the prediction included classroom reading level as indicated by teachers and performance on standardized tests of academic achievement. When children were assessed at the end of second grade, the battery, which had been administered during kindergarten, had accurately identified 91% of the children with severe learning problems and 66% of the mildly disordered group. Sixty-eight percent of the average and 97% of the superior readers had also been correctly identified. Prediction of performance six years after battery had initially been completed was virtually identical to the earlier followup (Satz et al., 1978). Again, the extreme ends of the continuum (superior readers and severely disabled readers) had been most accurately identified during the kindergarten assessment. Conditional probability values based upon the probability of test sign (i.e., true and false negatives, valid and false positives) and the base rate of reading disorders in the population were then calculated. Based upon this analysis, Satz and associates (1978) indicated that accuracy of prediction, suggesting the need for intervention, is increased over chance levels by using the screening tool for severe high-risk, low high-risk, and very low-risk children. By using the battery, an accurate response (i.e., provision of services) will result for at least 67% of the children who will develop severe learning disorders. Given the probability of identification using the screening device and base rates of learning disorders within the population, it is difficult to respond to low-risk children without treating large numbers of children who will not have learning problems.

SUGGESTIONS FOR THE PRACTITIONER

Experience in medical settings and a review of the literature suggest that a dual strategy for screening may be useful, given the probability of accurate identification using screening tests. Screening of children with no history predictive of learning difficulties might be accomplished using any of the tools previously discussed that can be consistently and comfortably given to children at the time of their physical evaluation prior to entrance in school. Time constraints suggest that exams such as the PEEX will not be consistently given in a busy medical practice. Tests with no cutoffs would be difficult to interpret. The diagnostic accuracy and the ease of the Kaiser Permanente exam, the Personality Inventory for Children, and the Florida Kindergarten Screening Battery suggest that they may warrant consideration.

A differential approach would seem appropriate for children with histories suggesting that they are at risk for the development of learning problems. Some of these children (e.g., those with severe birth anoxia or encephalitis) will have clear difficulties that will be recognized without recourse to screening. Another group at high risk secondary to medical disorders may have only subtle findings that may not be picked up by screening tools. Screening, by itself, does not appear justifiable in this group. Following such children by using a screening tool, plus a careful interview to ascertain if any concomitant problems are appearing (e.g., how is the child doing in preschool, does he/she get along adequately with other children, is the child's development commensurate with siblings' progress?), should assist the practitioner in deciding whether children in this high-risk, low-severity group require extensive evaluation. Any indicators of difficulty (e.g., the teacher has asked the mother to work with the child at home) should be attended to regardless of performance on the screening measures. Similarly, any indication of difficulty on the screening tool, regardless of how well the child appears clinically, should be responded to with appropriate referrals. It is inappropriate to use a developmental screening tool with children referred specifically for school-related difficulties. Those children should be referred for more comprehensive evaluations if such an assessment is not being satisfactorily completed at school.

Children considered to be at high risk for the presence of subtle learning difficulties as a consequence of medical disorders or treatments include those with traumatic, infectious, neoplastic, neurologic, and metabolic disorders. Most of these children will have no deficits, but some will have greater difficulty learning specific subjects than the majority of their peers. Others will be doing fairly well compared with peers, but may look deficient when compared with siblings and other family members, suggesting an alteration in their capacity to learn. It must be recognized that the latter pattern may be quite painful and demoralizing for the child and family despite the child's apparent success in most situations.

Children who have had severe neonatal problems, particularly respiratory failure or seizures, are a high-risk group. The presence of early seizures, whether generalized convulsive or focal, alerts the practitioner that a child is at risk for having school-related difficulties.

Some childhood disease processes seem to pose greater risks for later learning problems when they occur at a younger age. Data on the sequelae of encephalitis during childhood are not entirely clear but suggest that children ill prior to two years of age are especially vulnerable to learning problems. Similarly, children diagnosed as diabetic prior to age five are considered to have an unusually high incidence of learning disorders. The long-term consequences of cranial irradiation for treatment of leukemia are thought to be greater in children who are treated when they are younger; the incidence of learning difficulties, particularly difficulty with attention, concentration, arithmetic, has been reported to be unusually large in this group.

Though children with significant head trauma deserve careful follow-up, there is also evidence that mild head injuries in children may be detrimental to optimal school performance. Mild head injuries include those resulting in loss of consciousness for less than 15 minutes.

Clinically, my experience with children treated for subtentorial tumors suggests that these children also have an unusually high incidence of relatively mild, but academically debilitating, learning problems. Though children treated for cortical tumors may have normal neurologic evaluations, they often can be shown to have difficulties with higher-level cognitive problems that impair school learning. Similarly, children treated promptly for hydrocephalus, though most often of normal intelligence, should receive special attention as the practitioner considers the likelihood that they may require special assistance at school.

MORE INTENSE EVALUATION

Once the practitioner has decided that a child demonstrates behavior consistent with a learning disorder, the next step is to arrange for an evaluation that will result in the provision of the most appropriate services for that child. For many children and families, the best resource for further evaluation may be the teams that are provided by local school districts. The advantages of using such an approach are that evaluations completed by school district evaluators are free to the family and provide direct access to publicly provided therapeutic programs, if such a program is deemed necessary. The disadvantages include the heavy case loads handled by such teams (so that evaluations are not always completed in the most timely manner), the limitations on provision of services imposed by bureaucratic rules, and the discomfort some families feel in identifying a young child to school personnel as handicapped.

Regardless of whether the family seeks services within the private or the public sector, the purpose of further evaluation is to delineate more clearly how the child functions across a broad range of skills, to ascertain what the underlying dysfunctional process is that is impeding academic progress, and to establish what areas of strength and skill might be utilized to help the child progress. The second goal, that of identifying the basic area of deficit and predicting what other skills may be in jeopardy, is the most difficult aspect of such an evaluation, but can most readily be completed by using a neuropsychological battery.

The purpose of neuropsychological assessment in a learning-disabled child is to see if any pattern of deficit can be demonstrated that has been previously and empirically established in groups of learning-disabled children. Identification of patterns is useful, since specific patterns presumably have a relationship to similar findings that are seen as the sequelae of known focal brain lesions. For example, Mattis, French, and Rapin (1975) have identified three types of reading disorders (other authors identify other clusters of dysfunction, but have provided additional evidence that within the dyslexic population there are relatively homogeneous subtypes). The three groups can be typified as those reading-disabled children who have an underlying language disorder, those with visual-spatial and perceptual disorders, and those with articulatory and graphomotor dyscoordination. These subtypes represent groupings of depressed performance but also bear a striking similarity to the deficits produced as a consequence of focal damage to the left hemisphere, the right hemisphere, and the anterior left hemisphere, respectively. The identification of such patterns assists in diagnosis but is even more useful in that it suggests an optimal approach to and prognosis of treatment.

Neuropsychological batteries are similar to other psychological tests in requiring a behavioral response to specific, standardized stimuli on the part of the child. Unlike other psychological tests, however, they have been specifically validated to discriminate between normal children and those who have organic disorders. Because the effects of brain damage in children are mediated by a large number of variables, including age at onset, the effect of plasticity, greater frequency of diffuse injuries, and the interaction between development and the effects of injury, the types of judgments that can be made following a neuropsychological evaluation of a child are different from those that can be made subsequent to the same evaluation of an adult. Localization of the lesion is not often a goal in child neuropsychology. We are also less able, when evaluating a child, to describe the pathological process on the basis of neuropsychological data than we are in evaluating an adult. What can be done, however, especially in the learning-disabled population, is to describe, as specifically as possible, the child's strengths and weakness in those higher cognitive skills believed necessary for adequate achievement and to relate these problems to those seen in other learning-disabled children and to patterns seen subsequent to known brain damage.

The areas typically assessed within a neuropsychological evaluation include motor and sensory functions, receptive and expressive language skills, pitch and rhythm perception, problem-solving skills and strategies, academic skills, memory functions, nonverbal problem solving, attention and concentration, and new learning. Some pediatric neuropsychologists use batteries, while others perfer to use a series of tests put together for a specific population or to answer a specific question. Reviews of specific independent neuropsychological tools are available elsewhere (Lezak, 1983; Golden, 1981).

In this review, two frequently used neuropsychological batteries developed especially for use with children will be discussed. The Reitan–Indiana (for children 5–8 years) and the Halstead Children's (for children 9–14 years old) neuropsychological batteries follow the format of the Halstead–Reitan Neuropsychological Battery that is commonly used in adult assessment. The Children's Revision of the Luria–Nebraska Neuropsychological Battery (for children 8–12 years old) is similar to the adult form of the battery in terms of theory and content.

Validity studies of both batteries yield hit-rates in the 75–90% range of accuracy. Klonoff, Robinson, and Thompson (1969), using the Reitan–Indiana, reported hit-rates that varied between 80% in five-year-olds to 96% in eight-years-old children. Klonoff and Low (1974) reported an overall hit-rate of 80% in normal children and 75% in brain-injured children using the Reitan–Indiana Neurological Test Battery. Selz and Reitan (1979) developed a series of 37 rules using the Halstead Neuropsychological Test Battery for Children to differentiate normal, learning-disabled, and brain-injured children. They found an overall hit-rate of 73%. Initial validation studies with the children's revision of the Luria–Nebraska Neuropsychological Battery (Wilkening, Golden, MacInnes, Plaisted, & Hermann, 1981) yielded an overall hit-rate of 82%. The cross-validation (Gustavson, Wilkening, Hermann, Plaisted, & MacInnes, 1982) using the same discriminant function analysis yielded an overall hit-rate of 81%. The use of a decision rule yielded an overall hit-rate of 85%. Two of these studies, the Selz and Reitan study (1979) and the use of the critical cutoff with the Luria–Nebraska Neuropsychological Battery (Golden, Hammeke & Durisch, 1980) suggest how accurate one will be using only a decision rule. Some data (Heaton, Grant, Anthony, & Lehman, 1981) suggest that a well-trained, experienced clinician will be more accurate than a set of rules, since the clinician is able to attend to a greater number of subtle, but neurologically significant, variables.

A thorough neuropsychological evaluation of a child seldom involves only the administration of a set battery. Most neuropsychologists will include administration of a standardized test of intelligence (which is considered part of the Reitan–Indiana and the Halstead Children's Batteries) and measures of academic achievement. More in-depth evaluation of memory, problem-solving, and language skills is often included, thereby extending the accuracy of the batteries and their utility in describing how a child is functioning.

In many cases, an important issue is establishing whether a child's learning difficulties are primarily attributable to emotional factors. Neuropsychologists, who are most often trained and licensed as clinical psychologists but who have had additional training in neuropsychology, will include an assessment of psychological functioning so as to make the differential between primary learning and primary psychological disturbance, and in order to gain a fuller, more complete picture of the child.

The following brief write-up will help to elucidate the data that can be provided through a complete neuropsychological evaluation. This child's difficulties had initially been identified, not via screening, but secondary to chronic learning difficulties.

A.J. is an 11-year-five-month-old male. At the time of the evaluation he was enrolled in a fourth-grade program. The referral question concerned the etiology of A.J.'s learning difficulties. Though he was thought to be a bright child, he was having some behavioral difficulties, and the relationship between his behavioral disturbance and his learning problems was in question. During his evaluation, the Luria–Nebraska Neuropsychological Battery-Children's Revision, the Wechsler Intelligence Scale for Children–Revised, the Grooved Pegboard, the Wide Range Achievement Test–Revised, the Judgement of Line Orientation Test, and the Wisconsin Card Sorting Test were administered.

A.J.'s performance on the Wechsler Intelligence Scale for Children–Revised yielded a Full-Scale IQ of 95, with a Verbal IQ of 87 and a Performance IQ of 105. Though the verbal performance is within normal limits, it is suggestive of some language-related difficulties. A.J.'s performance on the neuropsychological battery corroborated the presence of deficits associated with left-hemisphere dysfunction. Indeed, his performance suggested a diagnosis of developmental Gerstmann's syndrome. His performance included bilateral finger agnosia, directional confusion, dysgraphia, dyscalculia, and difficulties in reading. Spatial difficulties pervaded his presentation. He was unable to copy large-motor movements and became confused about position in space when drawing figures. He continues to make reversals in writing letters. Spatial confusion interferes with his ability to write numbers, because he is not always sure which comes first when he is writing multidigit numbers. Spatial confusion is also evident in automatic expressive language, where A.J. is able to count forward, but unable to count backward without becoming confused. Other signs of dominant parietal lobe dysfunction include mild dysnomia.

In summary, this child is seen to be a child of normal intelligence, but one who is experiencing major difficulties in learning academic functions. Though he may have some psychological difficulties that contribute to his school problems, he has multiple signs of dominant parietal lobe dysfunction that is interfering with his ability to learn academic skills. His primary diagnosis is not one of emotional disturbance, but rather the presence of a learning disability.

Recommendations included acknowledging A.J.'s learning difficulty, despite his adequate intelligence, and providing alternative ways of both learning information and responding to tests. It was also suggested that he may be able to learn more easily if the emphasis is placed on his relatively better abstract reasoning skills, rather than on his learning academic skills (e.g., reading) per se.

CONCLUSIONS

This chapter opened by describing the problems presented by a local physician who was unsure how to help a family whose child had been screened. The information presented in this chapter suggests that the initial concern, that is, the adequacy of the screening tool, is a valid one and one that practitioners who practice in areas where multiple groups complete screenings, often for the purpose of directing patients to the services they are providing, need to be aware of. If the practitioner has assured himself of the adequacy of the screening tool, then the next major issue is where to refer the child. My predilection would be to have the child evaluated at a center that would not be involved in the provision of remedial services if such services were required. When questions about learning disabilities are paramount, neuropsychological evaluation, which focuses upon the elucidation of underlying deficits consistent with known brain processes, is recommended. For children who are at high risk, on the basis of medical histories, referrals should be made less stringently.

REFERENCES

Allen, C. M., Metz, J. R., & Shinefield, H. R. (1971). Test development in the Pediatric Multiphasic Program. *Pediatric Clinics of North America, 18,* 169-178.

Curry, J. F., & Thompson, R. J. (1982). Patterns of behavioral disturbance in developmentally disabled children: A replicated cluster analysis. *Journal of Pediatric Psychology, 7,* 61-73.

Golden, C. J. (1981). *Diagnosis and rehabilitation in clinical neuropsychology* (2nd ed.). Springfield, IL: Charles C. Thomas.

Golden, C. J., Hammeke, T. A., & Purisch, A. D. (1980). *The Luria-Nebraska Neuropsychological Battery.* Los Angeles: Western Psychological Services.

Gorrell, R. W. (1981). The validity and predictive efficiency of the North Carolina Psychoeducational Screening Test. *Journal of Pediatric Psychology, 6,* 435-449.

Gustavson, J. L., Wilkening, G. N., Hermann, B. P., Plaisted, O. R., & MacInnes, W. D. (1982, August). The Luria-Nebraska Neuropsychological Battery-Children's Revision: Validation with brain damaged and normal children. Proceedings of the American Psychological Association, Washington, DC.

Heaton, R. K., Grant, I., Anthony, W. Z., & Lehman, R. A. (1981). A comparison of clinical and automatized interpretation of the Halstead-Reitan Battery, *Journal of Clinical Neuropsychology, 3,* 121-141.

Hynd, G., & Cohen, M. (1983). *Dyslexia: Neuropsychological theory, research and clinical differentiation*. New York: Grune & Stratton.

Klonoff, H., & Low, M. (1974). Disordered brain function in young children and early adolescents: Neuropsychological and electrophysiological correlates. In R. M. Reitan & L. A. Davidson (Eds.), *Clinical neuropsychology: Current status and applications* (pp. 121-177). New York: Wiley.

Klonoff, H., Robinson, G. C., & Thompson, G. (1969). Acute and chronic brain syndrome in children. *Developmental Medicine and Child Neurology, II,* 198-213.

Levin, M. D., Meltzer, L. J., Busch, B., Palfrey, J., & Sullivan, M. (1983). The Pediatric Early Elementary Examination: Studies of a neurodevelopmental examination for 7- to 9-year-old children. *Pediatrics, 71,* 894-903.

Levine, M., Brooks, R., & Shonkoff, J. P. (1980). *A pediatric approach to learning disorders*. New York: Wiley.

Lezak, M. D. (1983). *Neuropsychological assessment* (2nd ed.). New York: Oxford University Press.

Mattis, S., French, J. H., & Rapin, I. (1975). Dyslexia in children and young adults: Three independent neuropsychological syndromes. *Developmental Medicine and Child Neurology, 17,* 150-163

Peats, J. E., Romine, J. S., & Dykman, R. A. (1975). A special neurological examination of children with learning disabilities. *Developmental Medicine and Child Neurology, 17,* 63-78.

Satz, P., & Fletcher, J. (1982). *Florida Kindergarten Screening Battery*. Odessa, FL: Psychological Assessment Resources, Inc.

Satz, P., Friel, J., & Rudegeair, F. (1979). Some predictive antecedents of specific reading disability: A two-, three- and four-year follow-up. In J. T. Guthrie (Ed.), *Aspects of reading acquisition* (pp. 111-140). Baltimore: Johns Hopkins Press.

Satz, P., Taylor, H. G., Friel, J., & Fletcher, J. M. (1978). Some developmental and predictive precursors of reading disabilities: A six-year follow-up. In A. Benton & D. Pearl (Eds.), *Dyslexia: Appraisal of current knowledge* (pp. 315-347). New York: Oxford University Press.

Selz, M., & Reitan, R. M. (1979). Rules for neuropsychological classification of brain function in older children. *Journal of Consulting and Clinical Psychology, 47,* 258-264.

Shaywitz, S. E., Shaywitz, B. A., McGraw, K., & Groll, S. (1984). Current status of the neuromaturational examination as an index of learning disability. *The Journal of Pediatrics, 104,* 819-825.

Sines, J. O., Pauker, J. D., Sines, L. K., & Owen, D. R. (1969). Identification of clinically relevant dimensions of children's behavior. *Journal of Consulting and Clinical Psychology, 33,* 728-734.

Thompson, R. J., Curry, J. F., Sturner, R. A., Green, J. A., & Funk, S. G. (1982). Missouri children's behavior checklist ratings of preschool children as a function of risk status for developmental and learning problems. *Journal of Pediatric Psychology, 7,* 390-316.

White, M., Batini, P., Satz, P., & Friel, J. (1979). Predictive validity of a screening battery for children "at risk" for reading failure. *British Journal of Educational Psychology, 49,* 132-137.

Wilkening, G. N., Golden, C. J., MacInnes, W. D., Plaisted, J. R., & Hermann, B. P. (1981, August). The Luria-Nebraska Neuropsychological Battery-Children's Revision: A preliminary report. Proceedings of the American Psychological Association, Los Angeles.

Wirt, R. D., Lachar, D., Klinedinst, J. K., & Soat, P. D. (1977). *Multidimensional description of child personality*. Los Angeles, CA: Western Psychological Services.

7

Brief and Comprehensive Neuropsychological Assessment of Alcohol and Substance Abuse

Ralph E. Tarter
and
Kathleen Lou Edwards

Alcohol and drug use are historically ingrained in Western society. Abuse of these substances is of epidemic proportions and estimated to involve 10–15% of the population. Indeed, alcohol and drug abuse are the greatest causes of morbidity and mortality in Western society, not only by directly causing medical illness (e.g., liver disease), but also by affecting persons victimized by alcohol and drug users through domestic violence, traffic accidents, and crime, as well as from deprivation and neglect of family and children.

Comparatively little attention has been given to the functional adaptive capacities of individuals having a long-standing history of alcohol and drug abuse. Neuropsychological assessment, by measuring cerebral integrity, provides an optimal basis for clarifying the adjustment potential, employability, and rehabilitation prognosis of chronic alcohol and drug abusers (Heaton & Pendleton, 1981; Walker, Donovan, Kivlahan, & O'Leary, 1983). As will be seen, however, there are numerous interacting factors influencing the neuropsychological status of substance abusers. This chapter will discuss the interrelationships among the manifold variables that influence neuropsychological capacity and describe the methods, both brief and comprehensive, that can be systematically applied to evaluate the substance abuser. In so doing, it is important to emphasize that early detection and intervention are critical so as to avert the debilitating consequences of progressive neurological and social deterioration. Inasmuch as all forms of treatment involve a high degree of both cognitive capacity and motivation on the part of the patient, it is apparent that the most cost-effective interventions would be for those individuals who still possess the required resources to participate actively in their rehabilitation. Alcohol and drug abuse are often chronic conditions that are well established in the person's lifestyle; hence, in order to maximize the recovery process and prognosis, it is essential to be able to acquire information that is pertinent to the intervention process and outcome. As will be seen below, the neuropsychological examination can substantially contribute to these objectives.

NEUROPSYCHOLOGICAL ASSESSMENT

Neuropsychological tests, as distinct from other forms of psychometric assessment, are validated measures of cerebral integrity. As such, poor performance on neuropsychological tests provides an accurate basis for inferring the presence of either brain damage or brain dysfunction. Diagnostic accuracy of neuropsychological test batteries, such as the Halstead–Reitan, exceeds that of the EEG, angiogram, and clinical neurological examination (Filskov & Goldstein, 1974). For conditions that are either too subtle to detect upon visual inspection (e.g., early stage dementia), or not involving histopathological changes (e.g., metabolic lesion), neuropsychological measures are also very useful, and are at least comparable for diagnostic purposes to neurophysiological and neuroradiological measures.

In addition to elucidating the presence or absence of brain lesions, neuropsychological procedures have also been demonstrated to be highly successful at lateralizing and localizing cerebral pathology (Lezak, 1983; Walsh, 1978). Through the selective administration of tests measuring functions known to be subserved by specific brain regions and systems, the neuropsychological assessment can, therefore, yield a detailed profile of the individual's cognitive strengths and weaknesses, as well as provide information to the skillful clinician regarding the locus of brain pathology.

Emotional disturbance is a frequent concomitant of cerebral pathology. Such disturbances may antedate, be concurrent with, or be a consequence of a neurological disorder. Inasmuch as psychopathological disruption is itself a militating factor in adjustment, this aspect of psychological functioning needs to be evaluated in the alcohol and drug abuser in tandem with a cognitive assessment. Virtually every major psychopathological disorder has been reported in the literature to accompany alcohol and drug abuse; therefore, it is important to evaluate emotional status, especially since psychiatric disturbance, in the absence of substance abuse, is associated with certain neuropsychological impairments.

Social functioning also needs to be evaluated in the alcohol and drug abuser. This aspect of the evaluation is very important inasmuch as cognitive capacity is, to some extent, predictive of employability and social adjustment (Heaton & Pendleton, 1981). Ultimately, all treatment efforts are aimed at improving the person's quality of social adjustment and restructuring a lifestyle that is not adversely affected by alcohol and drug consumption. Consequently, it is critical that social adjustment be objectively measured in order to identify the social factors that could have influenced the person's initial decision to use and abuse alcohol and drugs, as well as helped sustain such usage. Alcoholism and drug abuse are commonly found in conjunction with a major disruption in psychosocial adjustment that affects mental stability, employment, emotional well-being, legal status, friendship involvements, and social networks; it is therefore essential that a neuropsychological evaluation not only address the traditional domain of cognitive capacity, but also incorporate an assessment of psychopathology and social functioning. The primary objective of such an evaluation is to determine how cognitive, psychiatric, and social processes are synergistically interacting to determine the etiology and maintenance of maladaptive substance use.

Thus the neuropsychological assessment can be conceptualized as consisting of three spheres of functioning: cognitive, psychopathological, and social. As illustrated in Figure 7.1, each of these spheres can be represented in a Venn diagram, in which a disturbance in one area of functioning may (overlap) or may not (overlap) be associated with disturbances in another aspect of functioning. Therefore, in assessing the patient, it is essential that the information obtained enable a determination of cognitive, emotional, and social status and be of sufficient detail to explain the interplay of these latter processes in the individual with respect to the etiology, maintenance, and consequence of a substance abuse history.

An assessment of the alcohol or drug abuser can take one of two approaches. Typically, the needs of the particular situation, personnel resources, patient flow, financial considerations, and time constraints determine the assessment strategy. While a comprehensive assessment, because of its thoroughness, is preferred, it is suitable only in circumstances where it is feasible, justified on a cost-benefit basis, and probable that significant disruption in psychological functioning would result from an intake interview and medical examination. Central to the type of any assessment is the issue of what is to be done with the information obtained. If, for example, the objective of the assessment information is to plan and implement a rehabilitation program in a clinic setting, then a comprehensive evaluation is warranted. If, on the other hand, the information is to be used for military recruitment, then a screening approach will

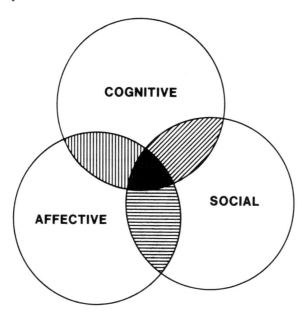

FIGURE 7.1 Component processes of comprehensive neuropsychological evaluation.

ordinarily suffice. The ensuing discussion examines both the screening and comprehensive assessment strategies and describes various selected instruments that can be of assistance in clarifying the etiology of the substance abuse disorder and its currently manifest cognitive, psychopathological, and social characteristics.

SCREENING ASSESSMENT

As already indicated, this type of evaluation is primarily of value in identifying the presence of cognitive, emotional, or social adjustment problems in high-volume, low-yield situations. The screening evaluation aims to accrue a maximum amount of general information, at a predetermined risk level of misclassification, that could either reject psychological problems as being associated with the substance use and abuse or suggest the need for further intensive inquiry into specific aspects of functioning. The screening evaluation contains as many measures as possible that allow the patient or client to self-administer the tests or to take the various tests in group settings. Indeed, the recent advent of microcomputers to the arsenal of neuropsychological assessment and rehabilitation techniques offers the promise, in the not too distant future, of a fully automated and integrated evaluation, test-scoring, and interpretation package.

Cognitive Assessment

A variety of clinically validated test measures have been employed in the assessment of alcoholics and drug abusers. The tests found to be most discriminative are usually very demanding, in that they require a high degree of cognitive efficiency (accuracy and speed) in performing the task. Hence, instruments such as the Trail-Making Test, Block Design Test of the WAIS, and the Category and Tactual Performance tests from the Halstead–Reitan Battery have been found to elicit impaired performance in unselected groups of alcoholics (Tarter, 1976, 1981). These latter tests have not been systematically studied with respect to drug-abusing individuals, but, as will be discussed subsequently, poor performance on these measures seems to characterize individuals with certain types of drug abuse.

One viable strategy for describing cognitive status in the context of a screening battery is to tap key areas of functioning by using an array of brief but validated objective measures. Goldstein, Tartar, Shelly, and Hegedus (1983) assembled and validated the Pittsburgh Initial Neuropsychological Test System (PINTS) so as to obtain age-corrected measures of performance in such diverse aspects of functioning as memory, psychomotor efficiency, language capacity, spatial capacity, and attention. The battery was initially designed for large-scale screening of psychiatric patients. This battery, containing approximately 35 performance indices, takes approximately 90 minutes to administer and yields a computer printout of a profile in standard T-scores. This type of assessment format, emphasizing expediency, enables a rather broad-based assessment of cognitive capacity, while simultaneously requiring little expertise for administration and no examiner time for conversion of raw data into standard scores. As a screening device, it therefore has a number of obvious advantages over neuropsychological procedures that employ only one or two tests.

A number of other screening tests have been developed. None of them, however, have been routinely applied to the alcohol- and drug-abusing population. Benton (1975) has proposed a battery of tests that can be flexibly applied to a number of situations, depending on the assessment objectives. Four major areas of functioning are covered: general intelligence, perception, learning and memory, and language. Lezak (1976) has also proposed a brief test battery consisting of certain WAIS subtests, the Symbol Digit Modalities Test, Rey-Auditory-Verbal Learning Test, Draw-a-Bicycle Test, Subtracting Sevens Test, Purdue Pegboard, Bender-Gestalt Test, Trail-Making Test, and Rorschach. Smith (1975) proposed a test battery comprised of several WAIS subtests, the Visual Organization Test, Benton Visual Retention Test, Raven's Progressive Matrices, Peabody Picture Vocabulary Test, and Symbol Digit Modalities Test.

Each of the above representative screening batteries have two features in common. First, they attempt to assess general level of functioning; second, they make an effort to identify specific areas of cognitive impairment. The particular instruments selected to achieve these measurement objectives are, however, variable, and a function of both the theoretical orientation and idiosyncratic preferences of the clinician.

Psychopathology

The second component of the evaluation, namely the measurement of personality and psychopathology, can be assessed using a variety of psychometric instruments. Traditionally, the Minnesota Multiphasic Personality Inventory (MMPI) has been used adjunctively with a cognitive assessment. In situations where the individual cannot be administered the complete 566-item questionnaire, a short form or mini-mult can be utilized to obtain preliminary information. Two positive features of the MMPI are that it requires very little of the clinician's time and that it contains quantitative measures of the most frequently occurring psychopathological conditions. The MMPI can also be computer scored and submitted to an actuarial interpretation. Because of the extensive research that has been conducted on the MMPI, there are also numerous specialized scales that could be of value in certain situations. For example, the MacAndrew Alcoholism Scale (MacAndrew, 1981) has not only been shown to be useful for the diagnosis of alcoholism, but also may have value in the prediction of subsequent drinking problems. Numerous other specialized scales have been developed. These can be found in Dahlstrom and Welsh (1960) and Dahlstrom, Welsh, and Dahlstrom (1975), who also present the scales' item composition. In situations where the client case-load is very large or where the expertise is unavailable to conduct in-depth clinical interviews, the MMPI can readily suffice in revealing the presence, severity, and type of psychopathology or personality disorder. With respect to alcoholics and drug abusers, the MMPI has been found to be valuable for elucidating personality and psychopathology disturbances; it has also been found capable of delineating subtypes among the substance-abusing population (Hoffman, 1976).

One instrument that is less demanding in time and effort than the MMPI, but also can indicate the presence of psychopathology, is the Symptom Checklist-90 (Derogatis, Rickels, & Rock, 1976). The SCL-90 is a 90-item questionnaire that the person can complete without clinician involvement and that also can be computer scored and profiled. Like the MMPI, it was designed to detect psychopathology, but does so in a more categorical fashion. Specific scales have been validated to diagnose various disorders in the SCL-90, whereas the MMPI requires a configurational analysis of the 10 basic and three validity scales in order to arrive at a clinical diagnosis. Hence, less expertise is required for interpretation of the SCL-90. There are nine primary dimensions assessed by the SCL-90: Somatization, Obsessive-Compulsive, Interpersonal Sensitivity, Depression, Anxiety, Hostility, Phobia, Anxiety, Paranoid Ideation, and Psychoticism. This scale also enables three general distress indices to be computed:

Positive Symptom Distress Scale, Positive Symptom Total, and Global Severity Index. Thus, where there is a need for preliminary information regarding the presence and severity of psychopathology, the SCL-90, by encompassing a broad range of emotional disorders while being brief and yielding easily interpreted results, can be routinely administered in conjunction with a cognitive evaluation. These attributes are particularly positive if applied, for example, in situations where one needs to determine if the substance abuse is associated with a psychopathological disturbance or where changes in clinical status need to be monitored concomitant to treatment. Furthermore, the assessment of psychopathological status affords the opportunity to ascertain if the manifest cognitive deficits are due to such emotional factors as anxiety, depression, or psychosis, which are often associated with significant distractibility, psychomotor retardation, concentration difficulties, and learning and memory problems.

Other test measures are also available, which, though more circumscribed than the MMPI and the SCL-90, may also provide useful information regarding the co-existence of psychopathological and cognitive disturbances. Several self-administered objective scales and interview-based rating scales for measuring anxiety and depression are commonly employed in clinical screening situations. The State-Trait Anxiety Inventory (Spielberger, Gorsuch, & Lashere, 1970) is a brief, self-administered test of current and dispositional anxiety. The Taylor Manifest Anxiety scale of the MMPI is another procedure for obtaining an estimate of a client's anxiety level. For screening for depression, the Beck Depression Inventory (Beck, 1972) is a commonly used, briefly administered, and easily scored test. Also, a number of health status questionnaires have been developed, which, if used in tandem with tests of psychopathology, can provide information that clarifies the association, if any, between emotional and physical well-being in the individual. The most promising of these instruments is arguably the Millon Behavioral Health Inventory (Millon, Green, & Meagher, 1982). This relatively brief (150 items) questionnaire was developed for application in medical settings, but it is equally useful in situations where coping style and stressors interact to culminate in adjustment failure, such as resorting to substance abuse. The test consists of two major components, these being measures of psychogenic attitude and of coping style. The individual scales are: Chronic Tension, Recent Stress, Premorbid Pessimism, Future Despair, Social Aberration, Gastrointestinal Susceptibility, Allergic Inclination, Cardiovascular Tendency, Pain Treatment Responsivity, Introversive, Inhibited, Cooperative, Sociable, Confident, Forceful, Respectful, Sensitive, Life Threat Reactivity, and Emotional Vulnerability. Although these latter measures have the advantage of brevity, taking 5–15 minutes to complete, it is important to note that, for relatively little added time, substantially more information can be derived from the MMPI or the SCL-90.

Social Adjustment

The third component of the neuropsychological evaluation addresses the current social functioning or adjustment of the individual. Of interest in this regard is the possibility that certain life stresses or events precipitated or currently sustain the alcohol or drug abuse. If such factors can be identified, interventions aimed at their amelioration or, alternatively, modification of the person's coping strategy, can be implemented; in the long term, these interventions would have prophylactic value with regard to neurological status. The Life Experience Survey (Sarason, Johnson, & Siegel, 1978) is one simple technique that can be used to obtain an indication of the relationship between social events (e.g., divorce, death of family member, etc.) and the onset and maintenance of alcohol or drug consumption. This 57-item instrument was designed to measure the occurrence and significance of events during the previous 12 months. The individual items are weighed according to the amount of readjustment that is required following the event. Somewhat different information can be obtained from the Sickness Impact Profile (Bergner & Gilson, 1981). This self-administered questionnaire evaluates the extent to which social and physical functioning are disrupted. A somewhat unique feature of this instrument is that it defines health status *behaviorally*, thereby enabling quantification of deficit in terms of percent of functional impairment. The dimensions of behavior assessed are quite broad and include: Social Interaction, Ambulation, Sleep and Rest, Eating, Work, Home Management, Mobility, Body Care and Movement, Communication, Recreation and Pastimes, Alertness Behavior, Emotional Behavior, Physical Dysfunction, Psychological Dysfunction, and Total Dysfunction.

In summary, there are a number of strategies that can be utilized for conducting a screening evaluation of alcohol and drug abusers. Because of the substantial overlap between cognitive, emotional, and social factors in substance abusers, it is necessary that the relationships among these variables be elucidated in the particular individual. The specific test measures described above provide a basis for efficient evaluation; that is, maximum information accrued per unit of time available for assessing the client.

COMPREHENSIVE NEUROPSYCHOLOGICAL ASSESSMENT

The comprehensive examination, though more demanding in terms of time, effort, clinical resources, and patient expense, is necessary if the assessment information is to be utilized for rehabilitation purposes. There are presently no packaged or commercially available assessment protocols for alcohol and substance abusers that can be systematically applied, that have established reliability and validity, and that have interpretative rules for implementing one or another treatment procedure. Thus the only avenue available to the clinician is comprehensively to evaluate cognitive, psychopathological, and social status and, by exercising clinical acumen, to derive inferences about the relationships among these areas of functioning in the individual. Hence, the unavoidable endpoint is at present a clinical judgment about the patient or client's functioning in developing a rehabilitative strategy.

Cognitive Assessment

The Halstead-Reitan Battery was the first standardized battery for evaluating the severity and location of cerebral lesions. As will be discussed subsequently, alcoholics and certain types of drug abusers have been found to perform in the neurologically impaired ranges on this test battery. In alcoholics, significant correlations have been observed between the magnitude of CT scan indices of atrophy and various test measures of cerebral pathology (Ron, 1983). Recently, the Luria-Nebraska Neuropsychological Battery has been administered to alcoholics and found to be sensitive to detecting impairment; studies of drug abusers other than alcoholics have yet to be conducted with this battery.

Both of the above batteries are sufficiently comprehensive so as to specify the severity of impairment as well as lateralize and localize cerebral lesions. The Luria-Nebraska is a rather recent addition, and while there are many advantages to employing this battery, its psychometric properties are still subject to debate and heated controversy. However, because administration time is about half that required by the Halstead-Reitan Battery and appears to cover essentially the same dimensions of cognitive functioning (Goldstein & Shelly, 1984), it promises to be a very important contribution to the clinical neuropsychology laboratory.

Psychopathology

Comprehensive assessment of psychopathology and personality disorder is possible only by means of a detailed interview. In order to standardize this process, several structured interview instruments have been developed and are presently in clinical use. These procedures are not only useful for arriving at a clinical diagnosis meeting DSM-III criteria (American Psychiatric Association, 1980), but are also amenable to yielding information regarding research diagnostic criteria (Feighner, Robins, Guze, Woodruff, Winokur, & Munoz, 1972). Currently, the Diagnostic Interview Schedule (DIS) (Robins, Helzer, Croughan, & Ratcliffe, 1981) and Schedule for Affective Disorders and Schizophrenia (SADS) (Spitzer & Endicott, 1978) are the most comprehensive psychiatric interview measures. Each of these instruments yields information about alcohol and drug use practices in addition to a broad range of psychiatric and personality disorders. Where the substance abuse is found in conjunction with another disorder, it is necessary to address these problems, inasmuch as they may be responsible for the drug use. For example, if a person drinks excessively in an effort to reduce anxiety, alleviate depression, or attenuate a phobia, the substance disorder may be related to the psychiatric disturbance. Individuals in the early phases of decompensation into a psychiatric episode may voluntarily attempt to self-medicate by abusing alcohol or other drugs. In addition, certain drugs, as a result of their chronic use, may induce personality and psychopathological disturbances. Amphetamine psychosis and amotivational syndrome are two well-documented reactions. Furthermore, it is important to document the extent to which substance abuse may be related to physical illness or injury. Finally, unlike any of the screening tests, the above structured interviews enable a determination of the time of onset and pattern of substance abuse both in the present and at any point in the person's lifetime.

The structured interview examination also assesses for a personality disorder underlying the substance abuse behavior. This information has relevance for both cognitive and social assessment. For example, an antisocial personality disorder places the person at elevated risk to incur head trauma from fights and accidents due to a deviant lifestyle characterized by poor self-control, excitement seeking, and behavioral lability. Consequently, in an effort to arrive at a perspective of the role of alcohol and drug abuse on cognitive status, it is also important to assess personality disposition. Both the DIS and SADS, by attempting to arrive at the time of onset of the various conditions, afford the opportunity to evaluate current and prior substance abuse behavior in relation to other personality and psychiatric disorders.

Social Adjustment

Remarkably little attention has been given to the development of comprehensive instruments for the assessment of social adjustment. Investigators in the field of behavioral medicine and health psychology have been in the vanguard of developing such instruments, but as yet these test measures have not been assimilated into routine clinical practice.

Among the more promising measures is the Social Behavior Adjustment Schedule (SBAS) (Platt, Weyman, Hirsch, & Hewitt, 1980). The data are acquired from an informant, usually a spouse, who verbally responds to a set of questions describing the onset and characteristics of the person's behavioral disposition and changes in social disposition, if any. The categories of behavior evaluated include: (1) general behavior (e.g., irritability, rudeness, self-neglect, indecisiveness, etc.); (2) person's social performance (domestic role, work, etc.); (3) adverse effects of the person's problem on others; (4) ongoing other events contributing to the overall social environment (e.g., health of other family members, legal problems, financial loss, etc.); and (5) support network available to relieve stress. A summary score, having a range of 0–44, indexes overall social adjustment. An especially attractive feature of the SBAS is that it links changes in social adjustment to a particular onset factor (e.g., drug use). Although a number of other social adjustment measures have been developed and promoted by their authors, the SBAS currently ranks among the most comprehensive and applicable to diverse situations.

NEUROPSYCHOLOGICAL CHARACTERISTICS OF ALCOHOLICS AND SUBSTANCE ABUSERS

The above discussion addressed the neuropsychological perspectives and methods used in the clinical neuropsychological assessment process. It was pointed out that the neuropsychological evaluation should consist of three broad components: cognitive, psychopathological/personality, and social adjustment assessments. The measurement of these three components can be conducted in the context of either a screening approach or, if conditions are amenable, a comprehensive evaluation. Depending on clinical needs, logistical realities, and economic considerations, a decision must necessarily be made about how best to maximize existing professional resources in the diagnosis and treatment of alcohol and drug abusing individuals.

Having considered the clinical methodological issues, this discussion will next review the neuropsychological findings pertinent to alcohol and drug abuse. Space limitation does not permit a review of the psychopathological and social manifestations; however, the interested reader is referred to Alterman (1985) for an extensive discussion of these topics.

Alcoholics

Alcoholics typically perform in the normal ranges on standardized tests of intelligence (Tarter, 1975). Specific aspects of cognitive functioning are, however, impaired. For example, abstracting ability is poor (Fitzhugh, Fitzhugh, & Reitan, 1965; Jones & Parsons, 1971). In addition, deficits have been noted in alcoholics on tasks requiring persisting with an acquired concept (Tarter, 1973), changing concepts when the current one is incorrect (Tarter & Parsons, 1971), and utilizing the information contained in an incorrect response in order to alter the problem-solving strategy (Tarter, 1973). Also, hypothesis-testing capacity (Klisz & Parsons, 1977), visual search (Bertera & Parsons, 1978), visuospatial sequencing, and integration (Jones, 1971) are impaired in alcoholics. Standardized memory tests do not consistently reveal deficits, but employing more demanding laboratory techniques reveals learning and short-term retention deficits.

Perception and basic sensory processes are not impaired in most detoxified alcoholics (Tarter, 1975). Tests requiring visual-motor integration and reaction time also do not appear to be disrupted (Callan et al., 1972; Tarter & Jones, 1971). On the other hand, tasks measuring goal persistence that employ perceptual and motor tasks are performed poorly by alcoholics (Tarter, 1973).

There is, at this time, substantial evidence implicating neuropsychological impairment in alcoholics who have been detoxified for about one month. While improvement in cognitive performance has been observed with continued sobriety, a complete amelioration of impairment is not typically observed (Goldman, Williams, & Klisz, 1983; Berglund, Leijonquist, & Horlen, 1977). In one study, memory deficits were found in alcoholics even after seven years of abstinence from alcohol (Brandt, Butters, Ryan, & Bayog, 1983).

Investigations of nonalcoholic social drinkers have revealed cognitive deficits in college-aged and middle-aged community-dwelling individuals (Parker, Birnbaum, Boyd, & Noble, 1980; Parker & Noble, 1977). Particularly interesting in these studies was the finding that the amount of beverage alcohol consumed per drinking occasion was predictive of cognitive performance. Individuals who consumed the most alcohol per drinking occasion performed the most poorly, whereas those who drank the least on a drinking occasion performed best on the cognitive measures. The above studies have two important ramifications. First, they suggest that the threshold for cerebral dysfunction measured by cognitive tests may be much lower than is generally suspected. Hence, the deleterious consequences exerted by alcohol on neurological functioning may not necessarily appear only after many years of abusive drinking. Second, the finding that it is the amount consumed per drinking occasion, and not chronicity of consumption, that best predicts cognitive capacity indicates that metabolic factors associated with acute intoxication may be responsible for the manifest cognitive deficits. Specifically, metabolic overload concomitant to acute intoxication may be one of the mechanisms responsible for inducing neurological disruption.

Neuropsychological capacity has been found in several studies to be related to treatment persistence (Walker et al., 1983) and prognosis (Gregson & Taylor, 1977; O'Leary, Donovan, Chaney, & Walker, 1979). Unfortunately, there is a dearth of systematic research on this topic, although the general thrust of the available findings indicates that the best prognosis is observed in persons with intact cognitive capacity. This finding is not particularly surprising, since the traditional modes of therapy, as well as the path to recovery prescribed by Alcoholics Anonymous, require competence in problem solving so as to achieve "insight" in pursuing a redirected lifestyle that is free from alcohol use. Only one study has explicitly examined level of cognitive capacity in relation to the type of treatment. Kissin, Platz, and Su (1970) observed that alcoholics who profited best from directed and pharmacological treatment were cognitively concrete, whereas those who responded best to didactic forms of therapy had an abstract cognitive orientation. These investigations, though preliminary, underscore the potential value of a comprehensive cognitive evaluation in maximizing the prognosis for rehabilitation from alcoholism.

Although there is extensive evidence pointing to significant cognitive deficit in alcoholics, comparatively little attention has been given to elucidating the underlying etiological mechanisms. Although alcohol is neurotoxic, the diverse impairments found in alcoholics probably involve the culmination of numerous interacting factors and not just ethanol acting on the brain. The factors most strongly implicated are discussed below.

Preexisting impairment

Evidence has recently been accrued indicating that children and adults at elevated risk for developing alcoholism, but not themselves suffering from this disorder, exhibit certain neuropsychological impairments (Schaeffer et al., 1984; Tarter, Hegedus, Goldstein, Shelly, & Alterman, 1984). These findings suggest that individuals who may eventually capitulate to alcoholism, have cognitive deficits prior to the onset of drinking. Interestingly, many of the same tests on which alcoholics are found to be impaired are also performed poorly by nonalcoholic high risk individuals.

Another condition which is associated with neurological and psychological disturbance is the fetal alcohol syndrome (Streissguth, Landesmann-Dwyer, Martin, & Smith, 1980). Women who abuse alcohol during pregnancy, particularly during the first trimester, are at increased risk for giving birth to a child with partial or extensive features of the fetal alcohol syndrome. This syndrome is characterized by craniofacial abnormalities, neurological pathology, and cognitive retardation. Inasmuch as alcoholism is often a transgenerational disorder, there is the strong likelihood that within the alcoholic population, there is a substantial segment who suffer, in varying degrees of severity, from the sequelae of the fetal alcohol syndrome. Hence, acquired neurological pathology, due to the teratogenic effects of alcohol, probably to some extent contributes to the overall pattern of neuropsychological deficits observed in alcoholics.

Lifestyle

A sociopathic behavior disorder is commonly found in conjunction with habitual alcohol abuse. This lifestyle, by virtue of placing the person in conflict with society's mores, increases the probability for conflict. Hence, cumulative head traumas from fights and accidents increase the likelihood of neurological injury. The neuropsychological disturbances commonly found in alcoholics may therefore, to some extent, be the result of brain injury that is not directly due to alcohol consumption.

Psychopathology

Cognitive deficits have been reported in nonalcoholics who are depressed or have an antisocial personality (Gruzelier & Flor-Henry, 1979). These latter conditions are also commonly found in conjunction with alcoholism. The degree to which the neuropsychological impairments found in alcoholics reflect cerebral dysfunction due to psychopathology has not been directly investigated, but in light of the above, this factor would appear to have a contributing impact on cognitive performance.

Nutrition

Poor diet, combined with chronic liver disease affecting the storage and utilization of essential vitamins, can induce avitaminosis and concomitant cognitive deficits. Chronic thiamin and niacin deficiency can cause dementia. These types of avitaminosis have been reported in alcoholics (Dreyfus, 1974; Reynolds, Rothfield, & Pincus, 1973). Thus vitamin deficiency is another factor that can contribute to the impaired cognitive capacities of alcoholics.

Hepatic pathology

Nonalcoholic cirrhosis is associated with neuropsychological impairment (Tarter, Hegedus, Van Thiel, Schade, Gavaler, & Starzl, 1984). The finding that cirrhotic nonalcoholics are more similar than dissimilar to alcoholic cirrhotics (Tarter, Hegedus, Gavaler, Schade, Van Thiel, & Starzl, 1983) indicates that hepatic pathology plays an important intervening role in the induction of cerebral pathology and the subsequent cognitive sequelae. However, the finding that alcoholics with cirrhosis perform more poorly than alcoholics without cirrhosis on the WAIS (Smith & Smith, 1977) and neuropsychological tests (Gilberstadt, Gilberstadt, Ziever, Buegel, Collier, & McClain, 1980) indicates that liver disease alone does not produce all of the manifest deficits.

Consumption pattern

Chronicity, frequency, quantity, and age of onset of alcohol consumption are related to neuropsychological test performance. These different aspects of alcohol consumption each affect cognitive functioning in different ways (Eckardt, Parker, Noble, Feldman, & Gottshalk, 1978). Inasmuch as no single consumption variable can account for even half of the variance on cognitive tests, it can be concluded that factors other than consumption history and pattern are more important in the induction of cognitive impairment.

Systemic illness

Alcoholism affects multiple organ systems. Disruption of these systems could exacerbate neuropsychological impairment found in alcoholics. Thus, pathology to the pancreas, cerebrovascular, endocrine, and cardiovascular systems could contribute to the cognitive deficits, since pathology to these systems in the absence of alcohol use is associated with reduced performance on neuropsychological tests.

Drug Abusers

Considerably less information is known about the effects of drug abuse on neuropsychological capacity than is known about alcoholism. Studies of the effects of drug abuse on cognitive processes are difficult to conduct because it is difficult to assess accurately quantity and frequency of usage and because most drug abusers consume more than one type of mood-altering drug. These limitations notwithstanding, it will be seen below that drug abuse is far from inconsequential with respect to its effects on cognitive functioning.

Sedatives

Bergman, Borg, and Holm (1980) found evidence for cerebral dysfunction in a group of patients who were abusers of only sedatives or hypnotics. Judd and Grant (1978) found that users of barbiturates obtained a Halstead–Reitan impairment index that was in the normal ranges, although deficits were noted on the Categories test, Trail-Making test (Part B), and the time measure of the Tactual Performance Test. Although a definitive conclusion cannot be advanced, these two studies suggest that sedative use is associated with certain cognitive deficits.

Inhalants

Administering the Halstead–Reitan Battery to a group of long-term heavy inhalant abusers, Bruhn and Maage (1975) found evidence for a borderline neuropsychological impairment. In a sample of psychiatric patients who were inhalant abusers, Bigler (1979) observed a generalized pattern of deficit on the WAIS and Halstead–Reitan Battery. Korman, Matthews, and Lovitt (1981) observed that inhalant abusers were more impaired than other drug abusers on 20 of 67 cognitive measures assessing intelligence, neuropsychological capacity, and educational achievement. Tsushina and Towne (1977) found that a sample of glue sniffers obtained Full-Scale IQ scores in the borderline ranges of retardation. Deficits were observed on the Trail-Making Test, and the impairment index of the Halstead–Reitan Battery implicated cerebral dysfunction. Berry, Heaton, and Kirley (1977) found that their group of chronic inhalant abusers obtained a Full-Scale IQ of 90 and were impaired on the Trail-Making test (Part B) and Categories Test. These latter studies, collectively considered, indicate that inhalant abusers suffer from cognitive impairments, although it cannot be discerned from these studies if any of the deficits preceded the onset of this form of substance abuse.

Heroin

Fields and Fullerton (1975) found that a group of heroin addicts performed identically to a control group of normals on the Halstead-Reitan Battery. Rounsaville, Novelly, Kelber, and Jones (1981) found that 53% of addicts, many of whom were also polydrug abusers, were moderately to severely impaired on a battery of neuropsychological tests. It should be pointed out, however, that the addicts who were most impaired tended to have a poor academic history and also a childhood history of hyperactivity, indicating that their cognitive deficits may have preceded their drug addiction. Based on these two studies, it does not appear that heroin use is associated with cognitive impairments in the majority of consumers.

Hallucinogens

In the first study reporting on the neuropsychological sequelae of LSD abuse, McGlothlin, Arnold, and Freedman (1969) found evidence for an abstracting impairment as indicated by performance on the Categories Test of the Halstead-Reitan Battery. None of the other tests were performed in the impaired ranges. Acord and Barker (1973) replicated this finding and additionally found that their sample performed in the impaired ranges on the Tactual Performance Test, a measure of constructional praxis capacity. In contrast to these latter studies, Wright and Hogan (1972) observed, in their sample of LSD abusers, that performance was intact on the Halstead-Reitan measures, as well as the Wechsler Memory Scale. Culver and King (1974) found that a group of 42 college seniors who used LSD/mescaline performed within the normal limits on a battery of neuropsychological tests, but on several measures obtained significantly lower scores than normal controls and marijuana users. Overall, these studies do not implicate significant neuropsychological impairment consequential to hallucinogenic drug abuse, even though certain rather isolated deficits have been reported.

Marijuana

Heavy and casual marijuana users were first studied by Mendelson and Meyer (1972), who found no evidence for impairment on the Halstead-Reitan Battery and Wechsler Memory Scale. Grant, Rockford, Flemming, and Stunkard (1973) also observed no signs of neuropsychological impairment in a group of medical students who were marijuana users. Similar negative findings were reported by Culver and King (1974) and Carline and Turpin (1977). In a group of ten subjects in whom cannabinol metabolites were present in the urine, Schaeffer, Andrysiak, and Ungerleider (1981) also found no evidence for impairment on a battery of neuropsychological tests. The results are therefore consistent in demonstrating normal cognitive functioning in marijuana users.

Polydrug Abuse

Judd and Grant (1975) observed evidence, based on the Halstead–Reitan Battery, for cerebral dysfunction in half of their sample of polydrug users. Adams, Rennick, Schoof, and Keegan (1975) tested a group of subjects who only two days previously had terminated drug taking. Deficits were found on the categories test, speech sounds test, and rhythms test of the Halstead–Reitan. Finger-tapping speed and performance on the Trail-Making Test (Part B) were also impaired. Bruhn and Maage (1975) studied a group of male prisoners having varying histories of drug abuse. Users of cannabis, amphetamines, opiates, and hallucinogens were not different from abstainers on a battery of neuropsychological tests. Grant and Judd (1976) found that 45% of polydrug abusers had neuropsychological impairments when tested three weeks after admission to treatment. In a subsequent report, Grant, Mohns, Miller, and Reitan (1976) studied 22 men who had been abstinent from drugs for 60 days. Ratings of the Halstead–Reitan test results by two experienced clinicians pointed to a 41–64% incidence of cerebral dysfunction. In another report, Grant, Mohns, Miller, & Reitan, (1976) concluded that the neuropsychological deficits in polydrug abusers were more pronounced than those found in psychiatric patients and were quite similar to those presented by schizophrenic patients. Drug-use style and life events are more predictive of neuropsychological impairment than actual quantity of drug consumption (Carline & Turpin 1977). Older and less-educated individuals who had abnormal medical and developmental histories were most likely to manifest deficits on neuropsychological tests (Grant et al., 1976).

The above studies indicate that up to 50% of polydrug abusers exhibit neuropsychological impairment, even after a period of abstinence. The deficits do not appear to be related in a simple cause-and-effect fashion to consumption history, but rather reflect the culmination of demographic, lifestyle, medical, and developmental variables, which, in combination, result in impairments in cognitive capacity for some individuals. It is not known, however, whether the deficits on neuropsychological tests reflect permanent histopathological alterations in the cerebrum or, alternatively, are the sequelae of reversible metabolic disruption involving multiple neurochemical systems. Thus while the results appear to indicate that certain vulnerable individuals may be prone to suffering neuropsychological deficits from polydrug abuse, they do not demonstrate that such abuse is by itself either causal to the manifest cognitive impairments or a product of permanent cerebral pathology.

CLINICAL CONSIDERATIONS

The most recent edition of the *Diagnostic and Statistical Manual* (DSM III) divides the substance-use disorders into two broad categories. These are substance abuse and substance dependence. Substance abuse features a pattern of pathological use, impaired social and occupational functioning, and a duration of disturbance lasting at least one month. Substance dependence is a more severe disorder and, for diagnosis, requires physiological indications of either tolerance or withdrawal.

Five general classes of drugs can be associated with either abuse or dependence; (1) alcohol, (2) barbiturates, (3) opioids, (4) amphetamines and other sympathomimetics, and (5) cannabis. Three classes of drugs are associated only with abuse, inasmuch as the capacity for dependence to these drugs has not been demonstrated. These drugs include hallucinogens, cocaine, and phencylidine (PCP).

Regardless of the particular drug, or class of drug, there are a number of important issues that need to be addressed with respect to the meaning and significance of neuropsychological information. These issues, discussed below, not only are relevant to appraising cognitive status, but also, within the broad assessment framework described in this discussion, have substantial bearing for understanding the emotional and social concomitants of substance abuse and dependency.

Pattern of Use

The pattern of substance abuse, consisting of the frequency and amount consumed per occasion, defines in broadest scope the severity of a problem, if, indeed, a problem exists. Occasional use of drugs for recreational, stress-relief, or other purposes has not been unequivocally shown to be related to either social maladjustment or psychiatric disturbance. Even "binge" use of drugs is typically featured by normal or optimal functioning during the intermittent periods of excess. Rather, cognitive impairments and associated psychiatric and social sequelae generally are manifest only after prolonged or habitual use. At present, it is not known where the transition point is between "safe" and "dangerous" patterns of consumption. In all likelihood, this is highly variable and is probably determined by factors both intrinsic (e.g., nutrition, systemic pathologic, premorbid vulnerability, etc.), and extrinsic (e.g., living conditions, social supports, etc.) to the particular person.

Recovery of Cognitive Capacity

Because of the direct and indirect consequences of drug usage on the central nervous system, the time of evaluation will significantly determine the quality of the clinical presentation. Hence, an assessment conducted during the toxic state will result in findings that are substantially different from those obtained if the person is in a state of withdrawal or detoxification, or if the person is evaluated after long-term abstinence, at which time acute metabolic disturbance has subsided. During the toxic state, depending on the class of drug consumed, the neuropsychiatric picture is likely to reflect the consequences of either central nervous system (CNS) stimulation or depression. Withdrawal is, typically, a state of CNS hyperexcitability, whereas the long-term abstinent person is likely to reflect the effects of permanent CNS changes, if any, from chronic drug use. Each of these stages can be associated with the so-called functional and organic types of symptoms; however, systematic examination employing the procedures previously described can facilitate arriving at a differential diagnosis.

Age of Onset

The circumstances surrounding substance abuse onset provide valuable information about the cognitive, psychiatric, and social functioning in the client. Not only does this information provide an index of chronicity of abuse, which in turn is related to severity, but this type of data could also reveal the life tasks that confronted the person at the time and prompted substance abuse. For example, drug or alcohol use initiated during adolescence has distinctly different motivational characteristics from use commenced after retirement. Not only are the cognitive sequelae different, since the brain is differentially susceptible to permanent impairment at each of the various life-cycle stages, but so, too, are the psychiatric and social characteristics of the user. Early-life onset is more likely to be associated with a nonconforming or antisocial propensity, whereas later-life onset is more likely to be associated with acute psychiatric disturbance, such as depression. With respect to social functioning, problematic substance use is commonly found in younger individuals who are immature and socially unskilled; whereas the older user is typically socially competent and employing drugs or alcohol in an effort to cope with an immediate life crisis.

Thus, the age of onset of drug or alcohol problems provides the clinician with clues about the direction the assessment process needs to take with regard to the interplay among cognitive, psychiatric, and social variables responsible for the initiation and maintenance of a pattern of abuse. This information can substantially assist in deriving a comprehensive picture of the etiology, as well as consequences, of the substance abuse.

Motivation for Drug Use

It is well documented that drug and alcohol use and abuse can serve a number of motivational needs for the individual. The desired effect to be achieved by persistent use of a drug could reflect the need to correct disturbed neurological functioning. For example, it has been hypothesized that many alcoholics, at least initially, use alcohol to control hyperactivity (Tarter, 1978), a finding that is supported by recent reports suggesting that stimulant medication is thera peutic for certain alcohol-abusing individuals (Wender, Reimherr, & Wood, 1981). Similarly, childhood hyperactivity has been shown to be associated with subsequent opioid use. Thus it appears that for some individuals, substance abuse is used to modify disturbed CNS functioning. In addition, substance abuse can be prompted by the need to manipulate affective states. Moreover, there are numerous social sanctions, both positive and negative, that press on the person to influence substance use and abuse.

It is not possible to divorce the cognitive, emotional, and social consequences of substance use from underlying motivational propensities that influence the selection of drugs and alcohol in the first place. The diversity of motivation for substance abuse is so manifold that it is inconceivable that one, or even a few, drive states can be concluded to predispose to alcohol and drug use. As noted above, the motivational origins can be any one or a combination of neurological, psychiatric, and social factors.

UTILIZING NEUROPSYCHIATRIC ASSESSMENT INFORMATION

Once having obtained a profile of the individual's cognitive, psychiatric, and social functioning, it is essential that this information be applied in a rehabilitation program. In effect, intervention requires implementing an optimal match between the person's neuropsychiatric status and the environment. If this is not obtained, maladjustment is likely to persist, thereby continuing the risk for relapse or persisting substance abuse.

A cardinal assumption in treating the alcohol or drug abuser is that the prolonged use of such substances is a coping strategy. To change this ultimately self-destructive strategy, it is necessary either to modify the environment so that this coping style is no longer necessary or to modify the individual so as to increase existing coping skills or acquire new ones. Viewed in an interactional context, the neuropsychiatric examination, employing the measurement techniques mentioned herein, affords the opportunity directly to incorporate assessment information into a comprehensive treatment plan.

CONCLUSIONS

Alcohol and drug use are deeply rooted in the sociocultural history of mankind. Throughout history, a segment of the population has been unable to regulate its consumption of such substances. In excess, cognitive, psychiatric, and social adjustment problems commonly ensue. However, the effects of substance abuse on the individual are not fixed or invariant, but rather are the culmination of numerous predisposing, concurrent, and consequential factors.

In conducting a neuropsychological evaluation it is therefore essential that the clinician obtain information about the individual that not only clarifies the temporal patterns of the substance-abuse history, but also elucidates how emotional, cognitive, and social variables interact to produce a coping style whereby substance abuse is the selected means of adjustment. Only after this information is obtained can treatment interventions that have a reasonable prospect for success be implemented.

REFERENCES

Acord, L., & Barker, D. (1973). Hallucinogenic drugs and cerebral deficit. *Journal of Nervous and Mental Disease, 156*, 281-283.

Adams, K. M., Rennick, P. M., Schoof, K. G., & Keegan, J. F. (1975). Neuropsychological measurement of drug effects: Polydrug research. *Journal of Psychedelic Drugs, 7*, 151-160.

Alterman, A. (Ed.). (1985). *Substance abuse and psychopathology.* New York: Plenum.

American Psychiatric Association, Committee on Nomenclature and Statistics. (1980). *Diagnostic and Statistical Manual of Mental Disorders* (3rd ed.). Washington, DC: American Psychiatric Association.

Beck, A. (1972). *Depression: Causes and treatment.* Philadelphia: University of Pennsylvania Press.

Benton, A. (1975). Psychological tests for brain damage. In H. Freedman, H. Kaplan, & B. Sadock (Eds.), *Comprehensive textbook of psychiatry* (Vol. 2) (pp. 530-538). Baltimore: Williams and Wilkins.

Berglund, M., Leijonquist, H., & Horlen, M. (1977). Prognostic significance and reversibility of cerebral dysfunction in alcoholics. *Journal of Studies on Alcohol, 38*, 1761-1769.

Bergman, H., Borg, S., & Holm, L. (1980). Neuropsychological impairment and exclusive abuse of sedatives or hypnotics. *American Journal of Psychiatry, 137*, 215-217.

Bergner, M., & Gilson, B. (1981). The Sickness Impact Profile: The relevance of social science to medicine. In L. Eisenberg & A. Kleinman (Eds.), *The relevance of social science for medicine* (pp. 135-150). Boston: D. Reidel Publishing Co.

Berry, G., Heaton, R., & Kirley, M. (1977). Neuropsychological deficits of chronic inhalants abusers. In B. Rumaek & A. Temple (Eds.), *Management of the prisoned patient* (pp. 59-83). Princeton: Sciences Press.

Bertera, J., & Parsons, O. (1978). Impaired visual search in alcoholics. *Alcoholism: Clinical and Experimental Research, 2*, 9-14.

Bigler, E. D. (1979). Neuropsychological evaluation of adolescent patients hospitalized with chronic inhalant abuse. *Clinical Neuropsychology, 1*, 8-12.

Brandt, J., Butters, N., Ryan, C., & Bayog, R. (1983). Cognitive loss and recovery in long-term alcohol abusers. *Archives of General Psychiatry, 40*, 435-442.

Bruhn, P., & Maage, N. (1975). Intellectual and neuropsychological functions in young men with heavy and long-term patterns of drug abuse. *American Journal of Psychiatry, 132*, 397-401.

Callan, J., Holloway, F., & Bruhn, P. (1972). Effects of distraction upon reaction time performance in brain damaged and alcoholic patients. *Neuropsychologia, 10*, 303, 370.

Carline, A., & Turpin, E. (1977). The effects of long-term cannabis use and neuropsychological functioning. *International Journal of the Addictions, 12*, 617-624.

Culver, C., & King, F. (1974). Neuropsychological assessment of undergraduate marijuana and LSD users. *Archives of General Psychiatry, 31*, 707-711.

Dahlstrom, W., & Welsh, G. (1960). *An MMPI Handbook*. Minneapolis: University of Minnesota Press.

Dahlstrom, W., Welsh, G., & Dahlstrom, L. (1975). *An MMPI handbook: Vol. 1. Clinical interpretation*. Minneapolis: University of Minnesota Press.

Derogatis, L., Rickels, K., & Rock, A. (1976). The SCL-90 and the MMPI: A step in the validation of a new self-report scale. *British Journal of Psychiatry, 128*, 280-289.

Dreyfus, P. (1974). Diseases of the nervous system in chronic alcoholics. In B. Kissin & H. Begleiter (Eds.), *The biology of alcoholism: Clinical pathology* (Vol. 3) (pp. 265-290). New York: Plenum.

Eckardt, M., Parker, E., Noble, E., Feldman, D., & Gottshalk, L. (1978). Relationship between neuropsychological performance and alcohol consumption in alcoholics. *Biological Psychiatry, 13*, 551-565.

Feighner, J., Robins, E., Guze, S., Woodruff, R. A., Winokur, G., & Munoz, R. (1972). Diagnostic criteria for use in psychiatric research. *Archives of General Psychiatry, 26*, 57-63.

Fields, F. R. J., & Fullerton, J. R. (1975). Influence of heroin addiction on neuropsychological functioning. *Journal of Consulting and Clinical Psychology, 43*, 114.

Filskov, S., & Goldstein, S. (1974). Diagnostic validity of the Halstead–Reitan Neuropsychological Battery. *Journal of Consulting and Clinical Psychology, 42*, 382-388.

Fitzhugh, L., Fitzhugh, K., & Reitan, R. (1965). Adaptive abilities and intellectual functioning of hospitalized alcoholics. *Quarterly Journal of Studies on Alcohol, 26*, 402-411.

Gilberstadt, S., Gilberstadt, H., Zieve, L., Buegel, B., Collier, R., & McClain, C. (1980). Psychomotor performance deficits in cirrhotic patients without overt encephalopathy. *Annals of Internal Medicine, 140*, 519-521.

Goldman, M., Williams, D., & Klisz, D. (1983). Recoverability of psychological functioning following alcohol abuse: Prolonged visual-spatial dysfunction in older alcoholics. *Journal of Consulting and Clinical Psychology, 51*, 370-378.

Goldstein, G., & Shelly, C. (1984). Relationships between language skills as assessed by the Halstead–Reitan Battery and the Luria–Nebraska Language-Related Factor Scales in a nonaphasic patient population. *Journal of Clinical Neuropsychology, 6*, 143-156.

Goldstein, G., Tarter, R., Shelly, C., & Hegedus, A. (1983). The Pittsburgh Initial Neuropsychological Testing System (PINTS): A neuropsychological screening battery for psychiatric patients. *Journal of Behavioral Assessment, 5*, 227-238.

Grant, I., Adams, K. M., Carlin, A. S., & Rennick-Phillips, M. (1977). Neuropsychological deficit in polydrug users. A preliminary report of the findings of the Collaborative Neuropsychological Study of Drug Users. *Drug and Alcohol Dependence, 2*, 91-108.

Grant, I., Adams, K. M., Carlin, A. S., Rennick-Phillips, M., Judd, L. L., Schooff, K., & Reed, R. (1977). Organic impairment of polydrug users: Risk Factors. *American Journal of Psychiatry, 135*, 178-184.

Grant, I., & Judd, L. L. (1976). Neuropsychological and EEG disturbances in polydrug users. *American Journal of Psychiatry, 133*, 1039-1042.

Grant, I., Mohns, L., Miller, M., & Reitan, R. (1976). A neuropsychological study of polydrug users. *Archives of General Psychiatry, 33,* 973-978.

Grant, I., Rockford, J., Flemming, T., & Stunkard, A. (1973). A neuropsychological assessment of the effect of moderate marijuana use. *Journal of Nervous and Mental Disease, 156,* 278-280.

Gregson, R., & Taylor, G. (1977). Prediction of relapse in men alcoholics. *Journal of Studies on Alcohol, 38,* 1749-1759.

Gruzelier, J., & Flor-Henry, P. (Eds.). (1979). *Hemisphere asymmetries of function in psychopathology.* New York: Elsevier/North Holland.

Heaton, R., & Pendleton, M. (1981). Use of neuropsychological tests to predict adult patients everyday functioning. *Journal of Consulting and Clinical Psychology, 49,* 807-821.

Hoffman, H. (1976). Personality measurement for the evaluation and prediction of alcoholism. In R. Tarter & A. Sugerman (Eds.), *Alcoholism: Interdisciplinary approaches to an enduring problem* (pp. 309-358). Reading, MA: Addison-Wesley.

Jones, B. (1971). Verbal and spatial intelligence in short- and long-term alcoholics. *Journal of Nervous and Mental Disease, 153,* 292-297.

Jones, B., & Parsons, O. (1971). Impaired abstracting ability in chronic alcoholics. *Archives of General Psychiatry, 24,* 71-75.

Judd, L. L., & Grant, I. (1975). Brain dysfunction in chronic sedative users. *Journal of Psychedelic Drugs, 7,* 143-149.

Judd, L., & Grant, I. (1978). Intermediate duration organic mental disorders among polydrug abusing patients. *Psychiatric Clinics of North America, 1,* 153-167.

Kissin, B., Platz, A., & Su, W. (1970). Social and psychological factors in the treatment of chronic alcoholism. *Journal of Psychiatric Research, 8,* 13-27.

Klisz, D., & Parsons, O. (1977). Hypothesis testing in younger and older alcoholics. *Journal of Studies on Alcohol, 38,* 1718-1729.

Korman, M., Matthews, R. W., & Lovitt, R. (1981). Neuropsychological effects of abuse on inhalants. *Perceptual & Motor Skills, 53,* 547-553.

Lezak, M. (1976). *Neuropsychological assessment.* New York: Oxford University Press.

Lezak, M. (1983). *Neuropsychological assessment* (2nd ed.). New York: Oxford University Press.

MacAndrew, C. (1981). What the MAC scale tells us about alcoholic men: An interpretive review. *Journal of Studies on Alcohol, 42,* 604-625.

McGlothlin, W., Arnold, D., & Freedman, D. (1969). Organicity measures following repeated LSD ingestion. *Archives of General Psychiatry, 21,* 704-709.

Mendelson, J., & Meyer, R. (1972). *Behavioral and biological concomitants of chronic marijuana smoking in heavy and casual users.* Technical Paper of the First Report of the National Commission on Marijuana and Drug Abuse. Washington, DC: U.S. Government Printing Office.

Millon, T., Green, C., & Meagher, R. (1982). *Millon Behavioral Health Inventory Manual.* Minneapolis: Minneapolis National Computer Systems, Inc.

O'Leary, M., Donovan, D., Chancy, E., & Walker, R. (1979). Cognitive impairment and treatment outcome with alcoholics: Preliminary findings. *Journal of Clinical Psychiatry, 40,* 397-398.

Parker, E., Birnbaum, I., Boyd, B., & Noble, E. (1980). Neuropsychological decrement as a function of alcohol intake in male students. *Alcoholism: Clinical and Experimental Research, 4,* 330-334.

Parker, E., & Noble, E. (1977). Alcohol consumption and cognitive functioning in social drinkers. *Journal of Studies on Alcohol, 38,* 1224-1232.

Platt, S., Weyman, A., Hirsch, S., & Hewitt, S. (1980). The Social Behavior Assessment Schedule (SBAS): Rationale, contents, scoring and reliability of a new interview schedule. *Social Psychiatry, 75,* 43–55.

Rehnstrom, S., Simert, G., Hansson, J., & Vang, J. (1977). Chronic hepatic encephalopathy: A psychometrical study. *Scandinavian Journal of Gastroenterology, 12,* 305–311.

Reynolds, E., Rothfield, P., & Pincus, J. (1973). Neurological disease associated with folate deficiency. *British Medical Journal, 2,* 398–400.

Robins, L., Helzer, J., Croughan, J., & Ratcliff, K. (1981). National Institute of Mental Health Diagnostic Interview Schedule. *Archives of General Psychiatry, 39,* 381–389.

Ron, M. (1983). The alcoholic brain: CT scan and psychological findings. *Psychological Medicine, 13* (Monograph Suppl.), 1–192.

Rounsaville, B. J., Novelly, R. A., Kelber, H. D., & Jones, C. (1981). Neuropsychological impairment in opiate addicts: Risk factors. *Annals of the New York Academy of Sciences, 362,* 79–90.

Sarason, I., Johnson, J., & Siegel, J. (1978). Assessing the impact of life changes. *Journal of Consulting and Clinical Psychology, 46,* 932–946.

Schaeffer, K., Parsons, O., & Yohman, J. (1984). Neuropsychological differences between male familial and nonfamilial alcoholics and nonalcoholics. *Alcoholism: Clinical and Experimental Research, 8,* 347–351.

Schaeffer, J., Andrysiak, T., & Ungerleider, J. T. (1981). Cognition and long-term use of Ganja (Cannabis). *Science, 213,* 465–466.

Smith, A. (1975). Neuropsychological testing in neurological disorders. In W. Friedlander (Ed.), *Advances in Neurology* (Vol. 7) (pp. 164–196). New York: Raven Press.

Smith, J., & Smith, L. (1977). WAIS functioning of cirrhotic and noncirrhotic alcoholics. *Journal of Clinical Psychology, 33,* 309–313.

Spielberger, C., Gorsuch, R., & Lushere, R. (1970). *The State-Trait Anxiety Inventory Manual.* Palo Alto, CA: Consulting Psychologists Press.

Spitzer, R., & Endicott, J. (1978). *Schedule for Affective Disorders and Schizophrenia* (3rd ed.). New York: Biometrics Research, New York State Psychiatric Institute.

Streissguth, A., Landesmann-Dwyer, S., Martin, J., & Smith, D. (1980). Teratogenic effects of alcohol in humans and laboratory animals. *Science, 209,* 353–361.

Tarter, R. (1973). An analysis of cognitive deficits in chronic alcoholics. *Journal of Nervous and Mental Disease, 157,* 138–147.

Tarter, R. (1975). Psychological deficit in chronic alcoholics: A review. *International Journal of the Addictions, 10,* 327–368.

Tarter, R. (1976). Empirical investigation of psychological deficit. In R. Tarter & A. Sugerman (Eds.), *Alcoholism: Interdisciplinary approaches to an enduring problem* (pp. 359–394). Reading, MA: Addison-Wesley.

Tarter, R. (1978). Etiology of alcoholism: Interdisciplinary integration. In P. Nathan, G. Marlatt, and T. Loberg (Eds.), *Alcoholism: New directions in behavioral research and treatment* (pp. 41–70). New York: Plenum.

Tarter, R. (1981). Brain damage in chronic alcoholics: A review of the psychological evidence. In D. Richter (Ed.), *Addiction: Biochemical aspects of dependence and brain damage* (pp. 267–297). London: Croom Helm.

Tarter, R., Hegedus, A., Gavaler, J., Schade, R., Van Thiel, D., & Starzl, T. (1983). Cognitive and psychiatric impairments associated with alcoholic and nonalcoholic cirrhosis: Compared and contrasted. *Hepatology, 3,* 830.

Tarter, R., Hegedus, A., Goldstein, G., Shelly, C., & Alterman, A. (1984). Adolescent sons of alcoholics: Neuropsychological and personality characteristics. *Alcoholism: Clinical and Experimental Research, 8,* 216-222.

Tarter, R., Hegedus, A., Van Thiel, D., Schade, R., Gavaler, J., & Starzl, T. (1984). Nonalcoholic cirrhosis associated with neuropsychological dysfunction in the absence of overt evidence of hepatic encephalopathy. *Gastroenterology, 86,* 1421-1427.

Tarter, R., & Jones, B. (1971). Motor impairment in chronic alcoholics. *Journal of Nervous Disease, 32,* 632-636.

Tarter, R., & Parsons, O. (1971). Conceptual shifting in chronic alcoholics. *Journal of Abnormal Psychology, 77,* 71-75.

Tsushina, W., & Towne, W. (1977). Effects of paint sniffing on neuropsychological test performance. *Journal of Abnormal Psychology, 86,* 402-407.

Walker, R., Donovan, D., Kivlahan, D., & O'Leary, M. (1983). Length of stay, neuropsychological performance and aftercare: Influences on alcohol treatment outcome. *Journal of Consulting and Clinical Psychology, 81,* 900-911.

Walsh, K. (1978). *Neuropsychology: A clinical approach.* New York: Churchill Livingstone.

Wender, P., Reimherr, F., & Wood, D. (1981). Attention deficit disorder ("minimal brain dysfunction") in adults: A replication study of diagnosis and drug treatment. *Archives of General Psychiatry, 38,* 449-455.

Wright, M., & Hogan, T. (1972). Repeated LSD ingestion and performance on neuropsychological tests. *Journal of Nervous and Mental Disease, 154,* 432-438.

8

Brief and Extended Neuropsychological Assessment of the Geriatric Patient

J. Michael Williams

Many diseases that affect the central nervous system are much more common among the elderly and are often directly or indirectly associated with advanced age. For example, cerebral vascular accident and multi-infarct dementia are often associated with arteriosclerosis and chronic heart disease in the advanced stages. As the circulatory systems deteriorate, the probability of embolic or thrombotic stroke increases. Of course, most dementing conditions, such as Alzheimer's disease, are almost exclusively confined to the older age groups. As our population of elderly increases over the coming decades, the diagnosis and treatment of these diseases will become increasingly important.

Neuropsychological assessment of the geriatric patient is made difficult by the extreme variability in performance present in the geriatric clinic population. At one extreme, normal aging or depression may result in a mild reduction of cognitive ability. In this situation, the person may be able and willing to take an extended battery of tests. At the other extreme, patients may exhibit the advanced cognitive symptoms of Alzheimer's disease or another dementing condition; the best these patients can tolerate are brief questions as to orientation or a simple three-item memory test that usually includes a five-minute delay. To add to these problems, most people suffering a dementing illness deny their symptoms and may be resistant to any questioning or testing, even when the clinician applies the kindest entreaties.

Dementia in this context is a relatively specific syndrome referring to the acquired decline of all or most intellectual functions. The onset of decline may be acute or insidious. It is primarily characterized by a general cognitive decline rather than the decline of specific cognitive functions that is characteristic of such disorders as aphasia or amnesic syndrome. Although some dementias may begin with a more severe decline in a particular function, such as language, other functions are also affected to some degree. If there is impairment of only a specific cognitive function, then the disorder is not usually classified as a dementia.

Dementia may result from a variety of diseases that affect the central nervous system (CNS). These include Alzheimer's disease, multi-infarction, Pick's disease, hypothyroidism, normal pressure hydrocephalus, and Huntington's disease (Joynt & Shoulson, 1979). All of these result in a generalized cognitive decline. Whether certain cognitive functions typically decline earlier than others is currently unknown, although patients and their families will often report memory difficulties as the first sign of the disease. Family members may observe that memory declines first because of the immediate practical consequences of memory disorder.

Alzheimer's disease is the most common form of dementia and follows a course that is typical of most dementing illnesses. Usually the behavioral manifestations of the disease begin with the observation of relatives that the patient's memory is poor. The patient may forget names, pay bills twice, misplace money, or manifest any of a number of everyday mistakes on tasks that require memory. It is rare for the patients themselves to report memory problems. Typically, patients will deny any problems and will often refuse diagnostic tests of any kind. Most cases have an extremely insidious onset, and the patients may well mask their difficulties until the deterioration of thinking and memory is so advanced that it can no longer be hidden. The brain deterioration continues to impair all cognitive functions severely, and such extreme symptoms as ataxia, aphasia, profound anterograde amnesia, and loss of the fundamental reflexes (e.g., swallow reflex) become apparent in the latter stages. Often the patient expires because of loss of the swallow reflex and consequent dehydration or aspiration pneumonia. This progression may take up to 20 years and severely stresses the family and other social institutions not typically designed to handle such chronic, problematic illness.

Although this is the usual progression of cognitive symptoms, there is considerable variability. For some, aphasic symptoms appear earlier. Many demented patients will lose social inhibitions and become irascible. Others will become socially withdrawn and isolated. Finally, some demented patients have a more rapid onset and progression of symptoms.

The neuropathology of dementing conditions is also varied. Most involve a degenerative process that affects the entire brain. In the case of Alzheimer's disease, there is widespread cell death with neurotransmitter depletion and the establishment of neurofibrillary tangles and plaques. Possible explanations for these changes include viral infection, toxic agents, and abnormalities in the production of proteins (Coyle, Price, & Delong, 1983).

DIFFERENTIAL DIAGNOSIS

The common diagnostic problem in geriatric neuropsychology is the discrimination of these dementing conditions from depression. Although the elderly are probably no more susceptible to depression than other groups, depressed affect, cognitive complaints, and psychomotor retardation can mimic dementing illnesses in this group, and it is often not immediately clear that an elderly person is suffering depression, dementia, or a combination of both. For a younger person, dementia would not be considered as a possible explanation for such symptoms.

The discrimination of dementias is accomplished through a wide array of examinations. These include CT scan, thyroid studies, investigation of medication dosage levels, and, in the case of Huntington's disease, study of the prevalence and incidence of the disease in the patient's family. When evaluated using neuropsychological tests, these diseases are similar in their cognitive and behavioral manifestations. However, it is important to note the history of cognitive symptoms. It is here that significant differences emerge. There are three relatively specific patterns of symptom development that characterize these diseases. The first of these results from conditions that have a recent or acute onset, such as hydrocephalus or medication-induced dementia. These conditions will often involve the decline of all or most cognitive functions in relative unison; family members usually do not report that one ability declined earlier than another. Onset, and the noticeable progression of cognitive symptoms, can range from a few days up to six months, varying with the underlying condition. Many of these conditions are treatable and may resolve within the same time interval in which they developed. Often, the proper medication changes or installation or a periventricular shunt will substantially improve the patient's cognitive functioning, and these changes can be noted using postintervention neuropsychological assessment.

The second major pattern is specific to multi-infarct dementia. This condition results in a stepwise progression of cognitive symptoms. The decline begins with the first stroke. As the patient recovers from this first one, it is apparent that specific cognitive functions have been impaired. This specific disability is associated with the site of the brain lesions; for example, aphasia usually develops if the left hemisphere is affected first. As more infarcts are created, more cognitive abilities become involved until generalized dementia is present. The important distinction between this form and others is that the progression into a dementia condition is stepwise and discontinuous. Often relatives and patients will report that there were definite points in the downward progression of symptoms. However, this progression is not characteristic of all multi-infarct cases. A subset of these cases will have small frequent strokes, an insidious onset, and gradual progression, closely resembling other forms of dementia. Hachinski, Linette, Zilhka, Doboulay, McAllister, Marshall, Russell, and Symon (1975) provide a summary and scoring system for evaluating the signs and symptoms of multi-infarct dementia.

The final pattern of dementia is the most prevalent and characterizes, most prominently, Alzheimer's disease and Huntington's disease. In this type of dementia, cognitive symptoms have a very gradual onset and progression paralleling the slow process of cell death and creation of lesions that are typical of these disease. Relatives of the patient have extreme difficulty placing the onset of thinking and memory difficulties. As months and years pass, the cognitive problems worsen and it becomes obvious to the family that the patient has serious problems. The patient is referred for assessment at this later point in the progression of the disease. Neuropsychological evaluation usually indicates that all cognitive functions are impaired at this stage. Usually memory scores are lower than measures of language, abstract reasoning, visuospatial processing, or other cognitive functions. As the dementing disease progresses, the patient becomes frankly aphasic, reasons at only the most concrete levels, becomes disoriented, and has a complete anterograde amnesia. Remote memories are often preserved but are often disorganized in retrieval. The patient will often apply his/her remote memories to current situations. For example, the patien may give the current hospital the name of one in which he/she received treatment many years before. As the patient's cognitive abilities deteriorate, assessment turns from more extended batteries to brief assessment techniques such as the mental status examination.

These three typologies, describing the different dementing illnesses using a neuropsychological perspective, are presented only as a convenient heuristic to aid the clinician in diagnosis. There are many exceptions to these categories, and certainly such diseases as multi-infarct dementia can follow the same pattern of cognitive decline as Alzheimer's disease. The following is a brief presentation of specific measures and techniques used in assessing these conditions.

NEUROPSYCHOLOGICAL ASSESSMENT

Aside from measuring a variety of cognitive functions, brief and extended assessment techniques are also characterized by the source of information about the patient. These sources are (1) the patient's family or friends, (2) clinical interviews and rating scales, (3) the self-report of the patient, and (4) the results of formal neuropsychological assessment. Another rule of thumb is that the clinician should utilize all these sources of information when making an assessment of cognitive functioning. Often the patient cannot report his/her history of symptoms and is unwilling or unable to take even the briefest neuropsychological tests. At this point, the reports of family members who have observed the progress of the disease and clinical rating scales completed by the clinician are the most important sources of information. Even if the patient is able to provide information, the observations of the clinician and family will corroborate the patient's report and increase the validity and reliability of the assessment.

BRIEF ASSESSMENT APPROACHES

The most popular method of evaluating cognitive function in the geriatric population is the mental status examination (MSE). All forms of the MSE exist as a collection of screening devices for the assessment of different cognitive functions organized into a short battery. For example, a popular mental status exam presented by Strub and Black (1977) consists of a collection of brief approaches for the measurement of orientation, attention, language, memory, construction ability, and other higher cognitive functions. Each sub-test consists of simple observations and descriptions of the patient's behavior when confronted with a cognitively demanding task or of actual measurements of certain abilities by quantification of the patient's level of response. For example, the presence of unilateral neglect is simply observed and described in the Strub and Black (1977) system; but memory ability is quantified in one test as the number of story segments a patient can recall after hearing a brief 3-to-4-sentence story. From these observations and measurements, the clinician is able to make a relatively formal appraisal of cognitive ability as it relates to history and other evidence of cerebral integrity.

One feature of the MSE makes it unique among brief assessment approaches and attractive to clinicians assessing geriatric patients: It is directed toward the lower levels of cognitive functioning. The obvious advantage of this approach is that the MSE does not usually confront the older person with tasks that are initially too difficult. The patient can usually perform at some level and provide the clinician with information. The obvious disadvantage is that the patient's functioning is not assessed at the upper levels and that more subtle aspects of cognitive dysfunction can go unnoticed. If the patient easily completes MSE items and cognitive disability is still suspected, then a more extended assessment should be used. For example, older patients who suffer a mild head injury or manifest milder signs of medication toxicity may experience a cognitive loss that will go unnoticed on the MSE. However, even mild cognitive dysfunction can be distressing to the patient, depending upon the cognitive demands of the patient's occupation and everyday life. Consequently, the full range of cognitive abilities should be assessed.

Brief assessment approaches that allow the clinician formally to test the patient (e.g., the MSE) come in many forms. One easily administered and widely used instrument is the brief Mental Status Questionnaire (Pfeiffer, 1975). It provides a quick measure of orientation and attention for the patient experiencing severe dementia or confusional state. Another brief approach that relies on the judgment or observation of the clinician is the Brief Cognitive Rating Scale (Reisbert, 1983). This measure requires the clinician to make global ratings of cognitive ability in the areas of concentration, recent memory, past memory, orientation, and self-care.

There exist two recently developed measures for assessing the self-report of cognitive problems in the elderly. These are the Cognitive Difficulties Scale (McNair & Kahn, 1983) and the Cognitive Behavior Rating Scale–Self-Report Form (CBRS) (Williams, Klein, Little, & Haban, in press). Both these measures allow the patient to report the extent of his/her difficulties in thinking and memory. Finally, the Relative Report Form of the CBRS allows the relatives of the patient to rate everyday symptoms of cognitive decline. The relatives of the patient can often provide valuable information about the progression of symptoms and their severity that can supplement the clinician's test results and observations.

There are also several rating scales that enables the clinician to assess depression in the elderly. Certainly the most widely used instrument utilizing the clinician's observations is the Hamilton Rating Scale (Hamilton, 1967). The Beck Depression Inventory (Beck, Ward, Mendelson, Mock, & Erlbaugh, 1961) and the Zung Self-Rating Depression Scale (Zung, 1965) allow the patient to report depressive symptomology. Other related measures that assess a wide range of psychological disorders and somatic concerns are the Brief Psychiatric Rating Scale (Overall & Gorham, 1962), the Inventory of Psychic and Somatic Complaints of the Elderly (Raskin & Rae, 1961), and the Sandoz Clinical Assessment–Geriatric Scale (Shader, Harmatz, & Salzman, 1974). These instruments allow the clinician to measure depressive and other psychiatric disorders in order to discriminate them from dementia-related illness.

EXTENDED NEUROPSYCHOLOGICAL ASSESSMENT

As previously mentioned, the extent and breadth of assessment of the elderly is extremely dependent upon the patient's overall level of functioning. The person must be able to attend and follow instructions, as well as simply cooperate with the examiner. From the initial contact with the patient, great attention must be paid to establishing rapport and eliciting cooperation. The examiner must encourage and reinforce the patient's efforts frequently throughout the examinations. Frequent breaks are important to maintain rapport, although such breaks can often encourage the patient's attention and conversation to wander. Usually the patient can be brought back on track with a firm suggestion or transition to the instructions for the next task.

Extended assessment techniques for the geriatric patient must be ranked in order of priority and administered accordingly. There will be a limit to the patient's endurance, and a point will be reached at which the patient's fatigue is so great that the test results are invalid.

After the assessment of basic orientation, attention, and global cognitive abilities using a brief assessment approach, the most important cognitive ability to measure in detail is memory functioning. This is adequately measured by the Wechsler Memory Scale (Wechsler, 1945). Although numerous criticisms have been leveled at this measure, it still remains the most popular general-purpose clinical memory scale (Erickson & Scott, 1977). Alternative measures are the Randt Memory Battery (Randt, Brown, & Osborne, 1980), the Cronholm Memory Battery (Cronholm & Ottoson, 1963), and the Vermont Memory Scale (Williams, Klein, Little, & Haban, in press). All of these techniques allow for the relatively comprehensive measurement of verbal and visuospatial memory ability. In the verbal sphere this is accomplished by asking the patient to remember a short list of words or a four- or five-sentence story. Visuospatial memory tasks require the patient to remember geometric designs or pictures of common objects. Verbal recall is measured by having the patient recite the lists or stories after a delay interval. Recall of visuospatial material most often requires the patient later to draw figures originally presented or recognize the correct figure out of an array of similar figures. Most of these batteries also include an assessment of immediate recall of verbal information. Elderly patients who have dementing illness will have extremely poor long-term memory for all types of information, but immediate recall will be preserved. It is important to note a dissociation between such immediate recall and long-term consolidation of information. Immediate recall is usually assessed with the Digit Span task, which requires the patient immediately to repeat successively longer number strings. The longest string the patient can repeat without error is recorded as the digit span.

In addition to memory batteries, there exist several self-report memory problem questionnaires that are helpful in evaluating the extent to which the patient is aware of possible memory difficulties and the manner in which such problems may affect everyday memory tasks. Most prominent among these is the Everyday Memory Questionnaire (Zelinski, Gilewski, & Thompson, 1980).

Extended assessment should also include an examination of basic sensory and motor abilities. Sensory examination is readily accomplished using the sensory-perceptual examination included in most neurological examinations or the Halstead–Reitan Neuropsychological Battery (Reitan & Davison, 1974).

These procedures allow for the examination of tactile, visual, and auditory suppressions, graphesthesia, finger agnosia, and tactile form recognition. Motor speed is adequately measured using the Tapping Test of the Halstead-Reitan Battery or Thumb-Finger Sequential Touch Test of the Luria–Nebraska Neuropsychological Battery (Golden, Hammeke, & Purish, 1978). Assessment of these abilities allows the examiner to determine the degree to which sensory and motor abilities may be influenced by the disease process and the manner in which the condition may be lateralized. Dementia-related illness that is vascular in origin will often affect one hemisphere more than another.

Extended assessment of language abilities can range from an aphasia screening test, like the Reitan–Indiana Aphasia Screening Test (Heimberger & Reitan, 1961), to extended aphasia batteries, like the Boston Diagnostic Aphasia Battery (Goodglass & Kaplan, 1972). Aphasia-related assessment often also includes the measurement of basic arithmetic ability and ideomotor apraxia. All of these abilities are often impaired with dominant-hemisphere lesions. Elderly patients with prominent aphasic symptoms who are also generally demented have probably suffered a cerebral vascular accident in the past. Aphasia is also a prominent symptom of the very late stages of dementing illness.

Abstract reasoning and complex problem solving should also be assessed. This is frequently accomplished through the use of a general intellectual battery like the Wechsler Adult Intelligence Scale (Wechsler, 1955). Verbal reasoning is measured by having the patient interpret proverbs, define words, and express the relationship between verbal concepts. Visuospatial problem solving is measured through asking the patient to solve puzzles that require sensorimotor manipulation and visuospatial analysis of an arrangement of objects. Additional measures of these constructs are the Raven Progressive Matrices (Raven, 1960) and the Category Test (Reitan & Davison, 1974), which require the patient to form an abstract principle or concept from an arrangement of stimuli and solve problems based upon these abstractions.

A final component of extended assessment should be the measurement of basic activities of daily living. Since the purpose of neuropsychological assessment often includes discharge planning, the clinician must have some knowledge of the patient's ability to function in everyday life. A popular method used to acquire this information is the clinical interview. Most patients will be able to answer basic questions about mobility in the home, accessibility of bathroom and kitchen, and the ability to dress and care for themselves. However, often the demented patient will deny or be unaware of his/her everyday problems. For this reason, the interview of the patient should be supplemented with an interview of a reliable observer, such as a spouse or other relative. This interview should be summarized using such instruments as the instrumental Activities of Daily Living Scale (IADL) (Lawton & Brody, 1969), the Multilevel Assessment Instrument (AMI) (Lawton, Moss, Fulcomer, & Kleban, 1982), or the Older Americans Resources and Service Questionnaire (OARS) (Fillen-baum & Smyer, 1981). All of these measures require a reliable observer or an interviewer to rate cognitive abilities and skills of everyday living. Such an assessment is necessary in the overall characterization of the patient and should be used whenever disposition or follow-up is important, especially when a brief assessment approach has been used to assess cognitive abilities.

CASE REPORT

The following case illustrates the application of these techniques with the elderly in a rehabilitation setting. Certainly the same techniques can be applied in other inpatient and outpatient settings. This particular example allows for the presentation of the full range of assessment techniques presented in the chapter.

Following admission to the hospital, B.W., a 67-year-old woman, was re-ferred for neuropsychological assessment for evaluation of family-reported symptoms of increased moodiness, poor memory, and disorientation. B.W. had been found by her family wandering in a nearby neighborhood, obviously lost. She was also having difficulty managing her money and preferred to have large quantities of cash sequestered in hiding places around the house. Since a dementing illness was suspected, a family member familiar with the patient's everyday behavior was interviewed and then asked to complete the Cognitive Behavior Rating Scale. Concurrent with this rating, B.W. was briefly inter-viewed and administered the Wechsler Memory Scale and the Zung Depres-sion Scale. The patient refused to complete the Wechsler Adult Intelligence Scale and the Cognitive Difficulties Scale but did respond to many items of the mental status examination. She was given a full range of other medical tests while in the hospital. These included a neurological examination, CT scan, EEG, and full hematological examination, all of which were read as essentially normal. She did not have a past history of high blood pressure, heart disease, or stroke.

The neuropsychological examination and interview revealed considerable anterograde memory disorder for verbal as well as nonverbal information. She was unable to remember more than five percent of a three-sentence story after a one-half hour delay. She scored very low on tests of memory for geometric designs. She was largely intact on tests of language and higher cognitive functions. She indicated mild depression on the Beck Depression Inventory. When asked about her difficulties in memory and managing money, she denied any problems and expressed some resentment at being asked to come into the hospital and take a lot of tests when there was nothing obviously wrong with her.

The responses of the patient's spouse to items of the Cognitive Behavior

Rating Scale revealed a consistent pattern of dementia-related everyday behavior. Most prominent of these behaviors was difficulty remembering the names of friends, misplacing objects, becoming lost in familiar places, losing the train of thought in conversation, and repeating the same story over and over again. The spouse did not indicate that cognitive problems were associated with depressed mood.

Through a combination of medical tests, the major treatable causes of dementia were ruled out. These included depression, hypothyroidism, and medication toxicity. Multi-infarct dementia and Alzheimer's disease were then considered the most likely of the remaining etiological explanations. Because B.W. had no previous history of stroke or heart disease, the most likely diagnosis was determined to be Alzheimer's disease. Her ischemia score using the Hachinski system was three, an extremely low score. Of course, a definitive diagnosis of Alzheimer's disease can currently be determined only by autopsy examination.

B.W. was followed after discharge for approximately nine months. The family was referred to a family support group sponsored by the local chapter of the Alzheimer's Disease and Related Disorders Association. The family was able to learn many practical techniques for the management of dementia-related behavior in the home. At the present time, the patient continues to live at home, and the family is able to manage her current level of everyday problems.

This case illustrates the usual evaluation history of the elderly demented patient. B.W.'s presentation of symptoms was relatively uncomplicated and clear-cut. Often such cases will present with greater depression, and this complicates the assessment of dementia-related cognitive decline. A great many elderly who are suspected of having dementia by their families will be depressed. This is one of the most important aspects to assess because it is imminently treatable. Successful treatment of depression will bring an immediate improvement in the patient's overall cognitive and adaptive functioning. Likewise, it is important to distinguish, as clearly as possible, between Alzheimer's disease and multi-infarct dementia, since this has consequences for the management of the patient by the family. Many cases of multi-infarct dementia will plateau after a series of strokes and decline no further. Alzheimer's disease involves a progressive decline of cognitive functioning and no marked plateaus. It is important for the families of multi-infarct cases to know that their family member may not decline in cognitive abilities beyond the present level and will probably recover some abilities as the stroke resolves. There may be more strokes in the future, but a steady pattern of cognitive disability is easier to manage than a persistent decline in functioning. As each month passes, the family of a patient with Alzheimer's disease is confronted with another or worse cognitive symptom to manage.

In summary, dementing conditions of the elderly are a considerable health problem and are difficult to diagnose, treat, and manage. Neuropsychological assessment of some type is important at every step in dealing with these diseases but is probably most important during the diagnostic phase. Dementia in the elderly represents a relatively well-defined syndrome that accompanies many diseases. Diagnosis of the proper etiological process depends greatly upon the history of symptom development as well as other signs unique to a particular disease (e.g., hypertension or low thyroxine level). For this reason, information provided by the family is extremely important in describing the history of dementia-related behavior.

In order to increase the reliability and accuracy of the assessment, information should be collected from many sources: formal neuropsychological assessment of the patient, observation by family members or other reliable observers, and the self-report of the patient. When necessary information is not available from one source, such as formal testing of the patient, it can be acquired in some form from other sources. Likewise, there is a spectrum of cognitive and self-care abilities to assess from these main points of view. These range from orientation and memory to activities of daily living. All of these may be assessed in some way by the family report, formal neuropsychological assessment, or the patient's self-report. Through combining these into a brief or extended assessment, a feasible and comprehensive measurement of the patient's neuropsychological functioning can be made to aid in diagnosis and management of the elderly patient.

REFERENCES

Beck, A. T., Ward, C. H., Mendelson, M., Mock, J., & Erlbaugh, J. (1961). An inventory for measuring depression. *Archives of General Psychiatry, 4*, 561-571.

Coyle, J. T., Price, D. L., & Delong, M. R. (1983). Alzheimer's disease: A disorder of cortical cholinergic inervation. *Science, 219*, 1184-1190.

Cronholm, B., & Ottosson, J. (1963). Reliability and validity of a memory test battery. *Acta Psychiatrica Scandinavica, 39*, 218-234.

Erickson, D. C., & Scott, M. L. (1977). Clinical memory testing: A review. *Psychological Bulletin, 84*(6), 1130-1149.

Fillenbaum, G. G., & Smyer, M. A. (1981). The development, validity and reliability of the OARS Multidimensional Functional Assessment Questionnaire. *Journal of Gerontology, 316*(4), 428-434.

Golden, C. J., Hammeke, T., & Purish, A. D. (1978). Diagnostic utility of a standardized neuropsychological battery derived from Luria's neuropsychological tests. *Journal of Consulting and Clinical Psychology, 46*, 1258-1265.

Goodglass, H., & Kaplan, E. (1972). *Assessment of aphasia and related disorders.* Philadelphia: Lea and Febiger.

Hachinski, V. C., Linette, L. D., Zilhka, E., Duboulay, G. H., McAllister, V. L., Marshall, J., Russell, R. W., & Symon, L. (1975). Cerebral blood flow in dementia. *Archives of Neurology, 32,* 632-637.

Hamilton, M. (1967). Development of a rating scale of primary depressive illness. *British Journal of Social and Clinical Psychology, 6,* 278-296.

Heimberger, R. F., & Reitan, R. M. (1961). Easily administered written test for lateralizing brain lesions. *Journal of Neurosurgery, 18,* 301-312.

Joynt, R. J., & Shoulson, I. (1979). Dementia. In K. Heilman & E. Vaslenstein (Eds.), *Clinical neuropsychology* (pp. 475-502). New York: Oxford University Press.

Kahn, R. L., Goldfarb, A. I., Pollack, M., & Peck, A. (1960). Brief objective measures for the determination of mental status in the aged. *American Journal of Psychiatry, 117,* 326-328.

Lawton, M. P., & Brody, E. M. (1969). Assessment of older people: Self-maintaining and instrumental activities of daily living. *Gerontologist, 9,* 179-186.

Lawton, M. P., Moss, M., Fulcomer, M., & Kleban, M. H. (1982). A research and service-oriented multilevel assessment instrument. *Journal of Gerontology, 37,* 91-99.

McNair, D. M., & Kahn, R. J. (1983). Self-assessment of cognitive difficulties. In T. Crook, S. Ferris, & R. Bartus (Eds.), *Assessment in geriatric psychopharmacology* (pp. 238-247). New Canaan, CT: Mark Dewley Associates.

Overall, J. E., & Gorham, D. R. (1962). The Brief Psychiatric Rating Scale. *Psychological Reports, 10,* 799-812.

Pfeiffer, E. (1975). A short portable mental status questionnaire for the assessment of organic brain deficit in elderly patients. *Journal of the American Geriatric Society, 23,* 433-441.

Randt, C. T., Brown, E. R., & Osborne, D. P. (1980). A memory test for longitudinal measurement of mild to moderate deficits. *Clinical Neuropsychology, 2,* 184-194.

Raskin, A. S., & Rae, D. W. (1981). Psychiatric symptoms of the elderly. *Psychopharmacology Bulletin, 17,* 96-99.

Raven, J. C. (1960). *Guide to the Standard Progressive Matrices.* London: H. K. Lewis; New York: Psychological Corporation.

Reisberg, B. (1983). The Brief Cognitive Rating Scale and Global Deterioration Scale. In T. Crook, S. Ferris, & R. Bartus (Eds.), *Assessment in geriatric psychopharmacology* (pp. 87-103). New Canaan, CT: Mark Powley Associates.

Reitan, R. M., & Davison, L. A. (1974). *Clinical neuropsychology: Current status and applications.* New York: Hemisphere.

Shader, R. I., Harmatz, J. S., & Salzman, C. (1974). A new scale for clinical assessment in geriatric populations: Sandoz Clinical Assessment-Geriatric (SCAG). *Journal of the American Geriatric Society, 22,* 107-113.

Strub, R. L., & Black, F. W. (1977). *The mental status examination in neurology.* Philadelphia: F. A. Davis Company.

Wechsler, D. (1945). A standardized memory scale for clinical use. *Journal of Psychology, 19,* 87-95.

Wechsler, D. (1955). *Wechsler Adult Intelligence Scale manual.* New York: Psychological Corporation.

Williams, J. M., Klein, K., Little, M., & Haban, G. (in press). The role of family observations in the description of dementia. *Archives of Clinical Neuropsychology.*

Zelinski, E. M., Gilewski, M. J., & Thompson, L. W. (1980). Do laboratory tests relate to self-assessment of memory ability in the young and old? In L. Poon, J. Fozard, L. Cermak, D. Arenberg, & L. Thompson (Eds.), *New directions in memory and aging.* Hillsdale, NJ: Lawrence Erlbaum Associates.

Zung, W. W. (1965). A self-rating depression scale. *Archives of General Psychiatry, 12,* 63-70.

9

Brief Neuropsychological Assessment of Memory

William D. MacInnes
and
Douglas E. Robbins

One of the most common sequelae of brain dysfunction is that of a memory disorder. The practicing clinician may be faced with making the differential diagnosis of whether the patient's presentation is indicative of a pathological process or represents a functional disturbance. Differentiating between normal aging and the onset of a dementing process, for example, may prove to be of great importance in terms of early intervention strategies. Similarly, the onset of an acute memory disturbance may be reflective of a severe neuropsychological disorder that warrants immediate attention.

It is the purpose of the following chapter to provide a synopsis of the clinical study of memory as relevant to the professional practicing in a medical setting. Although most clinicians receive training to assess relatively simple cognitive functions (e.g., sensory-motor abilities), very little attention is given to helping the clinician recognize the subtleties of higher-order pathologies. It is therefore the goal of this chapter to provide the clinician with a more thorough understanding of memory and memory processes, as well as the neuropsychological correlates manifested with various neurological and psychological conditions.

In any discussion of memory it is important to note that a certain degree of confusion exists in the terminology used to describe memory functioning. For example, neurologists classify memory as immediate, recent, and remote. Psychologists refer to immediate memory as short-term memory, that is, referring to information that exists in the subject's immediate awareness (e.g., memory for digits on the Digit Span Test). Recent memory is often referred to as long-term memory. Recent memory can be assessed by asking the subject what he/she had for breakfast or by administering a word-learning list. Remote memory is equivalent to distant memory and is assessed by asking questions that pertain to information that has been stored over an extended period of time. For the purpose of the following discussion, memory will be defined as being a complex higher-order process that includes the collection, storage, and retrieval of information (Erickson & Scott, 1977). Memory is also perceived as being a reconstructive process. As such, memories often do not constitute an accurate representation of a past event, since they are influenced by such variables as the emotional state of the subject and the congruity of the event with more-established memories. Memory, therefore, represents a reconstructive process in which the perceived event is integrated into the subject's frame of reference.

GENERAL MEMORY PROCESSES

Sensory Memory

Research and theory maintain that memory is not a unitary construct. Underlying every major model of memory today is not only the conceptualization that there appear to be different types of memory, but that a number of processes are involved in memory functioning. For example, the initial stage of this process involves the organism's attention to incoming sensations. This sensory input is transferred into an extremely short-term storage, the duration of which is measured in hundreds of milliseconds. It is at this stage that input sensations are transformed into coherent images that can then be transmitted to the sensory areas of the brain. Although the existence of sensory memory is generally accepted, there is argument as to whether this memory is located in the peripheral or central nervous system (Craik, 1979; Sakitt, 1976).

Short-Term Memory

From sensory memory, information is transmitted to short-term memory (STM). STM, which has been referred to as primary memory, immediate memory, span memory, and short-term store, has several characteristics. First, it is a system of limited capacity in which information is maintained by continued attention and rehearsal (Craik & Lockhart, 1972). Second, STM lasts 20–30 seconds (Norman, 1973). If rehearsal is introduced, the input will remain longer in STM but will gradually be replaced by new material (Drachman & Arbit, 1966). Third, the total of items that can be held in STM is seven plus or minus two (Miller, 1956; Norman, 1973).

It is now generally agreed upon that STM acts as the conscious processing unit of the brain (Atkinson & Shiffrin, 1971; Shiffrin, 1973; Shiffrin & Schneider, 1977). This process draws upon rehearsal, coding, decision making, thinking, and retrieval strategies in order to transfer the material to and from long term storage. Craik (1979) has postulated that stored past experiences helps to interpret the incoming information and infers missing information where necessary. If the stimulus event is common or overlearned, the cognitive processing is relatively automatic and only a minimal memory record remains. Novel events, however, may require extensive analysis, and, concomitantly, a distinctive memory trace may be established (Shiffrin & Schneider, 1977; Eysenck, 1978).

Long-Term Memory

The next stage in the memory process involves the encoding and consolidation of information into long-term memory (LTM). LTM begins after the first half-second in which the stimulus enters the realm of attention. Consequently, there is a 20–30-second overlap between STM and LTM. This overlap is clinically significant and should be taken into consideration when any assessment of STM or LTM is attempted, as one may be evaluating a combination of these two processes rather than either of the processes individually. LTM is recognized as having three separate stages: consolidation and transfer, storage, and retrieval (Russell, 1981).

Consolidation

Memory consolidation consists of (1) the transfer of material from STM to LTM or, in the case of theories that postulate independent, parallel processing in STM and LTM, direct access to LTM and (2) the consolidation of the memory in that storage (McGaugh, 1966). The transfer component is relatively rapid, on the order of one-half second. The consolidation component takes much longer (McGaugh, 1966; McGaugh & Herz, 1972) and involves a gradual strengthening of the memory trace. During the period of several minutes to several hours, the trace is highly unstable and easily subject to loss (e.g., as in anterograde amnesia in postconcussive syndrome) (Barbizet, 1970). Once information has entered LTM, whose capacity appears to be essentially unlimited, it is maintained by repetition or organization.

An essential element of the transfer process concerns how information to be learned is coded into memory (Kesner, 1973). LTM and STM are thought to have different organizations (Broadbent, 1969). Whereas STM is seen as being organized by time, LTM is organized by meaning and association. Information in STM is encoded according to the time that it was entered into memory, rather than being organized according to categories, as in LTM. Luria (1973) also argues that memorization requires the categorization of input and that the process of transfer is analogous to the process of categorization. Retrieval therefore requires the retracing of the code. The STM process of rehearsal may itself be a category in that items practiced can be coded and stored under the code "rehearsed."

Finally, as noted above, rehearsal plays an important role in the consolidation and transfer of information into LTM (Norman, 1973; Atkinson & Shiffrin, 1971). Traditionally, it has been maintained that rehearsal serves to increase the amount of attention paid to an item, thus reinforcing that item in memory. Current research now indicates that long-term retention may not be determined by either the sheer amount of rehearsal or the duration of an item's stay in STM. What appears to be critical is the type of rehearsal or processing that takes place during the input period. Rehearsal, such as simple repetition, which serves only to maintain the immediate availability of an item, does little if anything to enhance subsequent recall. Active processes such as elaboration, transformation, and recoding are activities that have been found to enhance recall (Postman, 1975, p. 301).

EPISODIC AND CATEGORICAL MEMORY

Information that is stored in LTM is stored in the same form as it was originally encoded. Two of the major forms of storage are episodic memory and semantic, or categorical, memory. Although this distinction is widely accepted in most research on memory (Craik, 1979; Tulving, 1972), it has received little attention in neuropsychology.

Episodic memory refers to memories that have been given a temporal and spatial coding. This is the type of memory associated with when and where something occurs. A temporal-spatial relationship exists among these events (Tulving, 1972); for example, the recall of the birth of one's first child would be an episodic memory.

In contrast to episodic memory, semantic memory lacks this emphasis on a spatial or temporal context. Instead, it is a verbally mediated memory. Norman (1973) has attempted to expand semantic memory to include all items, verbal and nonverbal, that a person remembers that are not attached to a particular time-space context. In other words, an item is repeated many times in different contexts until the context is no longer needed and only the item in relation to coded strategies remains. This conceptualization is similar to Luria's model of categorical memory. Categorical memory would thus be less restricted in definition than semantic memory and would refer to all LTM that is not episodic in nature and that can be placed into an abstract or nontime category.

Retrieval

Retrieval, the third process related to LTM, refers to the process of locating and retrieving information from long-term storage. Retrieval from LTM is of two types: (1) direct verbatim access to memory storage traces and (2) access to a general idea or gist of the original material and a reconstruction of the final output (Russell, 1981). The actual reconstruction of the memory may be influenced by a number of factors (e.g., how compatible this memory is to other memories, the context in which the memory occurred, and so forth). The cues necessary to retrieve information from memory are the same cues that were initially used to encode the material.

Recall and Recognition

Another important distinction related to the issue of retrieval is that between recall and recognition. Researchers question whether these are separate processes or different stages in one process. In support of the first view is the finding that retrieved information in recall is generally uncorrelated with that derived from recognition (Flexser & Tulving, 1978). In support of the latter view is the argument that recognition is easier than recall because the target word facilitates access to storage. Storage, however, is perceived as being the same for both recognition and recall (Brown, 1978). Support for the separation of recall and recognition has been made by Milner (1978). Using the Wada Test, patients with an anesthetized temporal lobe were presented sentences or picture. Recognition of the stimulus materials was possible later, whereas recall was not. Patients were not able to recall pictures when the right temporal lobe was inactivated and could not recall sentences when the left temporal lobe was inactivated.

MEMORY LOSS

For a memory to be lost, it must first have actually been stored. Testing may be utilized as a means of assessing whether a person's memory deficit is due to a storage or retrieval problem. In such an evaluation, the subject is first given a memorization task. Second, the subject is evaluated to see if this material was placed in storage. Third, the subject is given a test at a later date to see if there has been a loss between the two testings.

Theoretical explanations of memory loss are typically grouped into two broad categories: functional theories and structural theories. Functional, or information-processing models, state that memory failure is due to a functional defect in the process of memory storage or retrieval. For example, such models assume that for memory to become permanent some structural change in the brain is required. Memory failure occurs when the consolidation process is interrupted, thus preventing the structural change in the brain from occurring. More recent models take a slightly different version of memory failure by proposing that sensory experiences produce a structural change in the normal manner, but that access to the memory traces become compromised.

Structural models assume that memory failure results from a blockage in a particular form of memory. Impairment of a cognitive structure is expected to lead to deficits in certain types of memories but not in others (e.g., recognition failure).

A number of specific theoretical explanations have also been proposed to explain memory loss. Of course, the trace decay theory, the interference theory, the theory of consolidation failure, and the loss of intention theory have received the most attention. The decay theory states that over a period of time memory traces gradually deteriorate, that time alone does not produce change. Baddeley (1976) has proposed a more sophisticated version of this theory, which states that a memory trace may decay because of the neutral background activity, or "noise," that occurs in the brain.

A second explanation of memory loss is the interference theory. This theory states that memories do not decay, but that memory losses are due to interference by other memories. Interference can be either proactive (that is, previously learned material interferes with subsequent learning) or retroactive (subsequently learned material interferes with prior learning). Luria (1973) proposes that the proactive and retroactive interference that occurs is actually due to a failure in neural inhibition. He postulates that there is an inhibitory influence of prior memories on new traces that interferes with the retrieval of new information.

As stated earlier, there appear to be at least four possible explanations of memory loss. These explanations can easily be applied to explain memory loss in the case of brain damage. For example, the theory of trace decay would state that memory impairment is due to a loss of brain substance, associated with the actual physiological deterioration of memory traces. Very little research to date, however, has demonstrated a one-to-one relationship between the loss of a type of memory and the loss of brain substance.

The interference theory of memory suggests that insults to the brain overwhelm its ability to prevent interference from affecting memory traces (Russell, 1981). Findings derived from head-injury cases give support to this theory. For example, in cases of head trauma, memories gradually return after a period of retroactive amnesia, except for the few minutes or, in some cases, hours immediately preceding the head trauma itself. As this material gradually returns with time, it is clear that the information was retained but not retrievable at that time. The return of memories can be explained by a reduction of inhibition, which allows the retrieval process to occur.

A failure of consolidation has been noted as a third explanation for amnesia. Patients with Korsakoff's syndrome, as well as patients with bilateral lesions of the hippocampus, demonstrate such consolidation failure (Milner, 1959, 1978; Milner, Corkin, & Teuber, 1968). In cases of closed-head trauma, both inhibition and consolidation processes appear to be involved; that is, the retroactive amnesia, which gradually remits, is most likely caused by interference or inhibition. The few minutes or hours preceding the trauma never return, and the anterograde amnesia appears to be produced by a failure of consolidation.

A fourth cause of memory loss would be due to a loss of intention to memorize. Luria (1971, 1976) states that frontal damage may produce an inability to follow any intention for a length of time. As a result, the subject is unable to filter out irrelevant stimuli and is thus hampered in the ability to memorize material.

ETIOLOGIES OF SPECIFIC MEMORY DISORDERS

Closed-Head Injury

A cardinal feature of a closed-head injury is that of a memory disturbance. Recent evidence from neuropathological studies suggests that the primary mechanism of closed-head injury is mechanical shearing/stretching of nerve fibers immediately on impact (Levin, Benton, & Grossman, 1982, p. 7). These lesions are caused by microscopic tears to the fiber tracts and are often not fully disclosed by CT imaging. While an individual suffering a closed-head injury often experiences a variety of neuropsychological and emotional sequelae, memory dysfunction is probably the most commonly reported symptom.

Anterograde or posttraumatic amnesia concerns the loss of memory for events after a brain injury or disease. Amnesia concerns the failure to retrieve material from LTM. This is considered to be the most common memory problem after head injury. Levin and associates (1982) presented four stages of memory problems associated with closed-head injuries (see Figure 9.1). As can be seen, anterograde or posttraumatic amnesia can be much longer than the coma following a head injury. In fact, Russell (1971) suggests using duration of posttraumatic amnesia, rather than length of coma, as the index of the severity of the closed-head injury. Levin and associates (1982) reviewed the literature concerning this idea and concluded that posttraumatic amnesia is a better predictor of recovery than duration of coma.

Retrograde amnesia is often defined as the length of time preceding the head injury for which the patient has no recollection. It is not uncommon for an individual who has suffered a head injury, for example, to state that he/she cannot remember anything from earlier that same morning. Levin and associates suggest that retrograde amnesia is caused by the fact that "the cerebral insult disrupts consolidation of memory by blocking its transfer from labile

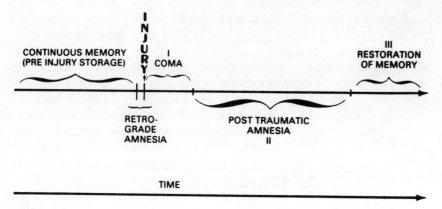

FIGURE 9.1 Early stages of recovery from closed-head injury.

Sequence of acute alterations in memory after closed-head injury. The periods of coma (I) and posttraumatic amnesia (II) have been traditionally combined to yield a total interval of impaired consciousness that extends until continuous memory for ongoing events (III) is restored. (From Levin, H. S., Benton, A. L., and Grossman, R. G. (1982). *Neurobehavioral consequences of closed head injury.* New York: Oxford University Press. Reprinted with permission.)

STM to permanent storage" (1982, p. 80). Unfortunately, there are serious methodological problems when one attempts to measure remote memory reliably. Attempts to standardize the assessment of remote memory have consisted primarily of recall and recognition tasks for current events and photographs of famous persons (Albert, Butters, & Levin, 1979; Warrington & Sanders, 1971). Most remote memory research assumes that a temporal gradient exists in remote memory; that is, the extent of a memory loss for any past event is inversely related to the time since it occurred (Ribot, 1982). However, this assumption may not always be true. Some events may be more difficult to remember than others. A person's cultural and socioeconomic background also complicates attempts to use public events and photographs in the evaluation of remote memory (Levin et al., 1982).

In summary, closed-head injury can cause a variety of memory deficits, which include retrograde and anterograde, or posttraumatic, amnesia. These memory deficits can be affected from a variety of modalities, depending on which fiber tracts in the brain are disrupted.

Korsakoff's Syndrome and Wernicke's Disease

These disorders have historically been considered separately. More recently, however, they have been described as representing different components of the same disease. Talland (1969) described six primary symptoms of the Korsakoff-Wernicke disease complex:

1. Anterograde amnesia—these individuals are unable to form new memories. A common consequence is that these individuals are often disoriented to time and place.
2. Retrograde amnesia—these persons exhibit faulty old memories.
3. Confabulation—these individuals will fabricate stories about the past rather than admit they cannot remember. Their stories may be based, in part, on past events and thus may be difficult to detect unless one has access to an independent source to confirm the accuracy of the recollection.
4. Meager content in conversation—these persons say very little spontaneously in conversation. This may be due to their amnesia and/or deficits in the frontal cortex.
5. Lack of insight—patients are often unaware of their own memory deficits.
6. Apathy—these individuals often exhibit indifference to their surroundings and are often unable to complete an ongoing task. They lose interest in most activities rather quickly (Kolb & Whishaw, 1980).

These previous symptoms are all observed in individuals who otherwise appear quite normal. They often have normal IQs, are alert, appear relatively motivated, and generally lack other neurological signs (Kolb & Whishaw, 1980). However, these individuals do not suffer severe memory deficits which cannot be reversed.

Dementias

While the aging process is associated with some declines in various cognitive abilities, these declines are qualitatively different from the declines seen in the various dementing illnesses (Goldstein & Shelly, 1975; MacInnes, Gillen, Golden, Graber, Cole, Uhl, & Greenhouse, 1983). There are numerous causes of dementia, the most common forms being Alzheimer's disease and multi-infarct dementia. Other nonreversible dementias include Pick's disease, dementia associated with Parkinson's disease, and Jakob-Creutzfeldt's disease. The classic hallmark of dementia is memory loss. Recent memory tends to deteriorate, while immediate recall can be quite good. Retention of more distant memories is more well preserved; however, as the dementing illness progresses, distant memories are also significantly impaired (Russell, 1981).

Amnesia Following Electroconvulsive Treatment

This technique is still employed in the treatment of severe intractable depression. Temporary memory impairment is a common consequence of electroconvulsive treatment (ECT). The particular variation of ECT employed will produce differential memory disturbances. For example, ECT is often given unilaterally. Memory functions associated with the hemisphere shocked are the most affected. If the right hemisphere is shocked, then nonverbal memory is more affected; if the left hemisphere is shocked, then verbal memory is more affected. The duration and intensity of the ECT affect both the extent and recovery period of the memory disturbance. The effect of a single ECT treatment is to produce confusion and disorientation that lasts several minutes. There is a temporary retrograde amnesia that gradually subsides, except for a permanent loss of a few seconds just prior to the ECT (Patterson, Lawler, & Rochester, 1978). During the brief period of confusion, the individual also suffers anterograde amnesia. There appears to be a total recovery from this procedure in approximately one hour (Russell, 1981).

Transient Global Amnesia

This is a syndrome in which the major symptoms are anterograde amnesia, with some retrograde amnesia. The onset is usually sudden, with some retrograde amnesia, no prodromal symptoms, and no apparent cause. There may be some confusion and disorientation of time and place, while most other cognitive functions are relatively unimpaired. The course of transient global amnesia is usually several hours, although it has been reported to last several days in some rare cases. Initially, the individual may exhibit mental clouding, manifested by some atypical behavior such as repeating the same questions and complaining of memory difficulties. The transient global amnesia usually ends rather abruptly. However, there can be some spotty periods of memory until the syndrome ends. Recovery is usually complete. There is usually some memory gap for the time of the episode, though this may shrink to some extent over time (Russell, 1981).

The etiology of transient amnesia is not known with any certainty. Russell (1981) suggests that the most likely cause is cerebral vascular in nature, for example, transient ischemic attacks. If the basilar or both of the posterior cerebral arteries are temporarily partially occluded, then the hippocampus and other structures can be compromised bilaterally. The hippocampus and/or other limbic system structures have often been associated with memory functions (Kolb & Whishaw, 1980). Another bit of evidence suggesting that transient global amnesia may be vascular in nature is that it often occurs in older adults with evidence of cerebral vascular disease (Russell, 1981).

Another possible etiology, particularly in younger adults, is temporal lobe epilepsy. A bilateral temporal discharge could produce the type of memory loss associated with transient global amnesia. Finally, hypoglycemia has also been suggested as another possible etiology for this disorder. While the cause is still not totally understood, the symptoms revolve around the inability to consolidate memory for some brief period of time (Russell, 1981).

DIFFERENTIAL DIAGNOSES

A variety of psychological and neuropsychological conditions may initially present as a memory disorder. Differential diagnoses include dissociative or hysterical amnesia, depression, malingering, somatization disorder, disorders of arousal, and attention and frontal lobe disorders.

Dissociative, or Hysterical, Amnesia

This is a loss of memory for emotional reasons with no known organic basis. For example, an individual may suffer an emotional trauma that is difficult for him/her to deal with effectively. The unconscious may refuse to accept the events, and an extreme form of denial is employed that results in memory and/ or identity loss for a variable period of time, from hours to years. This is often labeled a fugue state.

As Russell (1981) notes, although the theoretical distinction between an organic memory is clear, it is often difficult to separate the two in practice. There is no neuropsychological test battery or neurological test that alone can distinguish between transient global amnesia and a functional memory loss. Russell (1981) suggests that the best approach involves a combination of neuropsychological tests and tests of emotions, such as the Minnesota Multiphasic Personality Inventory (MMPI). Such combinations of tests can be helpful in determining the relative contributions of organic and emotional components to an individual's memory problems.

Depression

Memory and concentration problems, along with sleep disturbance, appetite changes, and alterations in mood, are often seen in depression and are diagnostic of this disorder. In such situations, a memory disturbance may be viewed as being symptomatic. (It is also recognized that severe depression may result in biochemical changes that compromise the brain's ability to function normally). Conversely, a depressive condition may represent a psychological reaction to the realization that one is no longer able to function in an adequate manner. In these situations, the depression is symptomatic of an underlying organic condition. The distinction between these two conditions is quite important, since they dictate very different treatment approaches.

From the above discussion, it is clear that symptoms of depression can often confound the assessment of memory functions. This is a problem that is commonly experienced in the assessment of the elderly. Elderly depressed patients, for example, often do not report the common symptoms of depression associated with younger adults. Their only complaint may be of memory problems. The inexperienced clinician might focus only on the assessment of memory and, indeed, discern short-term memory difficulties in such an individual. If the depression is treated, however, the short-term memory difficulties might also remit. If the clinician focuses only on the memory aspect of the assessment, it is possible to misdiagnose an elderly patient as having a progressive dementing illness when the problem is really depression. This last kind of assessment error can have a profound impact on the life of an individual so diagnosed.

Malingering

To diagnose a patient as malingering, one must be able to demonstrate that the memory complaints are for some type of secondary gain and that they are conscious in nature. Given the inherent complexity of memory, and the general level of understanding that most individuals have regarding this process, it is unlikely that a subject could successfully feign a memory disorder for an extended period of time. Whenever there is a question of malingering, neuropsychological and psychological testing should prove to be quite helpful in making a differential diagnosis. Claims of isolated memory disturbance, however, are the most difficult to disprove, and the diagnosis of malingering should only be made after all plausible explanations can be ruled out (e.g., temporal lobe epilepsy).

Somatization Disorders

Short-term memory problems, headaches, and stomach problems are just some of the common complaints voiced by subjects who are often diagnosed late as having a somatization disorder. These subjects typically present with complaints that are vague and difficult to document. As noted in the above discussion on hysterical amnesia and depression, a combination of psychological and neuropsychological testing is helpful in making such a differential diagnosis. Self-report inventories, such as the MMPI, and projective tests, such as the Rorschach, are often useful in such cases. Formalized memory testing typically fails to support the client's perception of memory impairment unless the client concomitantly presents with significant levels of anxiety or depression, which may compromise the patient's ability to perform adequately.

Disorders of Attention and Arousal

Disorders of the reticular activating system (RAS) can result in an inability to maintain sufficient cortical arousal. Neuropsychological functioning in such individuals therefore tends to be globally impaired. As the patient's level of consciousness may vary quite significantly across testings, so may the pattern of deficits demonstrated by the patient. The delineation of specific deficits in such cases should therefore be avoided, since such deficits are only a manifestation of the client's underlying arousal disorder.

Numerous symptoms have been associated with frontal lobe lesions. Of importance to the following discussion of memory functioning is the observation that frontal lobe patients often demonstrate an impaired ability to organize information in a useful or meaningful manner. In severe cases, the patient's presentation may be that of a memory disorder in which daily events become isolated occurrences that are not interrelated to any long-term plan or goal. An illustrative case study of such a patient is reported by Robbins (1985a). The role of the frontal lobes in memory will be discussed in greater detail later in this chapter.

LOCALIZATION AND NEUROPSYCHOLOGICAL DEFICITS

Research indicates that different aspects of memory functioning are disrupted under a variety of clinical conditions. In functional disorders such as severe depression, for example, deficits are usually only seen on tests of immediate memory and learning (Henry, Weingartner, & Murphy, 1973; Sternberg & Jarvik, 1976). In contrast, neurologically based disorders may manifest in a variety of patterns.

A synopsis of the literature on memory impairment and localization is provided below. It is important to note that although there has been an attempt to associate different areas of the neocortex with different types of memory functioning (e.g., parietal lobe is equated with STM), the conclusions based on this research are tentative. Luria's concept of a functional system, to be discussed later, would seem to offer the most parsimonious explanation for such findings.

Parietal Lobe

Warrington and Weiskrantz (1968, 1973) maintain that there is evidence that the parietal lobe is involved in STM. For example, left parietal temporal lesions impair the ability to recall strings of digits (Kolb & Whishaw, 1980). Whereas the left parietal-temporal region is involved primarily in processing verbal material, the right parietal-temporal region is involved primarily in processing nonverbal material.

Temporal Lobe

Lesions of the temporal lobes are associated with deficits in LTM (Meyer & Yates, 1955). Left temporal lobe damage often impairs the recall of verbal material, whether presented visually or aurally (Blakemore & Falconer, 1967; Meyer & Yates, 1955; Milner, 1958) and regardless of whether retention is tested by recognition or recall (Milner & Kimura, 1964). In contrast, lesions of the right temporal lobe result in impaired recall of nonverbal material, such as geometric drawings, faces, tunes, and similar material, while verbal skills remain intact (Kolb & Whishaw, 1980; Shankweiler, 1966). Milner (1962) notes that such subjects may be poor at analyzing changes in melodic patterns, although they can discriminate pitch. Subjects may also be poor at the recall and recognition of recurring nonsense figures (Kimura, 1963; Milner, 1968b). See Kolb and Whishaw (1980) for an excellent summary of the effects of left or right temporal lobectomies on various tests of memory.

Unlike parietal lobe lesions, temporal lobe lesions do not disturb the immediate recall of material, such as strings of digits. The temporal and parietal lobes, therefore, appear to have complementary rather than redundant roles in memory. *Frontal – memory for recency*

Frontal lobe lesions do not generally interfere with the long-term storage of material. However, a function that is mediated by the frontal lobes is the memory for recency. Subjects with frontal lobe lesions show a deficit in the ability to remember the order of events, although the memory of the events themselves remain intact (Prisko, 1963; Corsi, 1972).

From the literature reviewed, it would appear that certain memory processes are lateralized between the two hemispheres. In general, the left hemisphere controls the acquisition and reproduction of verbal material, while the right hemisphere reflects the learning and retention of nonverbal material. Researchers have also attempted even more refined localization, identifying certain memory deficits within certain areas of the brain. Deficits have typically been defined as being either modality specific or material specific.

From the literature reviewed there appears to be significant support for the theory that brain damage is not a unitary construct. Research findings are consistent with Luria's observation that a localized brain lesion in any one area of the brain may disrupt any number of functional systems in a variety of deficits. Studies by Kear-Colwell (1973) and Black (1973) support Luria's observations that brain damage is not unitary. Black's research, in particular, has shown that very similar types of brain insults can result quite differently in performances on tests of memory functioning.

Our discussion to this point has outlined the complexities of the study of mnestic processes and would argue for the employment of assessment procedures that recognize the multidimensionality of memory.

FUNCTION OF CLINICAL MEMORY TESTING

Russell (1981) outlines five functions of clinical memory testing. It (1) contributes to understanding the pattern of neurological deficits; (2) aids in the localization of damage; (3) assists in the diagnosis of a specific organic condition, since various kinds of memory are affected differently by different kinds of neurological conditions [e.g., in Korsakoff's syndrome, recent memory is severely impaired, while immediate memory is less affected (Barbizet, 1970)]; (4) assists in rehabilitation and management; and (5) is vital for research, that is, it has proven helpful in clarifying our understanding of such processes as LTM versus STM. Psychometric testing also provides a methodology for studying such specific issues as forgetting, the differentiation of storage and retrieval problems, and input and output modality differences as studied by parallel techniques.

It is not within the scope of this chapter to provide a comprehensive review of the available test instruments for memory assessment. It is clear, however, that although there has been a proliferation of experimental and clinical tests developed for assessing specific areas of memory functioning [e.g., the Benton Visual Retention Test (Benton, 1963, 1974) and the Memory for Designs Test (Graham and Kendall, 1960)], only a limited number of test batteries have been developed with the intent of providing more than just a cursory evaluation of mnestic processes. Examples of these memory batteries include the Wechsler Memory Scale (Wechsler, 1945; Wechsler & Stone, 1972), the Wechsler Memory Scale–Revised (Russell, 1975), the Williams Scale for the Measurement of Memory (Williams, 1968), the Guild Memory Test (Gilbert, Levee, & Catalano, 1971), the Memory Scale of the Luria–Nebraska Neuropsychological Battery (Golden, Purisch, & Hammeke, 1979), and the Randt Memory Test (Randt, Brown, & Osborne, 1980). A review of the relative strengths and weaknesses of these batteries can be found in Erickson and Scott (1977) and in Robbins (1985b).

It is clear that, to date, there is no universally accepted battery of memory functioning. The ideal battery, however, would provide a comprehensive assessment of memory, including tasks that: (1) are modality specific and representative of all areas of the brain; (2) assess a variety of memory functions, such as STM, LTM, consolidation, and episodic memory; (3) include a test of learning, preferably more than one trial or exposure in order to facilitate understanding of the learning process; (4) assess recall and recognition for both verbal and nonverbal materials; and (5) should be fairly independent tests of memory and not correlated so highly with tests of intelligence as to be redundant. Similarly, the ideal memory battery should possess good psychometric properties, should be based upon a unified theory of brain functioning, should assess both verbal and nonverbal memory, and should provide separately normed subtests for each area of mnestic processing.

A NEUROPSYCHOLOGICAL MODEL OF MEMORY FUNCTIONING

A comprehensive theoretical model of memory, which appears to offer promise for the neuropsychological assessment of memory dysfunction, has been proposed by A. R. Luria (1976). An integral component of Luria's (1976) theory of brain functioning in general, and memory in specific, is the concept of functional systems. According to Luria's theory, the functional units of the brain serve to (1) maintain and modify cortical tone, (2) receive, analyze, and integrate sensory information, and (3) organize, evaluate, and execute voluntary behavior.

The first functional unit is composed primarily of the reticular activating system. Attention and cortical tone are regulated by this unit. The second functional unit analyzes and integrates sensory information from the first functional unit into perceptions. While the first functional unit activates the appropriate cortical areas, which selectively attend to relevant incoming sensory information, the second functional unit integrates this information into complex perceptions. The third functional unit, corresponding to the parietal area, is then charged with the function of organizing voluntary behavioral programs. Sensory impressions are thus translated into meaningful actions.

Although these three functional units appear to be distinct and anatomically separate, Luria argues that complex psychological functions are not. The integrated action of all three units is necessary for the successful working of a single neuropsychological ability. Therefore a functional system is perceived as being the aggregation of several basic cognitive skills that, when combined, make up a complex neuropsychological ability. Each separate area contributes some elementary component to the complex ability. It is the concerted interaction of several cognitive areas that comprise any complex neuropsychological ability.

It should be noted that any one area of the brain may be involved in a number of functional systems. Therefore damage to a specific area may result in the disruption of a number of functional systems and the concomitant neuropsychological ability associated with this area.

In terms of memory functioning, neuropsychological deficits may be categorized as being modality specific (auditory, visual, or sensorimotor) or global. Modality-specific deficits represent gnostic dysfunctions resulting from a disruption of the relevant functional systems. Global deficits, however, occur because of a disruption of the basic cognitive functions that underlie the storage and retrieval processes of memory. All sensory modalities are therefore affected. These two types of memory deficits are best explained within the context of Luria's conceptualization of the functional unit.

Modality-specific memory problems are a result of damage to the second functional unit. When the reception and integration of a specific sensory modality is disrupted, memory for that modality is affected. However, it is important to note that memory deficits are not generally restricted to one modality.

Global memory problems encompass deficits in all aspects of memory, including all sensory modalities as well as short- and long-term phases of recall. These global problems arise from dysfunction of the first and third functional units. Damage to the limbic and reticular activating systems give rise to difficulties in the registration of sensory information and in the selective attention to the relevant information.

From this discussion, Luria's theory of memory is seen as a dynamic process. Memory is not a separate neuropsychological ability, but an integrative functioning of the entire brain. The level of cortical tone and arousal, the stability of intention and behavioral programs, as well as the integrity of gnostic activity, are variables that mediate this process.

LURIA-WISCONSIN MEMORY BATTERY (LWMB)

The Luria-Wisconsin Memory Battery (Robbins, 1985b) was developed in response to the need for both a theoretically derived and a comprehensive test battery. The LWMB, which allows for both a qualitative and quantitative assessment of memory functioning, is based upon Luria's (1976) theory of brain functioning. The LWMB was developed as a means of standardizing and operationalizing Luria's neuropsychological investigative technique.

Ten general scales of mnestic functioning make up the LWMB: (1) Audio-Verbal Retention, (2) Word and Design List Learning, (3) Haptic Retention, (4) Visual Retention, (5) Motor Response Learning, (6) Visual Learning, (7) Kinesthetic Learning, (8) Sentences, (9) Stories, (10) Indirect Memorizing. Each of these areas is assessed under the conditions of immediate recall, delayed recall, and following the presentation of heterogeneous and homogenous interference procedures. Episodic-incidental memory is also evaluated. An optional Intermediate Memory scale is available, as well.

Preliminary research in terms of reliability, validity, and discriminative ability of the LWMB has been quite promising. The major strength of the LWMB over its predecessors is, first, that it is based upon a comprehensive theory of brain functioning. Second, the type of tests and procedures employed in this battery have been developed using both experimental and clinical research. Third, the LWMB is based on the conceptualization that memory impairment is not a unitary function. A variety of mnestic processes are evaluated under a variety of conditions. Similarly, an attempt is made to differentiate verbal and nonverbal memory. Fourth, separate normative data for individual subscales are provided. Fifth, learning, retention, recognition, and recall are each evaluated within the LWMB.

SUMMARY

From the present discussion it is clear that memory represents a dynamic and complex neuropsychological process that is composed of numerous stages. It is apparent, however, that many clinicians fail to recognize the inherent complexities in evaluating this neuropsychological process. This problem appears to be due in part to the fact that, at first glance, the assessment of memory functions seems simplistic and rather straightforward. For example, the assessment of a gross-memory disturbance may be done in a similar manner as the mental status exam. That is, the subject may be evaluated for orientation, long-term memory, mental control, and remembering isolated series of three-to-five words with interference. Such gross assessments, however, provide only the most rudimentary indication that a memory disorder may or may not exist. Evaluations of this type do not delineate the parameters of the memory disturbance. It is of clinical importance, for example, to distinguish between the parent's ability to recall information versus his/her ability to recognize this same information. Similarly, it is important to assess the input and output differences between different sensory modalities as related to memory functioning. Finally, immediate, intermediate, and remote memory should be evaluated.

In addition, the brief assessment of memory can lead the clinician to erroneous conclusions if not followed by more extensive evaluation. For example, confounding factors in the assessment of memory (e.g., depression, anxiety, aphasia, hearing loss) might be overlooked. Thus, any evaluation of memory by the family practice physician should be considered a screening test, not a diagnostic evaluation.

Neuropsychologists have available numerous tests that have been developed for assessing different aspects of memory functioning. Most tests developed to assess memory are not practical for general clinical use by a physician because they involve an impractical amount of administration time (Lezak, 1983). A limited number of memory batteries have been developed as well, with the goal of providing a more extensive evaluation of memory processes.

In conclusion, it is important to reiterate that an essential aspect of recognition of or treatment for any memory disorder entails that an adequate assessment of the patient be performed so that not only the etiology of the memory disturbance can be determined, but the parameters of the dysfunction as well. Given the inherent complexity of the study of memory, as well as the potential ramifications of a memory disorder, appropriate consultation should be sought when there is any question as to whether a pathological process or condition exists after an initial screening assessment by the physician.

REFERENCES

Albert, M. S., Butters, N., & Brandt, J. (1981a). Development of remote memory loss in patients with Huntington's disease. *Journal of Clinical Neuropsychology, 3*, 1–12.
Albert, M. S., Butters, N., & Brandt, J. (1981b). Patterns of remote memory in amnesic and demented patients. *Archives of Neurology, 38*, 495–500.

Albert, M. S., Butters, N., & Levin, J. (1979). Temporal gradients in the retrograde amnesia of patients with alcoholic Korsakoff's disease. *Archives of Neurology, 36,* 221-216.

Atkinson, R. C., & Shiffrin, R. M. (1971). The control of short-term memory. *Scientific American, 225,* 82-90.

Baddeley, A. D. (1976). *The psychology of memory.* New York: Basic Books.

Barbizet, J. (1970). *Human memory and its pathology.* San Francisco: W. H. Freeman.

Benton, A. L. (1963). *The Revised Visual Retention Test.* New York: Psychological Corporation.

Benton, A. L. (1974). *The Revised Visual Retention Test* (4th ed.). New York: Psychological Corporation.

Black, F. W. (1973). Cognitive and memory performance in subjects with damage secondary to penetrating missile wounds and closed head injury. *Journal of Clinical Psychology, 29,* 441-442.

Blakemore, C., & Falconer, M. A. (1967). Long term effects of anterior temporal lobectomy on certain cognitive functions. *Journal of Neurology, Neurosurgery and Psychiatry, 30,* 364-367.

Broadbent, D. E. (1969). Communication models for memory. In G. A. Talland & N. C. Waugh (Eds.), *The pathology of memory* (pp. 167-171). New York: Academic Press.

Brown, G. G. (1978, August). *Rehearsal and recall in Korsakoff and leucotomy patients.* Paper presented at the annual convention of the American Psychological Association, Toronto, Canada.

Butters, N., & Albert, M. S. (1982). Processes underlying failures to recall remote events. In L. S. Cermak (Ed.), *Human memory* and *amnesia* (pp. 257-273). Hillsdale, NJ: Lawrence Erlbaum Associates.

Corsi, P. M. (1972). *Human memory and the medial temporal region of the brain.* Unpublished doctoral dissertation, McGill University, Montreal.

Craik, F. I. M. (1979). Human memory. *Annual Review of Psychology, 30,* 63-102.

Craik, F. I. M., & Lockhart, R. S. (1972). Levels of processing: A framework for memory research. *Journal of Verbal Learning and Verbal Behavior, 11,* 671-684.

Drachman, D. A., & Arbit, J. A. (1966). Memory and the hippocampal complex. II. Is memory a multiple process? *Archives of Neurology, 15,* 52-61.

Erickson, R. C., & Scott, M. L. (1977). Clinical memory testing: A review. *Psychological Bulletin, 84* (6), 1130-1149.

Eysenck, M. (1978). Levels of processing: A critique. *British Journal of Psychology, 69,* 157-169.

Flexser, A. J., & Tulving, E. (1978). Retrieval independence in recognition and recall. *Psychological Review, 85,* 153-171.

Gilbert, J. G., Levee, R. F., & Catalano, F. L. (1971). *Guild Memory Test manual.* Newark, NJ: Unico National Mental Health Research Center.

Golden, C. J., Purisch, A., & Hammeke, T. A. (1979). *The Luria-Nebraska Neuropsychological Battery, a manual for clinical and experimental uses.* Lincoln: University of Nebraska Press.

Goldstein, G., & Shelly, C. H. (1975). Similarities and differences between psychological deficit in aging and brain damage. *Journal of Gerontology, 30,* 448-455.

Graham, F. R., & Kendall, B. S. (1960). Memory for Designs Test: Revised general manual. *Perceptual and Motor Skills, II,* 147.

Henry, G. M., Weingartner, H., & Murphy, D. L. (1973). The influence of affective states and psychoactive drugs on verbal learning and memory. *American Journal of Psychiatry, 130,* 966-971.

Kear-Colwell, J. J. (1973). The structure of the Wechsler Memory Scale and its relationship to "brain-damage." *British Journal of Social and Clinical Psychology, 12*, 384–392.

Kesner, R. (1973). A neural system analysis of memory storage and retrieval. *Psychological Bulletin, 80*, 188–203.

Kimura, D. (1963). Right temporal lobe damage. *Archives of Neurology, 8*, 264–271.

Kolb, B., & Whishaw, I. Q. (1980). *Fundamentals of human neuropsychology.* San Francisco: W. H. Freeman and Company.

Levin, H. S., Benton, A. L., & Grossman, R. G. (1982). *Neurobehavioral consequences of closed head injury.* New York: Oxford University Press.

Levin, H. S., Grossman, R. G., & Kelly, P. J. (1977). Assessment of long-term memory in brain-damaged patients. *Journal of Consulting and Clinical Psychology, 45*, 684–688.

Lezak, M. D. (1983). *Neuropsychological Assessment* (2nd ed.). New York: Oxford University Press.

Luria, A. R. (1971). Memory disturbances in local brain lesions. *Neuropsychologia, 9*, 367.

Luria, A. R. (1973). *The working brain.* New York: Basic Books.

Luria, A. R. (1976). *The neuropsychology of memory.* Washington, DC: V. H. Winston & Sons.

MacInnes, W. D., Gillen, R. W., Golden, C. J., Graber, B., Cole, J. K., Uhl, H. S. M., & Greenhouse, A. H. (1983). Aging and performance on the Luria-Nebraska Neuropsychological Battery. *International Journal of Neuroscience, 19*, 179–190.

McGaugh, J. L. (1966). Time dependent processes in memory storage. *Science, 153*, 1351–1358.

McGaugh, J. L., & Herz, M. J. (1972). *Memory consolidation.* San Francisco: Albion.

Meyer, V., & Yates, A. J. (1955). Intellectual changes following temporal lobectomy for psychomotor epilepsy. *Journal of Neurology, Neurosurgery, and Psychiatry, 18*, 44–52.

Miller, G. A. (1956). The magical number seven, plus or minus two: Some limits on our capacity for processing information. *Psychological Review, 63*, 81–97.

Milner, B. (1958). Psychological defects produced by temporal lobe excision. *Research Publications of the Association for Research in Nervous and Mental Disease, 36*, 244–257.

Milner, B. (1959). The memory defect in bilateral hippocampal lesions. *Psychological Research Report, 11*, 43–52.

Milner, B. (1962). Laterality effects in audition. In V. B. Mountcastle (Ed.), *Interhemispheric relations and cerebral dominance* (pp. 177–195). Baltimore: John Hopkins University Press.

Milner, B. (1968a). Disorders of memory after brain lesions in man. Preface: Material-specific and generalized memory loss. *Neuropsychologia, 6*, 175–179.

Milner, B. (1968b). Visual recognition and recall after right temporal lobe excision in man. *Neuropsychologia, 6*, 191–209.

Milner, B. (1978). Clues to the cerebral organization of memory. In P. A. Buser & Rougeal-Buser (Eds.), *Cerebral correlates of conscious experience* (pp. 139–153). (INSERM Symposium No. 6). Amsterdam: Elsevier/North Holland Biomedical Press.

Milner, B., Corkin, S., & Teuber, H. L. (1968). Further analysis of the hippocampal amnestic syndrome: 14 year follow-up study of H. M. *Neuropsychologia, 6*, 215–244.

Milner, B., & Kimura, D. (1964, April). *Dissociable visual learning defects after unilateral temporal lobectomy in man.* Paper read at the 35th Annual Meeting of the Eastern Psychological Association, Philadelphia, PA.

Norman, D. A. (1973). What have the animal experiments taught us about human memory? In J. A. Deutsch (Ed.), *The physiological basis of memory* (pp. 397–417). New York and London: Academic Press.

Patterson, K. E., Lawler, E., & Rochester, S. R. (1978). Retrograde amnesia from electrovulsive therapy. *Neuropsychological, 16,* 91–97.

Postman, L. (1975). Verbal learning and memory. *Annual Review of Psychology, 26,* 291–335.

Prisko, L. (1963). Short-term memory in focal cerebral damage. Unpublished doctoral dissertation, McGill University, Montreal.

Randt, C. T., Brown, E. R., & Osborne, D. P. (1980). A memory test for longitudinal measurement of mild to moderate deficiences. *Clinical Neuropsychology, 2,* 184–194.

Ribot, T. (1982). *Diseases of memory: An essay in the positive psychology.* New York: Appleton.

Robbins, D. E. (1985a, May). *Forensic issues symposium: A case of a frontal-subcortical disorder.* Paper presented at the third annual conference on the Luria–Nebraska Neuropsychological Battery, Omaha, NE.

Robbins, D. E. (1985b). *The Luria–Wisconsin Memory Battery: A neuropsychological assessment of memory dysfunction.* Unpublished doctoral dissertation, University of Wisconsin, Milwaukee.

Russell, E. W. (1975). A multiple scoring method for the assessment of complex memory functions. *Journal of Consulting and Clinical Psychology, 42* (6), 800–809.

Russell, E. W. (1981). The pathology and clinical examination of memory. In S. Filskov & T. Boll (Eds.), *Handbook of clinical neuropsychology* (pp. 287–319). New York: Wiley.

Russell, W. R. (1971). *The traumatic amnesias.* New York: Oxford University Press.

Sakitt, B. (1976). Iconic memory. *Psychological Review, 83,* 257–276.

Shankweiler, D. (1966). Effects of temporal lobe damage on perception of dichotically presented melodies. *Journal of Comparative and Physiological Psychology, 62,* 115.

Shiffrin, R. M. (1973). Information persistence in short-term memory. *Journal of Experimental Psychology, 100,* 39–49.

Shiffrin, R. M., & Schneider, W. (1977). Controlled and automatic human information processing: II. Perceptual learning, automatic attending, and a general theory. *Psychological Review, 84,* 127–190.

Squire, L. R., & Slater, P. C. (1975). Forgetting in very long-term memory as assessed by an improved questionnaire taxonomy. *Journal of Experimental Psychology: Human Language and Memory, 104,* 50–54.

Sternberg, D. E., & Jarvik, M. E. (1976). Memory functions in depression: Improvement with antidepressant medication. *Archives of General Psychiatry, 33,* 219–224.

Talland, G. A. (1969). *The pathology of memory.* New York: Academic Press.

Tulving, E. (1972). Episodic and semantic memory. In E. Tulving & W. Donaldson (Eds.), *Organization of memory* (pp. 381–403). New York: Academic Press.

Warrington, E. K., & Sanders, H. I. (1971). The fate of old memories. *Quarterly Journal of Experimental Psychology, 23,* 432–442.

Warrington, E. K., & Weiskrantz, L. (1968). New method of testing long-term retention with special reference to amnesic patients. *Nature, 217,* 972–974.

Warrington, E. K., & Weiskrantz, L. (1973). An analysis of short-term and long-term memory defects in man. In J. A. Deutsch (Ed.), *The physiological basis of memory* (pp. 365-395). New York: Academic Press.

Wechsler, D. (1945). *The Wechsler Memory Scale.* New York: Psychological Corporation.

Wechsler, D., & Stone, C. (1972). *Manual: Memory Scale.* New York: Psychological Corporation.

Williams, M. (1968). The measurement of memory in clinical practice. *British Journal of Social and Clinical Psychology, 7,* 19-34.

10

Neuropsychological Assessment of Sensory and Physically Impaired Patients

Dennis P. Swiercinsky

Neuropsychological assessment of patients with a major sensory or physical limitation presents special concerns for appropriateness, selection, and interpretation of testing instruments. Most neuropsychological tests have been constructed for sighted and hearing persons, and norms reflect this assumption. Similarly, tests for laterality of hemisphere impairment are inappropriate with those patients exhibiting peripheral impairments, for example, paralysis of an arm or hand sustained independently of central nervous system etiology.

Three groups of special patients are discussed here: those with major physical, visual, and auditory impairments. Issues that apply to all special patient groups relative to appropriate test instruments and the use of norms are discussed first.

There is probably no such thing as a *routine* neuropsychological assessment, owing to the complexity and multiplicity of psychometric, procedural, and patient factors that contribute to test results. Thorough neuropsychology is more an art than a science, in that integrating these factors simultaneously has not, as yet, been reduced to scientific formulae. The rules for deriving a comprehensive neuropsychological status description are unspecified. (The best we have been able to accomplish are formulae for considering only a few factors, such as have been derived from multiple-discriminant analysis research.) Examining the sensory or physically impaired patient becomes an even more imposing task, since many of the traditional neuropsychological tests are inappropriate or their results must be interpreted much differently than for the nonimpaired patient. Not only are the norms of little direct value for inferring the presence or absence of brain impairment, but most clinicians have had limited experience with such patients, making qualitative inferences from test performance difficult as well.

The purpose of this chapter is to offer both general guidelines and appropriate test procedures or modifications to use when examining the peripherally impaired client. The term *peripherally impaired* is used here to include all types of special patients mentioned above for whom the impairment is not considered merely a symptom of an organic brain dysfunction. Rather, the impairment is peripheral—albeit essential to consider in determining procedures—when performing a neuropsychological assessment, whether for neurological or behavioral diagnostic interest. In other words, the sensory or physical impairment is peripheral to the context of evaluating the brain's condition.

With the introduction of many new assessment instruments and batteries in neuropsychology within the last few years, questions of validity and standards for test development and publication are frequently raised. Whenever there is a proliferation of techniques, all purported to do essentially the same thing, one must question why the wheel needs re-inventing so many times. In neuropsychology, as in clinical psychology generally, this may reflect lack of a sound theoretical base as well as haphazard standardization and development of measurement techniques. The type of patient discussed in this chapter complicates matters further, since there are virtually no tests specifically created and normed for this group. Consequently, other tests must be adapted. Before focusing specifically on the assessment of special patients, then, it is useful to reflect briefly on the state of the art in neuropsychology to underscore the need for conceptual understanding of psychosocial-neurobehavioral relationships and the limitations our assessment techniques place on evaluating these relationships in a single parent.

ART AND SCIENCE IN NEUROPSYCHOLOGY

For neither the routine patient nor the one presenting special assessment considerations (such as the blind or deaf) is there a quantitative test or battery in neuropsychology that can yield a formulation of the complexities of neurobehavioral interactions and consequences independent of the clinician's experience, theoretical understanding, and ability to integrate divergent data into a comprehensive description. Although an actuarial personality test can tell a clinician how strongly a patient matches criterion clinical groups along a few dimensions, it requires clinical judgment to derive a practical and comprehensive statement about the unique individual. A wealth of other qualitative and impressionistic data must be employed, the rules for which are only loosely defined at best.

Neuropsychology has developed largely as an empirical but atheoretical effort. Tests demonstrated as sensitive to brain damage are administered, and the extent to which these tests collectively match responses by independently confirmed brain-damaged patients provides data for diagnosing the presence or absence of intracranial pathology. This actuarial method has been refined somewhat by using criterion groups whose location of damage is known so that test scores can then be identified as sensitive to a particular location or kind of brain damage. Unfortunately, the clinical application is usually lengthy, the tests retain considerable susceptibility to error variance, and the original criterion groups have been notoriously questionable regarding their homogeneity. This actuarial technique has characterized the development and application of the Halstead-Reitan Battery (Reitan & Davison, 1974) and its many modifications (e.g., Russell, Neuringer, & Goldstein, 1970; Swiercinsky, 1978). Attempts have been made to streamline testing, applying a more or less theoretical model to the selection or construction of tests, and to quantify behaviors, previously considered only qualitative, observed during testing. This latter approach characterizes the Luria-Nebraska Neuropsychological Battery (Golden, Hammeke, & Purisch, 1980). The hosts of individual tests, as opposed to batteries, for "organicity" represent attempts to isolate rather general (factorially complex) behavioral characteristics seen in many forms of brain impairment, to quantify these, and to validate the predictability of the scores for heterogeneous groups of brain-damaged persons and normal persons.

It is unfortunate that so much of what used to characterize neuropsychology—blind prediction of brain damage based on individual test scores or patterns of scores—continues to condition our thinking. Brain damage is much too complex a concept to be predicted blindly, based on one or a few test measures. Systematic combinations of test scores (as in the Halstead Impairment Index, or from factor scores, for example) attempt to account simultaneously for greater information but still fall short of being anywhere near complete. Nowhere is this approach more obviously inappropriate than when using the familiar neuropsychological tests or batteries to work with sensory or physically impaired patients. Not only are the norms useless for predicting blind diagnosis, but the presence of a physical or sensory disability adds considerable emotional and psychological (in addition to neurological) complexity to the behaviors elicited by structured tests.

Wright (1960) and Stubbins (1977), in their discussions of the thinking and emotional processes associated with a physical disability, make it abundantly clear that qualitative observations from testing do not always have the same meaning when used to describe the nondisabled patient, on whom the tests were standardized. For example, negativism in the recently disabled person can be an important part of mourning a physical loss, rather than evidence of an insidious frontal lobe degeneration. Thus a significant initial step in assessing a physically impaired patient is to appreciate the correlation of behaviors and attitudes with the emotional and psychological processes employed in coping with a disability or with the neuropathology of certain diseases. In addition to negativism, other characteristics that may be the product of either disability or disease include depression, attentional problems, denial (or other defensiveness), communicative resistance, disorientation in space (especially with the newly visually or hearing impaired), and amotivation. It is essential to make the distinction between emotional and neurological etiology. The point is that the psychological reaction to a physical or sensory disability must be understood prior to interpreting behaviors and test scores.

Deriving inferences from a typical neuropsychological assessment is a two-staged process. First, a global determination is made to determine whether there is central nervous system pathology. Second, a positive diagnosis is fine-tuned for understanding both neurostructural and functional consequences. This procedure is appropriate for all types of patients. An exception occurs when using normed tests or observing well-established patterns of behavioral symptoms that suggest neuropathology. Then the information must be considered for appropriateness and context, given a sensory or physical abnormality. Consider the following example.

Problems with abstract or conceptual reasoning are a well-documented symptom indicating almost any form, type, or location of brain damage. Presumably this results from an interruption in the complex and spatially diversified neural interconnections necessary to search and synthesize vast memories. Thus there is an interruption in the ability to relate current thinking on a topic to relevant memories about that topic. Such a neurologically complex function is disturbed in nearly any case of brain neuropathology. An individual who has been deaf all of his or her life will likely fail Proverb Interpretations miserably, whether the person is brain impaired or not. For similar reasons, such a person will most certainly fare poorly on a Word Similarities test (such as from the WAIS or WISC). Since the English language cannot rightly be considered native to the congenitally deaf, only those concept-reasoning tests that make minimum demands on language-structured thinking can be used. Even then, issues of social deprivation might be problematic. Thus, although such tests might be administered to a deaf patient, their usefulness must be considered in a much narrower context. Certainly they must not be used as a part of the first stage in the diagnosis. Without an appreciation of psychological processes and sociocultural/educational background, neuropsychological interpretations can be seriously biased.

In summary, a set of structured observations (i.e., obtained through empirical tests) is usually invaluable for deriving a standardized, normative-based judgment of a person's brain state. Simultaneous observation of process, as well as product, is essential to a complete evaluation. Then, assuming appropriate instruments have been selected in the first place, both the qualitative and quantitative data must be interpreted within the context of the special psychological, physical, and social characteristics relevant to the disability. Whereas this conceptualization of the neuropsychological evaluation process is appropriate for all patients, it is especially important in acknowledging the special problems of assessing the sensory or physically impaired patient.

USING NORMATIVE DATA

Debate has been spirited among neuropsychologists regarding the appropriateness of normative data in interpreting individual neuropsychological test profiles. Many of the more popular neuropsychological batteries, including the Luria-Nebraska and Halstead-Reitan, and various modifications, including the Russell, Neuringer, and Goldstein (1970) approach, rely rather extensively on norms to derive empirical predictions. This reliance on norms to make an initial diagnosis of the presence of a central nervous system lesion has been paramount in objective assessment.

The appropriate application of norms has been questioned repeatedly. Skepticism usually relates to the nature of the population from which the norms were derived in comparison with the patient to whom the norms are applied. The issue of how heterogeneous or homogeneous normative samples should be always confronts test constructers.

Regardless of the composition of normative samples, subjects contributing data to norms must always be able to participate in the testing that complies with the original adminstration standards for the tests. Thus, deaf individuals would not have been included in the norming of the Wechsler scales, hemiplegics in the norming of the Tactual Performance Test, or the visually impaired in the norming of spatial orientation tests. Thus, when considering standardized norms, it is always important to recognize the composition of the normative samples and to note how closely a particular client matches the characteristics of the normative group.

The use of norms that are not derived from the same types of subjects with whom the neuropsychologist is working does not necessarily invalidate the norms. It merely means that the reason for using the norms in the first place must be clearly understood. It is not inherently wrong to compare a patient who has a disability with patients who do not share the disability. But the extent to which the disability influences the normed behavior must be considered, and the purpose of the comparison must be appropriate.

ASSESSING THE PERIPHERALLY IMPAIRED PATIENT: GENERAL PRINCIPLES

Regardless of the specific peripheral disability a patient presenting for neuropsychological assessment may exhibit, at least five principles must be considered in the course of choosing appropriate neuropsychological tests and in interpreting their results.

Norms

The preceding discussion of appropriateness of norms suggests the first general principle. Norms based on the non-peripherally impaired are generally used when evaluating a patient's behavior to compare it with the behavior expected of a non-peripherally impaired patient. For example, a blind client who has been neuropsychologically evaluated and found to be only moderately brain impaired may still be evaluated for the appropriateness of his/her continued performance in an occupation. If the job requires the individual to navigate a rather large and spatially complex office building, then evaluation of the patient's visual-perceptual skills relative to his or her brain impairment would be essential. Aside from observing the natural environment, correct assessment of visuospatial reasoning would be difficult given the blindness. Such an instrument as the Tactual Performance Test from the Halstead–Reitan Battery might be an appropriate method for assessing one kind of spatial recognition and learning. Certainly such a test would be appropriate for evaluating the spatial skills of the patient whether blind or not. But the final stage in the usual procedures of the Tactual Performance Test—having the individual, with the blindfold removed, draw a picture of the formboard to evaluate spatial memory—would obviously be inappropriate. However, the blind patient's spatial memory, the practical question at hand, can still be assessed by having the individual trace, with his or her finger on a surface, the layout of the formboard in lieu of drawing a picture on paper. Thus, although it may be dangerous to use existing norms from the location and memory scores obtained with sighted individuals to evaluate the presence or absence of brain damage (or to use such a score in a summary impairment index), such a modality change would still be useful for evaluating the practical issue; and the use of existing norms might be helpful, since there are no other norms based on finger tracing and since the patient will be working with sighted persons.

In making modality changes in either test administration or response recording, norms must be used cautiously for inferring the presence or absence of brain injury. However, using those norms for inferences that do not bear on the etiological diagnosis per se may be the only source of comparison for evaluating functional capability where no other method exists. Individuals with peripheral injuries are often integrated into the normal work world, to the extent that any intracranial pathology will allow. In this context, understanding how the patient performs compared with people in general becomes relevant for predicting his or her ability to perform alongside others irrespective of their neurological impairment. This is the practical and safe application of norms for such patients.

Native Communication

Another general principle to consider is the patient's native communication. Individuals who have had visual impairments for a long time have probably relied on their auditory communication modality more than any other. Similarly, hearing-impaired individuals have probably relied on visuospatial communication rather than language-oriented or oral communication. Thus, the individual who has been visually impaired for a long time may do poorly on the Tactual Performance Test or modifications of any other spatially oriented test. Individuals who cannot hear and have thus developed their communication around a spatial symbolic system, through sign language for example, may not relate well to such language-oriented tests as Proverb Interpretation, Verbal Memory, Verbal Abstractions, or even vocabulary tests. Thus, the native communication modality, whether it is basically language-symbolic or visuospatial, must be considered in selecting tests or weighing the importance of their results.

Similarly, although not in the realm of communication, individuals with upper extremity limitations, the cause of which is ancillary to the assessment of current neuropsychological abilities, must be administered tests that do not assume bilateral dexterity. For example, the Block Design Test from the Wechsler scales clearly assumes bilateral dexterity. Many neuropsychologists have observed performance characteristics in patients completing the Block Design Test that suggest the nature of brain functioning. Most bilaterally dextrous individuals will use both hands in completing the Block Design and either work from left to right and top to bottom or will manipulate blocks symmetrically with both hands, the left working on the left side of the design and vice versa. The individual who is only unilaterally dextrous, through either amputation or some other peripheral injury of one limb, is forced to work in a nonsymmetrical fashion and hence may also be a little slower. Thus it is important to evaluate the use of norms and the observation of process more critically in such tests as the Block Design than in other spatial tests, such as the Raven Progressive Matrices, where a related neurofunctional characteristic is being assessed but where bilateral dexterity is certainly not an assumed factor.

In general, tests must not assume a realm of experience—whether the use of English, spatial navigation, or bilateral manipulation of objects—with which the patient is unfamiliar. Respecting the native capabilities and experiences of the patient helps prevent inference bias. Each test must be evaluated with this in mind.

Time Since Impairment

The length of time since the onset of a peripheral impairment has significant effects on psychological adjustment and the consequent reaction to neuropsychological testing. As mentioned earlier, an individual who is still undergoing significant adjustment to a disability, particularly one who is mourning for the recent loss of a function, may be only marginally attentive, somewhat negative, or noticeably defensive in learning to cope with the disability; such factors can complicate the interpretation of neuropsychological test results.

In the case of a congenital or early-age impairment, particularly blindness or deafness, there is some question about whether the brain develops in the normal manner with regard to the functional separateness of the cerebral hemispheres. There is a significant modality dependence; and elimination of, or a major reduction in, the availability of a modality will undoubtedly alter the functional development.

The left hemisphere, typically the language-dominant hemisphere, is auditorially dependent because that is how we first learn to use language. Congenitally hearing-impaired persons do not initially use a sound-symbolic language and use only a limited visual-symbolic language.

Right-hemisphere functions, typically spatial-constructional, are visually dependent. We learn to navigate space, to understand mechanical things, and to construct objects by sight, not by hearing or by language. Congenitally blind individuals learn language much more easily than the deaf because their initial exposure to language is more normal.

One of the methods for assessing brain functioning is to compare relative functional characteristics of the right and left hemispheres. This would usually be perfectly appropriate for motor and sensory tasks, but would be inappropriate, for the reasons suggested above, for assessing higher cognitive skills of deaf or blind individuals. Since the lateral functional pattern may be quite biased in the first place, due to modality impairment during formative years, examining cognitive functions stemming independently from the two hemispheres is also inappropriate. (Research is needed to evaluate the consequences of this brain-developmental abnormality on the motor and tactile systems.)

Socialization Background

For any patient undergoing a neuropsychological examination, the sociocultural background is considered in any interpretation of test findings. However, it is of particular importance in the peripherally impaired patient, because the nature of the disability may have produced subtle changes in social experiences that may not always be apparent. This is particularly the case if an individual with a peripheral impairment comes from a family where other members have peripheral impairments; this is sometimes the case among the hearing impaired, whose families might have a history of some cultural deprivation simply by virtue of the social isolation brought about by the communication limitation. This is true for any disability, but seems to be more prevalent for the sensory impaired, who are essentially cut off from many cultural interactions and sometimes lead rather reclusive lives. Some hearing-impaired individuals, for example, will be much less worldly with respect to history or current events simply because they lack the passive exposure to information that is characteristic of hearing individuals. A hearing-impaired individual should not be expected to know who Louis Armstrong was, and obviously not just for reasons of possible social isolation. A congenitally blind individual may not be practically aware of why dark clothes might be warmer than light colored clothes. These examples of Wechsler Information subtest items suffice to warn about the complexity of interpretation that must be considered in the results of the neuropsychological testing of a peripherally impaired client.

As with any other patient group, there are heterogeneous psychological and cognitive characteristics among the blind or deaf groups. Some are socially deprived, others are not. For example, with the advent of closed captioning on television, the passive exposure of the hearing impaired to visual language will soon change the importance of some of the previous comments regarding English-language deprivation. However, the emphasis is still relevant because of the sociocultural development of the sensory impaired that does not apply to the nonimpaired patient.

Relation of Impairment to Brain Damage

A final general principle to consider in interpreting neuropsychological tests is how much time has elapsed between the onset of the impairment in question and the diagnosis of brain damage. In other words, if an individual is blinded at the time of a brain injury, the psychological effects of that blindness are certainly going to be much different than for the individual who has been blind for many years and only recently has exhibited symptoms of a central nervous system impairment. The time between the two phenomena is relevant not only for overall psychological adjustment but also for cognitive-functional adjustment. Persons who have had a disability for a long time, whether loss of limb or loss of sensory input, usually learn to adjust to that loss and compensate for it. For example, blind individuals who undergo extensive mobility training and practice can often learn to navigate spatially quite well despite total lack of visual input. Such an individual's performance on a spatial task would be quite different from that of an individual who has recently been blinded in connection with a brain injury or disease. In the latter case, difficulty in performing spatially oriented tasks may reflect psychological resistance, inexperience in compensatory coping, or a direct effect of the brain damage.

These general principles must always be kept in mind in evaluating the test results of peripherally impaired patients.

In the following discussion of groups of special patients, the emphasis in examples will be on the more familiar neuropsychological tests, including the Wechsler Intelligence scales and tests often used in the Halstead-Reitan or similar batteries. The principles, however, apply to many other tests, and the examiner must assume responsibility for the appropriateness of a test or the limits of inferences that might be drawn.

THE HEARING-IMPAIRED PATIENT

The single most important principle to remember in evaluating the hearing impaired is that the English language is typically not native to them. The usual form of communication for the congenitally hearing impaired is American Sign Language (ASL). Certainly there are other communication skills, such as lip reading or finger spelling, but the typical language is ASL. It is clearly a language in its own right and, like English, is conceptually oriented as opposed to object oriented. But English syntax is irrelevant in American Sign Language; one does not sign using a string of words making up a sentence ending with a period. Signs in ASL are broader in meaning and leave much more to contextual interpretation. Thus, vocabulary is significantly reduced.

Although ASL is conceptually oriented, abstract meanings are not easily conveyed, due to the interpretation necessary on the part of the sign reader. For example, the proverb, "A bird in the hand is worth two in the bush," would be signed literally and interpreted literally. Such abstract thought communication is not a part of ASL or its syntax. Proverbs such as this are not typically a part of the conversation of the deaf.

Whereas vocabulary resources are seen as the most stable sign of premorbid and long-standing intellectual potential, application of an English-language vocabulary test to a congenitally deaf individual, even one with significant education, would be unfair. The typical hearing-impaired individual reads English at a sixth-grade level. This is not due to educational deprivation but rather to the preferred form of communication, which is much more economical in vocabulary and in number of words—i.e., gestures—used to express a thought.

Except in the cases of deaf individuals who have had extensive special training in the English language, general mathematics ability might be a better indicator of premorbid and general intellectual functioning than English vocabulary. Actually, a comparison of vocabulary and arithmetic, via the Wechsler scales, for example, might provide an adequate basis for judging premorbid intelligence.

Evaluating concept learning is valid with a hearing-impaired individual as long as it is not English-language based. The Halstead Category Test, the Block Design subtest of the Wechsler scales, and the Wisconsin Card Sort (Berg, 1948) are relatively free of language contamination. In contrast, proverb interpretations, verbal similarities, or verbal sequences, such as the Abstraction portion of the Shipley Scale (Shipley, 1946), are generally inappropriate for neurodiagnosis of the hearing impaired; these may, however, be entirely appropriate for certain functional evaluations or comparisons.

Neuropsychologists who are unfamiliar with sign language sometimes use interpreters when evaluating the hearing impaired. Although this is quite useful for communication of test instructions, it is invalid for actual test-item administration. Even such apparently innocuous tests as Information from the Wechsler scales would be inappropriate when using an interpreter. An interpreter would ask the question "What is the apocrypha?" by signing in such a way that the word "apocrypha" would have to be defined within the question. In other words, there is no convenient way to ask that question in sign language without defining it in the first place.

Similarly, if the interpreter were to ask an even simpler question, "How are a ball and a wheel alike?" the interpreter must describe, through gesture, a specific ball and a specific wheel. Again, the specific nature of the gestures would destroy the intent of eliciting a general characteristic for all balls and all wheels. Thus the introduction of the interpreter confounds the testing by requiring the hearing-impaired person not only to extract the concept but to go beyond the specific examples of the interpreter in order to arrive at the concept. In other words, for the hearing-impaired patient being administered the test through an interpreter, the Similarities Test becomes a more complex task than for the hearing individual.

Memory functions are best examined through nonlanguage tests such as the figural memory portion of the Wechsler Memory scales, the Wechsler Digit Symbol (including free recall), and the Memory and Location portions of the Tactual Performance Test. Word-learning or associate-learning tests may be modified for visual presentation. Again, however, norms based on oral presentation are not definitive. Also, if English is not a native language, apparent problems with word lists or word-association tests may be a function of experience and not of brain damage. Contamination with an unnatural language must always be suspect in testing the hearing impaired.

Spatial-constructional functions can be evaluated with familiar tests such as the Wechsler Block Design and Object Assembly, Raven Progressive Matrices, Tactual Performance Test, mazes, hidden figures, and so forth. There is typically no contamination of these results as long as test instructions can be effectively communicated.

Good tests for evaluating overall brain functioning of the hearing-impaired individual would include most of the Wechsler performance subtests, the Raven Progressive Matrices, the Halstead Category Test (making sure, of course, to offer visual as opposed to auditory feedback), the Tactual Performance Test, the Hooper Visual Orientation Test (Hooper, 1958), or any of the other non–language-oriented general tests sensitive to organic impairment.

Another consideration in examining the hearing impaired is that many deaf individuals, particularly if deaf from an early age, do not have good articulatory skills and often prefer not to attempt to vocalize responses. Thus, even though many tests can be given with no requirement of auditory comprehension, some form of verbal response from the patient is necessary. The Hooper Visual Orientation Test is one such test. Because the stimuli are pictures of familiar objects, generally culturally fair, its only obstacle for use with the hearing impaired is in obtaining a response. Responses through sign language, finger spelling, or writing would be acceptable since the test is not timed.

THE VISUALLY IMPAIRED PATIENT

Nearly every neuropsychology test available requires some visual processing. And since visuospatial functions are among the most sensitively affected by broad types of brain damage, assessment of the visually impaired patient is particularly difficult.

Recall from previous discussion that, with long-standing visual impairment, and particularly congenital blindness, the spatial-constructional functions may never have developed well due to the modality impairment, despite an otherwise intact and normal brain. Thus, assessing spatial-constructional skills in the visually impaired may be best accomplished for practical reasons of predicting functional capability than for contributing to neurological diagnosis.

The more familiar neuropsychological tests that are appropriate for use with the visually impaired and that present minimal concern for altered interpretation are, nevertheless, essentially language bound. As with sighted individuals, the best estimate of premorbid intelligence can probably be inferred from such tests as Vocabulary or Information from the Wechsler scales. Add Comprehension and these three tests offer good opportunity to evaluate intelligence, language fluency, long-term memory, verbal judgment, and thought organization. The standard scores are obtained, as well as a wealth of opportunity to observe pathognomonic signs.

Probably the best-known and best-normed test for spatial skill (as well as lateral motor functioning) that requires no vision is the Tactual Performance Test (TPT). It is recommended because it also offers the opportunity to get relative right-side and left-side spatial-manipulative scores. It also is an excellent test to determine spatial-manipulative learning potential. Additionally, by having the patient finger-trace the shapes and configurations of the formboard on a large surface, an assessment may be made of the mental-spatial imaging capability of the patient. (The examiner, using pencil and paper, must imitate the patient's finger tracing to preserve a record of the patient's response. However, as pointed out earlier, the change in modality of the Memory and Location tasks from the TPT makes the currently available norms of limited use for neurodiagnostics.)

Assessing conceptual and abstract reasoning should be essentially language dependent. Analogies and Proverb Interpretations are good for evaluating thinking organization and ability to go beyond concrete stimuli. The Similarities subtest from the Wechsler scales also reflects the patient's ability to analyze essential and nonessential characteristics to come up with a commonality. Object-sorting tests where the patient can clearly tactually identify each object presented—as in a pretest examination—is about the only nonlanguage concept reasoning test appropriate for the visually impaired. A test of this type should be used to balance the verbal tests that will otherwise predominate in the examination of such patients.

Memory is tested by any existing test for this purpose that does not rely on visual input. Semantic (i.e., paragraph or word associations), memory, Digit Span from the Wechsler scales, or a variety of word-learning tasks (see Lezak, 1983) can be used.

The tests discussed for use with the hearing- or visually impaired patient are summarized in Table 10.1.

THE PHYSICALLY DISABLED PATIENT

Occasionally a patient with an amputated arm or hand, or some other disability that imposes a lateral handicap in motor performance, will require neuropsychological testing when the disability antedates or is otherwise ancillary to the issue of neurofunctional diagnosis. Muscular dystrophy, arthritis, amputation, or peripheral neuromuscular injury must be clearly discerned prior to administration of neuropsychological tests so that the disability does not contaminate the interpretation of test results.

Tests that are particularly contaminated are those involving lateral comparisons in time or error scores, such as finger tapping, pegboard speed, or the Tactual Performance Test. The examiner, in using these test scores, must evaluate the extent to which a disability presents a handicap to infer either general brain damage or laterality of damage.

Tests that do not involve lateral comparison, but that do consider time scores based on psychomotor performance, must likewise be avoided or else some allowance must be made for the motor disability. Many of the Wechsler performance subtests, for example, award bonus points for faster completion of tests. Certainly, the norms for these tests are inappropriate in the case of either lateral or bilateral motor dysfunction.

Whereas with the visually or hearing impaired caution needs to be exercised

TABLE 10.1 Suggested Tests

Hearing impaired	Visually impaired
Premorbid intelligence	
Arithmetic (WAIS)	Auditory vocabulary
	Information store
Language (left hemisphere)	
Picture-vocabulary	Oral vocabulary
	Verbal comprehension
	Information store
Spatial–constructional (right hemisphere)	
Block designs	Tactual performance test
Raven progressive matrices	
Object sorting	
Hidden figures	
Conceptual–abstract–analytical	
Halstead category	Proverb interpretations
Picture arrangement (WAIS)	Similarities (WAIS)
Object sorting	Analogies
	Object sorting
Memory	
Figural design memory	Semantic memory
Digit symbol (WAIS)	Tactual performance test
Word learning	memory/location traced
Tactual performance test	Word learning
memory/location scores	
Psychomotor	
Finger-tapping speed	Finger-tapping speed
Pegboard tests	Pegboard tests

with the selection and interpretation of higher cognitive tests, with the physically disabled, the concern is usually more at the motor-tactile level. Cognitive tests involving language or visuospatial processing are usually appropriate if allowance is made for slower motor responses, as noted above.

Frequently, individuals with cerebral palsy, a congenital brain impairment usually involving neuromuscular abnormalities, are neuropsychologically examined in order to assess cognitive potentials. In this case of physical disability, there is a direct link between the brain condition and the motor symptoms. However, the nature of cerebral palsy does not easily allow strong inferences about localization of cerebral damage based on the motor symptoms simply by nature of the diffuse characteristics of the disorder. Therefore motor testing should be minimally weighed for neurodiagnosis of the cerebral palsy patient.

With any patient exhibiting motor dysfunction, whether clearly lateralized or not, several cognitive tests present special problems, particularly in the application of norms. If one can be more sensitive to process rather than to profile patterns or normative level of performance, greater accuracy in understanding cognitive characteristics can be realized.

Among the Wechsler scales, Picture Arrangement, Object Assembly, Digit Symbol, and Block Design are the most susceptible to problematic interpretations using norms. However, each of these tests is entirely appropriate as long as the interpretation is based on observations of process. Persons with relatively recent onset of an upper extremity disability may also require extra encouragement to complete these motor tasks if they fatigue easily or are depressed over their self-perceived disability.

CONCLUSION

Although in the discussion of specific disability groups some suggestions were offered for appropriate neuropsychological tests, neuropsychologists should be aware of the wealth of tests that can be more or less informally adopted for neuropsychological assessment. These take on particular importance and sensitivity given the several qualifications previously discussed relative to most standardized neuropsychological tests. Lezak (1983) offers a tremendous compendium of tests relevant for neuropsychological assessment. Given all of the qualifications for considering whether to include particular tests for use with a given impaired patient, her work is invaluable in assessing the unique needs and characteristics of a peripherally impaired patient and then selecting the most appropriate tests to derive a well-balanced and fair neuropsychological assessment.

Although hundreds of tests have been identified as relevant for evaluating neurofunctional characteristics, they have nearly all been normed on persons without brain damage. Or, if they have been normed on brain-damaged persons, the norming groups have typically been heterogeneous, but have not included the types of patients discussed in this chapter.

Inference about brain state is largely based on an analysis of the relative functional state derived from tests measuring a broad spectrum of neurofunctional behaviors. Of course, to do this adequately, scores from the tests must be equated on some common scale.

REFERENCES

Berg, E. A. (1948). A simple objective test for measuring flexibility in thinking. *Journal of General Psychology, 39*, 15–22.

Golden, C. J., Hammeke, T. A., & Purisch, A. D. (1980). *Manual for the Luria-Nebraska Neuropsychological Battery.* Los Angeles: Western Psychological Services.

Hooper, H. E. (1958). *The Hooper Visual Organization Test.* Los Angeles: Western Psychological Services.

Lezak, M. (1983). *Neuropsychological assessment* (2nd ed.). New York: Oxford University Press.

Reitan, R. M., & Davison, L. A. (1974). *Clinical neuropsychology: Current status and applications*. Washington, D.C.: Winston.

Russell, E. W., Neuringer, C., & Goldstein, G. (1970). *Assessment of brain damage: A neuropsychological key approach*. New York: Wiley.

Shipley, W. C. (1946). *Institute of Living Scale*. Los Angeles: Western Psychological Services.

Stubbins, J. (Ed.). (1977). *Social and psychological aspects of disability*. Baltimore: University Park Press.

Swiercinsky, D. P. (1978). *Manual for the adult neuropsychological evaluation*. Springfield, IL: Charles Thomas.

Wright, B. A. (1960). *Physical disability—A psychological approach*. New York: Harper & Row.

11

A Descriptive Summary of Essential Neuropsychological Tests

Edward A. Peck, III,
Valerie Stephens,
and
Michael F. Martelli

This chapter provides only a brief survey of the possible tests that are available to the neuropsychologist. For further information, the reader is urged to consult one of several texts that provide comprehensive listings and descriptions of the more than 150 tests available (e.g., Lezak, 1983).

As with any test list, individual readers may or may not see their favorites included for comment. Each experienced examiner has developed a particular group of tests that he/she employs on a regular basis; these tests typically comprise a core battery. The Halstead-Reitan and Luria-Nebraska are two well-known and popular test batteries. Many groups and/or laboratories have developed their own particular sets of tests that approach the level of a formal test battery (e.g., Benton & Hamsher, 1983; Benton, Hamsher, Varney, & Spreen, 1983). Finally, there are versions of tests and test batteries for children of various ages (e.g., Reitan & Davison, 1974). The authors have restricted the focus here to those tests that are appropriate for adults.

The following pages contain a list of tests organized according to the main area of function that each is considered to measure. Although one test can often be classified under more than one category, space limitations preclude multiple classifications. In compiling these tests, the authors have relied heavily upon the following sources: Benton and associates (1983), Boll (1981),

Butcher and Keller (1984), Filskov and Boll (1981), Golden (1978), Golden, Hammeke, and Purisch (1980), Goldstein (1984), Goldstein and Hersen (1984), Gronwall and Wrightson (1974, 1975), Jarvis and Barth (1984), Lezak (1983), Lindemann and Matarazzo (1984), Mesulam (1985), Reitan and Davison (1974), Reitan and Wolfson (1985), Weintraub and Mesulam (1985), and Zimmerman and Woo-Sam (1973).

TESTS OF LANGUAGE ABILITY

Aphasia Screening Test (Halstead–Reitan Battery)

This screening test briefly measures the various major language functions as well as visual-constructional and motor apraxia. The major language functions surveyed include naming, spelling, repetition, reading, writing, enunciation, and calculation. There are tasks that assess left–right orientation and the ability to follow oral commands. The patient is also asked to demonstrate the use of a familiar object and to copy simple geometric designs. Test administration requires 10 to 15 minutes.

Findings obtained with this screening instrument provide information regarding the functioning of the right and left hemispheres. Specific signs of deficiencies usually warrant a more thorough investigation.

Multilingual Aphasia Examination (1983 Edition)

This is a collection of individual tests designed to assess the presence and severity of a variety of language dysfunctions. Three of the subtests (Visual Naming, Sentence Repetition, Controlled Oral Word Association) measure various aspects of oral expression. Two subtests (Aural Comprehension of Words and Phrases, Token Test) assess aural comprehension. Reading comprehension is also assessed. Spelling ability is measured by tests of oral, written, and block letter manipulation. Qualitative ratings of speech articulation and writing praxis can be carried out as well. It is quite common to administer only those subtests that are deemed necessary. Each subtest requires approximately 10 minutes to complete with a reasonably intact patient.

This series of subtests focuses upon different aspects of language-mediated ability. Impairment in selected areas may be associated with dysfunction involving certain portions of the language-dominant hemisphere.

Wechsler Adult Intelligence Scale–Revised (WAIS–R) Information Subtest

This test consists of 29 items that assess general verbal knowledge in five content areas: general information, current information, cross-cultural information, scientific information, and role-related information. The items are arranged in order of difficulty from simple to complex. The entire test usually can be administered in five minutes.

The information scale is a good measure of verbal fund of knowledge and information. It also reflects verbal communicative skills and is sensitive to education and motivation. In addition, remote memory is a basic requirement for what is being examined by this test. Disruption of information storage must occur at an early stage or deterioration must be very severe to have a profound effect on this measure. Since this scale is one of the WAIS–R subtests least affected by brain injury, it provides a useful estimate of premorbid intellectual functioning. Low scores obtained on this test that are inconsistent with the patient's history may be indicative of problems in the dominant hemisphere.

WAIS–R Comprehension Subtest

[handwritten: sensitive to dominant hemisphere dysfunction]

This scale consists of 14 open-ended questions that assess commonsense judgment and practical reasoning (11 items), and understanding of proverbs (three items). The questions are arranged in order of difficulty, and the patient can earn one or two points for responses, depending on whether they are more concrete or abstract. The scale usually takes 10 minutes or less to administer.

The Comprehension subtest is a measure of verbal intellectual ability, since it relates to comprehension and appreciation for common cultural practices and customs as well as social knowledge and judgment. The responses to the three proverb items allow for comparison of the patient's concrete versus abstract reasoning skills. Like the Information scale, Comprehension also appears to measure remote memory and is generally resistant to deterioration. However, this test is especially sensitive to dominant-hemisphere dysfunction. When the dominant hemisphere is relatively unaffected, then Comprehension is one of the better indicators of premorbid ability.

WAIS–R Similarities Subtest

[handwritten: sensitive to brain injury]

This scale consists of 13 paired items, and the patient must explain the similarity for each pair (e.g., how are an apple and a pear alike?). The items are arranged in order of difficulty, and abstract responses are given more credit than concrete responses.

Similarities is a test of verbal concept formation and associative thinking that also serves as a good measure of general verbal intellect. It is sensitive to brain injury in general. Low scores on this scale may be indicative of brain dysfunction involving either the left hemisphere (due to impaired verbal functions) or the frontal lobes (due to impaired concept formation).

WAIS-R Vocabulary Subtest

This scale consists of 35 words that the patient is asked to define. The words are arranged in order of difficulty, and correct responses are scored according to quality, with content-impoverished responses receiving less credit. This scale is the most time consuming of the WAIS-R subtests and can take anywhere from 15 to 25 minutes to administer.

Vocabulary is a very good measure of both verbal and general intellectual ability. It may reflect social, economic, and cultural origins. This subtest is considered to be somewhat less sensitive to lesions in the left hemisphere than the Comprehension or Similarities subtests, and is one of the subtests least affected by diffuse or bilateral brain dysfunction. Thus, Vocabulary scores can provide useful information about premorbid intellectual level. Finally, this subtest has shown clinical utility in the differential diagnosis of brain damage from thought disorder, as the latter is often revealed in the form of the patient's verbalizations.

Speech Sounds Perception Test (Halstead–Reitan Battery)

This test requires that the subject listen to an audio tape consisting of a series of 60 nonsense syllables (e.g., *preeng*). On each trial, a single stimulus is presented and the patient matches that sound to one of four choices on the answer sheet. The score consists of the number of errors. Test administration usually takes 10 to 15 minutes.

The Speech Sounds test is essentially an auditory verbal test that assesses the ability to discriminate between similar sounding syllables. It is sensitive to brain damage in general, but is more affected by dominant-hemisphere involvement. It should be noted that since this test requires patients to attend to a mechanically delivered and somewhat repetitious task, performance also reflects attention and concentration ability.

TESTS OF NONVERBAL ABILITY

Reasoning and Problem Solving Skills

Categories Test (Halstead–Reitan Battery)

This test is a concept-identification procedure in which the patient must discover the concept or principle that governs the relationship between various series of geometric forms. The stimuli (which can be presented through the use of a projection screen or in a booklet format) are presented visually to the patient. The patient is told that the point of the test is to see how well he or she can learn the concept, idea, or principle that underlies the geometric forms in each of the seven subgroups. The patient's effort is facilitated by the provision of feedback concerning the correctness of responses. The test is scored for number of errors, and administration time can vary from 30 to 60 minutes.

Categories is a nonverbal test of abstract reasoning, logical analysis, cognitive flexibility, and conceptual problem-solving ability. The patient is required to generate possible solutions based upon concepts that he/she formulates and then modifies based upon corrective feedback from the examiner. This test is a very good discriminator of neurologically impaired versus intact individuals. It is also considered to be a good predictor of everyday problem-solving skills involving the ability to learn and benefit from situational feedback. It does, however, require visual-spatial perception and color discrimination abilities and is not appropriate for individuals with deficits in these areas.

Wisconsin Card Sort Test

This test employs 64 cards, each consisting of one of four shapes (triangle, cross, star, or circle) and varying in number (one through four) and color (red, green, yellow, or blue). The patient must place these cards one at a time next to one of four stimulus cards (all four shapes and colors are represented on these stimulus cards). The patient must deduce a particular principle (e.g., shape of design) on the basis of examiner feedback about the correctness of each placement. After the patient achieves 10 consecutive correct responses (based on the current principle), the examiner shifts to one of two other possible principles. Common scoring practices include the number of principles completed as well as specific error types (e.g., number of perseverative errors). Total time for the administration of this test is approximately 10 to 30 minutes. A shorter, modified version is also available.

This test was designed to assess abstract reasoning ability and cognitive flexibility, or the ability to shift cognitive sets. As in the Category Test, the ability to generate concepts and to modify these concepts based on examiner feedback is required. This test also shows good discrimination between normal and brain-damaged individuals and is considered to be a good predictor of everyday problem-solving skills and ability to adapt to situational feedback.

Visual-Spatial and Constructional Performance

WAIS-R Block Design Subtest

This scale requires that patients assemble blocks in a two-dimensional pattern as presented in a test booklet. Ten designs are presented in order of difficulty, with the first five requiring four blocks (two-by-two matrix) and the last five requiring nine blocks (three-by-three matrix). The test is timed, and no formal credit is given for partial completion at the time limit. Total administration time varies from 10 to 15 minutes.

Block Design is a measure of visual-spatial construction organization. Block Design performance is sensitive to brain damage in general. However, it is most strongly affected by nondominant, right-hemisphere lesions, especially when there is parietal lobe involvement. In addition, observations regarding organizational style frequently provide insight about thinking processes and problem-solving style.

WAIS-R Object Assembly Subtest

Object Assembly is a puzzle assembly task using figures of familiar objects. This timed test measures speed as well as accuracy of performance. However, unlike Block Design, bonus points are given for very quick performance and partial credit is given if the design is not completely finished within the time limit. This subtest requires about 10 minutes to administer.

Object Assembly, like Block Design, is a measure of visual organization and construction ability. While this scale is sensitive to posterior nondominant-hemisphere dysfunction, lesions in other regions of the cortex can result in significant impairment as well.

WAIS-R Picture Arrangement Subtest

This scale consists of 10 sets of cartoon-type pictures, each of which is presented in a scrambled order. The patient must arrange the pictures in a sequential order that results in the most sensible story. The sets are presented in order of difficulty, and each set contains between three and six pictures with a time limit of either one or two minutes. The test takes approximately 15 minutes to administer.

Picture Arrangement evaluates the ability to detect nonverbal social cues and to think in a logical and sequential manner. It is sensitive to brain damage, and variations and performance errors may reflect particular patterns of brain dysfunction.

WAIS-R Picture Completion Subtest — *good indicator of premorbid functioning*

This scale consists of a series of 20 pictures, each of which is missing a relatively important detail (e.g., tail missing from a cat). The pictures are presented in order of difficulty, and the patient is permitted 20 seconds in which to identify the missing detail. Administration time of this test is approximately five minutes.

Picture Completion is a test of visual perception and recognition that requires remote memory and judgment concerning relevance of practical and conceptual detail. This scale is generally resilient to the effects of brain damage and is one of the best test indicators of premorbid ability, particularly when left-hemisphere damage has resulted in impaired ability.

Rey-Osterrieth Complex Figure Test—Copying Mode

The copying portion of this test involves the visual presentation of a complex design, which the patient is instructed to copy as accurately as possible. In order to evaluate effectively the patient's approach to the test, the examiner notes where the patient begins and has him or her switch to different-colored pencils at various points during the task. The order of colors used and the time needed to complete the drawing are also recorded, and then the original copy is removed. Some examiners use an alternate procedure of sketching out the pattern development themselves as the patient proceeds through the task. The copying task usually takes no more than five minutes.

This test assesses visual-motor copying and visual-spatial construction. In addition, perceptual organization and problem-solving approaches (e.g., copying via detail by detail, external boundaries versus internal detail, systematic versus nonsystematic) are informally evaluated with this test. The recall portion of this test will be discussed below under the section dealing with tests of memory and learning ability.

Tactual Performance Test (Halstead-Reitan Battery)

This test utilizes a formboard and 10 blocks (e.g., square, star, cross, half-circle, etc.) that fit into cut-out recesses. The patient is blindfolded and never allowed to see the board. The formboard is placed at an angle on a stand in front of the patient, and the examiner familiarizes the patient with the board and blocks by guiding the patient's hand across them. The patient is then instructed to place each block in the proper space as quickly as possible. The task is repeated three times, first with the preferred hand, then with the nonpreferred hand, and then finally with both hands. The time to completion as well as sequence of block placement is recorded for each trial. A maximum of 10 minutes is usually allowed for each trial.

After the three trials are completed, the formboard and blocks are removed. The blindfold is removed, and the patient is asked to draw a picture of the formboard, including the shape and location of the blocks. Maximum time for administration is approximately 35 minutes.

This test is a discriminator of neurologically intact versus impaired individuals. It appears to be particularly sensitive to parietal lobe dysfunction. In addition, time differences between trials for preferred and nonpreferred hands provide clues regarding lateralization. Scores for memory and localization will be discussed below under the section dealing with tests of memory and learning ability.

Benton Visual Form Discrimination Test   *Posterior Rt hemi. damg* [handwritten]

This is a multiple-choice test presented in a spiral booklet. It includes a series of 32 designs, generally involving two major figures and one peripheral figure. For each item, the patient is instructed to note a design on the top page and find the identical match from four choices presented on the page below it. There is no time limit on responses, and the test usually takes about 10 minutes to administer.

This test assesses the ability to discriminate complex visual stimuli independent of memory. It is sensitive to neurological impairment in general and to posterior right-hemisphere damage in particular. Concentration problems, visual-perceptual, scanning, or field-related problems, and visual neglect can also result in impaired performance on this test.

Benton Facial Recognition Test

This test is presented in a format similar to that of the Benton Visual Form Discrimination test, with the exception that patients must match photographs of faces instead of designs. This test evaluates the ability to recognize unfamiliar faces, a task which requires complex visual-spatial processing independent of memory. It is sensitive to parietal lobe dysfunction. Visual neglect problems as well as other forms of visual-spatial and visual search difficulties also can affect performance on this test.

Motor Skill Tests

Grooved Pegboard Test

For this test, patients must place pegs into a board containing grooved slots that are oriented in different directions. The test is administered in two trials, one for each hand. Time required for each trial and the number of pegs dropped during each trial is recorded. Test administration time is approximately five minutes.

This test assesses fine-motor dexterity and accuracy and allows for comparison of right- and left-hand performance. Deviations from the expected pattern of performance with the preferred hand versus nonpreferred hand also provide lateralization indicators.

Finger-Tapping Test (Halstead–Reitan Battery)

This test requires that patients tap as rapidly as possible with their extended forefinger on a telegraph key–like lever attached to a mechanical counter. Several series of 10-second trials are run with both the right and left hands. The scores are the average number of taps for each hand. The test requires approximately five minutes to administer.

Finger Tapping is a test of motor speed and coordination and allows for comparison of relative performance with right and left hands. Deviations from normal performance with the preferred versus the nonpreferred hand offer good lateralizing indicators.

Grip Strength (Halstead-Reitan Battery)

This test employs a calibrated hand dynamometer that is individually adjusted for hand size. The patient stands with the dynamometer held straight down at his or her side and then squeezes as hard as possible. Two or three trials (depending upon examiner approach) are conducted for the right and left hands. Test administration time is less than five minutes.

This test assesses motor strength for each hand. As with the Grooved Pegboard and Finger-Tapping tests, deviations from the expected pattern of performance for preferred versus nonpreferred hand may reflect lateralizing signs. In interpreting motor strength scores, factors such as sex, occupation, and history of peripheral injury to the upper extremities must be taken into consideration.

TESTS OF MEMORY AND LEARNING ABILITY

Rey Auditory Verbal Learning Test (RAVLT)

This test consists of a 15-item word list that is read to the patient. There are seven trials. After each of trials one through five, the patient is asked to recall as many words as he or she remembers. The recalled words, their order of recall, and any intrusion errors are recorded. Trial Six includes presentation of a second 15-item word list, after which the patient is asked to recall the words from the first list. Words from the second list that interfere are recorded. After a three-minute delay, a recognition trial is administered in which the patient is asked to recognize words from the first list contained in a paragraph that he or she is given to read. This test requires approximately 10 minutes to administer.

The RAVLT assesses immediate memory span for recall of words (Trial 1) as well as short-term memory following subsequent repetition (Trials 2-5). This test provides information about the patient's capacity for new learning. Organizational learning strategies, as well as the patient's susceptibility to retroactive/proactive interference, are also assessed. Finally, the delayed paragraph recall section provides a measure of long-term recognition memory.

WAIS-R Digit Span Subtest

This measure consists of two parts, each involving the presentation of random number sequences that are read aloud at the rate of one number per second. For digits forward, the examiner reads two trials of number sequences, beginning with a span of three and progressing to a span of nine digits (or until a patient is unable to repeat the exact sequence for both trials of the digit span). For digits backward, the patient must repeat the sequence in reverse, and the presented digit span lengths vary from two to eight. Total time for administration of this test is less than five minutes.

Digits Forward and Digits Backward involve somewhat different mental operations. Digits Forward is a measure of immediate auditory memory span and attention. Digits Backward is a measure of active or working memory, involving both the storage and the manipulation of information. Variations from the expected pattern of Digit Span Forward/Backward (e.g., forward approximately two greater than backward) are suggestive of attention, concentration, and/or sequencing problems that may reflect organic and/or emotional factors.

Rey–Osterrieth Complex Design Test–Recall Mode

The direct copy portion of this task was described earlier in the section on visual-spatial and constructional performance tests. The recall portion of the test can be conducted at varying time intervals (3, 30, or 60 minutes) after the completion of the copying portion of the task. At the specified time delay, the patient is asked to re-create the original design. This portion of the test requires approximately 10 minutes to complete. This portion of the test assesses long-term visual-motor/visual-spatial memory.

Tactual Performance Test–Memory and Localization

The performance section of this test was described earlier in the section on visual-spatial and constructional performance tests. The memory and localization scores are derived from the final portion of the Tactual Performance Test, subsequent to the removal of the formboard and blocks. The patient's blindfold is removed, and he/she is instructed to draw the outline of the formboard and the individual shapes in their respective locations. The memory score of the TPT refers to the number of correctly shaped blocks the patient is able to draw from memory. The localization score refers to the number of forms correctly located on the formboard. Thus, the memory score reflects tactual memory for the shapes, while the localization score reflects complex tactual-spatial memory. Performance on these two tasks is sensitive to brain injury, particularly lesions in the temporal-parietal region.

Benton Visual Retention Test

This paper-and-pencil task involves the visual presentation of a series of 10 cards, each containing one-to-three geometric designs. The patient must look at each card and then draw the design. There are four administrative procedures, three of which are normed. Administration A provides for a 10-second exposure followed by immediate recall; Administration B is like A, only it has a five-second exposure; Administration C is a direct copying test with no memory involvement; Administration D has a 10-second exposure followed by a 15-second delayed recall. There are several different series of geometric designs, so that more than one administration form may be given without concern for stimulus familiarity. Each series requires approximately 10 to 15 minutes to complete.

This test assesses visual-perceptual as well as visual memory abilities. Visual-spatial organization, visual inattention, and visual neglect problems may be demonstrated on this test, along with deficiencies in memory and recall. Perseverative tendencies may also be observed. This test is sensitive to the presence of brain dysfunction and is useful in differentiating patients with psychiatric disorders from those with organic dysfunction.

Wechsler Memory Scale

This scale was introduced as an assessment instrument intended to evaluate a variety of memory functions. It generates a Memory Quotient that was originally considered to be an overall memory score. As will be noted below, the various subtests also assess cognitive functions other than memory and learning. Many clinicians prefer to look at the individual scores of the various subtests rather than relying upon the Memory Quotient.

It consists of seven subtests. The Personal and Current Information (I) and Orientation (II) subtests assess information and orientation levels in a manner similar to that noted in a mental status examination. The Mental Control (III) subtest is a timed test of simple mental operations and attention (i.e., counting backwards, alphabet recital, counting by serial threes). The Logical Memory (IV) subtest requires the free recall of paragraph-length information. There are two paragraphs presented orally to the patient. The Digit Span (V) subtest is a standard digit span forward/backward task. The Visual Reproduction (VI) subtest involves the presentation of three designs, one at a time, each for 10 seconds. Following the visual presentation, each design is removed and the patient is asked to draw the design. The Associative Learning (VII) subtest consists of a list of 10 orally presented word pairs. Six of these word pairs are easily associated (e.g., gold–silver), and four are not (e.g., boat–giraffe). The list is presented for three trials. Each trial is followed by the oral presentation of the first word in each pair, for which the patient must provide the second or associative word.

The complete Wechsler Memory Scale requires approximately 20 minutes to administer. There is a delayed recall version for the Logical Memory and Visual Reproduction subtests. Parallel forms of the entire Wechsler Memory Scale are available.

TESTS OF ATTENTION, CONCENTRATION, AND CONCEPTUAL TRACKING

Paced Auditory Serial Addition Test (PASAT)

This test utilizes a standardized tape-recorded verbal presentation of a series of numbers that are presented at a progressively more rapid rate across four series of trials (from 2.4 to 1.2 seconds between numbers). The patient's task is to add each number to the immediately preceding number. For example, given the series, "3, 1, 5, 8," the patient should respond "4" after the number "1," "6" after the number "5," and "13" after the number "8". The test usually takes 10 to 15 minutes to complete. Basic addition skills are required for this task.

The PASAT is a sensitive measure of rate of information processing as well as sustained attention, concentration, and conceptual tracking. It also evaluates the ability to focus attention purposely on a prolonged task. It is thought to be extremely sensitive to minor alterations in general brain function, such as those demonstrated following minor head injury.

WAIS-R Arithmetic Subtest

This test consists of 14 arithmetic questions, arranged in order of difficulty, that require oral solution. The patient's responses are timed, with limits ranging from 15 to 120 seconds, and bonus points can be earned for fast performance on the final four problems. Total test administration time is approximately 10 to 12 minutes.

This subtest is a measure of concentration, immediate memory, and conceptual manipulation and tracking. Because of the oral format and timed nature of responses, scores do not reflect arithmetic skills alone.

WAIS-R Digit Symbol Subtest   *- very sensitive to Brain Dysfunction*

This symbol–number substitution task consists of four rows of 100 divided boxes. Each box has a randomly assigned number (1 to 9) in the top half, and the bottom half is empty. There is a separate key in which each of the numbers is associated with a specific simple geometric design. The patient's task is to fill in as many of the blank bottom spaces with the symbol it is paired with in the key. There is a 90-second time limit. This test takes less than five minutes to administer.

Digit Symbol is a psychomotor performance test that requires motor speed, persistence, visual-motor coordination, and sustained attention. This subtest is very sensitive to brain dysfunction. Emotional problems such as depression may also affect performance on this subtest.

Trailmaking Test—Parts A and B (Halstead–Reitan Battery)

This is a timed paper-and-pencil test with two parts. Part A consists of circled numbers randomly scattered over a sheet of 8×11 paper. The patient is instructed to connect, in order, the series of numbers without lifting his or her pencil. Part B includes circled numbers and letters, and the patient's task involves alternating between numbers and letters in serial order (e.g., 1–A–2–B, etc.). The time to completion and number of errors are recorded for each trial. Test administration is usually less than five minutes.

Trailmaking Part A provides a measure of attention and concentration abilities involving visual-motor, conceptual tracking, and sequencing skills. Part B measures attention and concentration processes involving more complex sequencing tasks where cognitive flexibility is required.

Seashore Rhythm Test (Halstead–Reitan Battery)

This test consists of a standardized, tape-recorded auditory presentation of 30 pairs of rhythmically patterned sounds. The patient is provided with a response sheet and asked to indicate whether each pair is the same or different by writing an "S" or a "D". Performance is scored in terms of either number correct or the number of errors. The test takes approximately 10 minutes to administer.

The Seashore Rhythm Test is a sustained attention and concentration task. It requires recognition, perception, and discrimination of symbolic sound patterns.

COMPREHENSIVE NEUROPSYCHOLOGICAL TEST BATTERIES

At this time, there are only two well-known, comprehensive neuropsychological test batteries: The Halstead–Reitan and the Luria–Nebraska. Most of the tests that comprise the Halstead–Reitan have been reviewed above in their relevant sections. For reasons noted below, tests comprising the Luria–Nebraska have not been included.

At the present time, the Luria–Nebraska consists of 11 clinical scales as well as three scales of overall impairment (Pathognomonic, Right Hemisphere, and Left Hemisphere). The 11 clinical scales are as follows: Motor, Rhythm, Tactile, Vision, Receptive Speech, Expressive Speech, Writing, Reading, Arithmetic, Memory, and Intellectual Processes. Subsequent research (McKay & Golden, 1979a, b; Golden, 1979; Golden & Berg, 1983; Moses, Johnson, & Lewis, 1983; Moses, 1985, to cite only a very few references) has led to the development of a number of other empirically derived scales dealing with localization, double discrimination, and other factors. Extensive factor-analytic work has also been carried out on this test battery.

The Luria–Nebraska has been controversial since it was first published [see Goldstein (1984) and Lezak (1983) for extensive reviews and comments]. The consensus of these two authors' reviews and comments is that while many studies have supported this battery's statistical validity and reliability, other studies have been extremely critical of its theoretical and statistical assumptions [see Stambrook (1983) and Kane, Parsons, & Goldstein (1985)]. They also note some apparently significant methodological difficulties involved in the standardization of the procedure (Adams, 1980). Other criticisms have focused upon deficiencies in assessment and diagnosis of language disorders (Delis & Kaplan, 1982). While many of these criticisms have been defended by Golden and his co-workers, the debate continues (Golden, 1980).

OBJECTIVE PERSONALITY TESTING

Minnesota Multiphasic Personality Inventory (MMPI)

The MMPI is a 566-item true–false personality questionnaire that is suitable for administration to older adolescents and adults having at least a sixth-grade education. It is considered to be the most commonly used self-report personality inventory used in this country. This measure consists of 10 clinical scales, comprised of items that empirically discriminate various psychiatric groups. It also includes four validity scales that assess test-taking attitudes. There are separate norms for males and females. Interpretation is usually based on multiple-scale configurations. The test requires approximately 90 minutes to administer.

The MMPI is frequently employed as part of a comprehensive neuropsychological examination, since it provides useful information regarding emotional distress and personality disturbance. It is used to determine not only patient adjustment to current problems, but also personality characteristics that facilitate/hamper adjustment in functioning. When interpreting MMPI profiles of neurologically impaired individuals, it is important to take into consideration that many of the feelings, symptoms, and complaints reported accurately reflect symptoms of brain dysfunction.

CONCLUSIONS

This chapter has provided a descriptive summary of many of the tests used in neuropsychological assessment. The number and variety of psychological tests available for use in neuropsychological assessment is considerable. Which tests are selected for administration to a particular patient will probably depend upon the referral question, individual patient characteristics, and the clinician's preference for certain individual tests and/or test batteries.

REFERENCES

Adams, K. M. (1980). In search of Luria's battery: A false start. *Journal of Consulting and Clinical Psychology, 48,* 511-516.

American Psychological Association. (1977). *Ethical standards for psychologists.* Washington, DC: Author.

Benton, A. L., & Hamsher, K. deS., (1983). *Multilingual Aphasia Examination. Manual of instructions.* Iowa City: AJA Associates.

Benton, A., Hamsher, K. deS. Varney, N., & Spreen, O. (1983). *Contributions to neuropsychological assessment.* New York: Oxford University Press.

Boll, T. J. (1981). The Halstead-Reitan Neuropsychological Battery. In S. B. Filskov & T. J. Boll (Eds.), *Handbook of clinical neuropsychology* (pp. 577-607). New York: Wiley-Interscience.

Butcher, J. N., & Keller, L. S. (1984). Objective personality assessment. In G. Goldstein & M. Hersen (Eds.), *Handbook of psychological assessment* (pp. 307-331). New York: Pergamon Press.

Delis, D. C., & Kaplan E. (1982). The assessment of aphasia with the Luria–Nebraska Neuropsychological Battery: A case critique. *Journal of Consulting and Clinical Psychology, 50,* 32-34.

Filskov, S. B., & Boll T. J. (Eds.). (1981). *Handbook of clinical neuropsychology.* New York: Wiley-Interscience.

Golden, C. J. (1978). *Diagnosis and rehabilitation in clinical neuropsychology.* Springfield, IL: C. C. Thomas.

Golden, C. J. (1979). Identification of specific neurological disorders using double discrimination scales derived from the standardized Luria Neuropsychological battery. *International Journal of Neuroscience, 10,* 51-56.

Golden, C. J. (1980). In reply to Adams' In search of Luria's battery: A false start. *Journal of Consulting and Clinical Psychology, 48,* 517-521.

Golden, C. J., & Berg, R. A. (1983). Interpretation of the Luria–Nebraska Neuropsychological Battery by item intercorrelation: The Memory Scale. *Clinical Neuropsychology, 5,* 55-59.

Golden, C. J., Hammeke, T. A., & Purisch, A. D. (1980). *Manual for the neuropsychological battery.* Los Angeles: Western Psychological Services.

Goldstein, G. (1984). Comprehensive neuropsychological assessment batteries. In G. Goldstein & M. Hersen (Eds.), *Handbook of psychological assessment* (pp. 181-210). New York: Pergamon.

Goldstein, G., & Hersen, M. (Eds.). (1984). *Handbook of psychological assessment.* New York: Pergamon Press.

Gronwall, D., & Wrightson, P. (1974). Recovery after minor head injury. *Lancet, 2,* 1452.

Gronwall, D., & Wrightson, P. (1975). Cumulative effect of concussion. *Lancet, 2,* 995-997.

Jarvis, P. E., & Barth, J. T. (1984). *Halstead-Reitan Test Battery: An interpretive guide.* Odessa, FL: Psychological Assessment Resources, Inc.

Kane, R., Parsons, O., & Goldstein, G. (1985). Statistical relationships and discriminative accuracy of the Halstead-Reitan, Luria-Nebraska, and Wechsler I.Q. scores in the identification of brain damage. *Journal of Clinical and Experimental Neuropsychology*, 7, 211-223.

Lezak, M. D. (1983). *Neuropsychological assessment* (2nd ed.). New York: Oxford University Press.

Lindemann, J. E., & Matarazzo, J. D. (1984). Intellectual assessment of adults. In G. Goldstein and M. Hersen (Eds.), *Handbook of psychological assessment* (pp. 77-99). New York: Pergamon Press.

McKay, S., & Golden, C. J. (1979a). Empirical derivation of neuropsychological scales for the lateralization of brain damage using the Luria-Nebraska Neuropsychological Battery. *Clinical Neuropsychology*, 1, 1-5.

McKay, S., and Golden, C. J. (1979b). Empirical derivation of experimental scales for localizing brain lesions using the Luria-Nebraska Neuropsychological Battery. *Clinical Neuropsychology*, 1, 19-23.

Meier, M. J. (1981). Education for competency assurance in human neuropsychology: Antecedents, models and directions. In S. B. Filskov & T. J. Boll (Eds.), *Handbook of clinical neuropsychology* (pp. 754-781). New York: Wiley-Interscience.

Meier, M. J. (1984). Report of the Division of 40/INS joint task force on education, accreditation and credentialing. *APA Division of Clinical Neuropsychology Newsletter*, 2, 3-8.

Mesulam, M. (Ed.). (1985). *Principles of behavioral neurology*. Philadelphia: F. A. Davis.

Moses, J. A. (1985). Replication of internal consistency reliability values for the Luria-Nebraska Neuropsychological Battery Summary. Localization, factor and compensation scales. *The International Journal of Clinical Neuropsychology*, 7(3), 200-203.

Moses, J. A., Johnson, G. L., and Lewis, G. P. (1983). Reliability analysis of the Luria-Nebraska neuropsychological battery summary, localization and factor scales. *International Journal of Neuroscience*, 20, 149-154.

Reitan, R. M., & Davison, L. A. (Eds.). (1974). *Clinical neuropsychology: Current status and applications*. Washington, DC: V. H. Winston & Sons.

Reitan, R. M., & Wolfson, D. (1985). *The Halstead-Reitan Neuropsychological Test Battery: Theory and clinical interpretation*. Tucson: Neuropsychology Press.

Stambrook, M. (1983). The Luria-Nebraska Neuropsychological Battery. A promise that may be partly fulfilled. *Journal of Clinical Neuropsychology*, 5, 247-269.

Weintraub, S., & Mesulam, M. (1985). The mental state assessment of young and elderly adults in behavioral neurology. In M. Mesulam (Ed.), *Principles of behavioral neurology* (pp. 71-115). Philadelphia: F. A. Davis.

Zimmerman, I. L., & Woo-Sam, J. M. (1973). *Clinical interpretation of the Wechsler Adult Intelligence Scale*. New York: Grune & Stratton.

Index

Index

Abstraction, 107–108, 120
Activity, programming, regulation and verification of, brain unit for, 16–17
Age of onset, in alcohol and substance abuse, 156
Aggramatic speech, and telegraphic, 63
Alcohol abuse, neuropsychological assessment in, 138–141
  clinical considerations in, 155–157
  comprehensive, 145–148
  screening in, 141–145
  utilizing information in, 157
Alcoholics, neuropsychological characteristics of, 148–152
Allen, C. M., 127–128
Amnesia
  dissociative or hysterical, 185
  following electroconvulsive treatment, 183–184
  transient global, 184
Anatomic and functional differences, in brain hemispheres, 17–18
Anomic aphasia, 55
Aphasia Screening Test, 214
Arithmetic scale, 97–101, 118–119
Arithmetic Subtest, WAIS-R, 224
Arousal, disorders of, 186–187
Arousal unit, 14–15
Art, and science, in neuropsychology, 198–201
Articulation disturbance, fluent speech without, but impaired content, 63
Assessment, see Neuropsychological assessment

Assessment approaches, other than neuropsychology, 1–3
Attention
  disorders of, 186–187
  tests of, 224–225
Audition change, 65; see also Hearing
Auditory Perception, 85, 115
  and expression, nonverbal, 79, 113
Automatic Series Repetition, 88–89, 117

Behavior, relationship of brain to, see Brain–behavior relationships
Behavioral indices, of hemispheric specialization, 18–20
Benton, A., battery of, 71
Benton Facial Recognition Test, 220
Benton Visual Form Discrimination Test, 220
Benton Visual Retention Test, 222–223
Bergner, M., 145
Bilateral Rapid Alternating Movements, 77, 112
Block Design Subtest, WAIS-R, 217–218
Blood pressure, in physical examination, 34
Brain, units of, 14–17
Brain–behavior relationships, 12–28
  early theories on, 12–13
  scientific progress in, 13
Brain damage, relationship of impairment to, 205–206
Brain pathology, characteristics of, 21–22
Broca, P., 13, 32